The Characters of Oz

The Characters of Oz

Essays on Their Adaptation and Transformation

Edited by DINA SCHIFF MASSACHI

Afterword by Robert Baum

McFarland & Company, Inc., Publishers
Jefferson, North Carolina

This book has undergone peer review.

ISBN (print) 978-1-4766-8797-1
ISBN (ebook) 978-1-4766-5047-0

LIBRARY OF CONGRESS AND BRITISH LIBRARY
CATALOGUING DATA ARE AVAILABLE

Library of Congress Control Number 2023028272

On the cover: L. Frank Baum, half-length portrait, seated, facing right,
hand raised to chin, circa, 1908 (Library of Congress); Illustration from
The Wonderful Wizard of Oz L. Frank Baum. Chicago and New York:
G.M. Hill, 1900, William Wallace Denslow (Library of Congress)

Printed in the United States of America

*McFarland & Company, Inc., Publishers
Box 611, Jefferson, North Carolina 28640
www.mcfarlandpub.com*

With love to
my parents, for watching the MGM film repeatedly with me,
my husband, for listening to all of my adventures in Oz,
and Judah, for letting me pass Oz on to the next generation

Acknowledgments

This book wouldn't exist without the support and encouragement of so many people. Dr. Mark I. West, who generously contributed an essay to this collection, provided crucial help throughout the entire process of editing this collection, and I thank him for his endless support. Jane Albright and the International Wizard of Oz Club also lent their help in working through the bumps that this collection inevitably stumbled across on the journey to becoming a book, and I am grateful for the collective patience and support from the Oz Club community. Mark I. West, Jane Albright, and Michael Patrick Hearn were all kind enough to let me use their names, and their address books, as I assembled this amazing collection of authors. I am in awe to be editing such a fine group of writers and thankful for each and every one of their contributions. Marcus D. Mébes generously provided all of the high-resolution scans of the Neill and Denslow art that accompanies each essay, and I am grateful for his willingness to jump right in to help a fellow Ozian. Susan Diamond Riley went above and beyond with copy editing and John Schacht proved to be the best beta reader a person could hope for; I am endlessly thankful for their willingness to read (and correct). A handful of Oz friends I've met at conventions—Colin Ayres, Jay Davis, Nathan DeHoff, Sam Milazzo, and Erica Olivera—were kind enough to brainstorm different adaptations for various characters, and I thank you for letting me pick your collective brains. Finally, I thank my colleagues and students at the University of North Carolina at Charlotte and my friends in the Children's Literature Association.

Table of Contents

Introduction

DINA SCHIFF MASSACHI

Once upon a time, in 1900, L. Frank Baum wrote something unique—a story of self-reliance that was also a buddy tale, a fantasy land that has been described as both utopian and dystopian, and well-rounded characters that remained abstract enough that W.W. Denslow drew a Dorothy with brown hair while John R. Neill drew his Dorothy as a blonde, and yet neither contradicted the text. When L. Frank Baum wrote *The Wonderful Wizard of Oz*, he created a uniquely American fairy tale myth with archetypal characters that have not only endured the test of time but have also been adapted and readapted many times over. Baum's characters remain timeless. We see echoes of Dorothy and her friends everywhere: popular television shows often have an Oz episode, novelists like William Goldman, Madeleine L'Engle, and Francesca Lia Block pay subtle tributes by borrowing character types and echoing familiar scenes while other writers like Gregory Maguire, Danielle Paige, and Eric Shanower find overt ways to modernize and continue Oz. In fact, every medium—from Broadway to the Muppets—has some variation or continuation of Baum's work.

As Richard Tuerk notes in his 2007 book *Oz in Perspective*, "Serious literary critics and scholars tend to neglect Baum" (3). This slight, if one wants to view it that way, is more about the history of how scholarship has looked at children's literature and less about Oz and, fortunately, is changing with time. Tuerk lists a history of book-length publications about Baum and Oz shortly after this claim, including Edward Wagenknecht's *Utopian Americana* (1929), Raylyn Moore's *Wonderful Wizard Marvelous Land* (1974), Michael O. Riley's *Oz and Beyond* (1997), Suzanne Rahn's *The Wizard of Oz: Shaping an Imaginary World* (1998), and the centennial edition of Michael Patrick Hearn's *The Annotated Wizard of Oz* (2000). There are a few titles published after Tuerk's book, including Kevin Durand and Mary Leigh's *The Universe of Oz: Essays on Baum's Series and Its Progeny* (2010), Alissa Burger's *The Wizard of Oz as American Myth* (2011), and Danielle Birkett and Dominic McHugh's *Adapting the Wizard of Oz: Musical Versions from Baum to MGM and Beyond* (2019). Nevertheless, Tuerk's general statement still applies. While academics have explored a variety of themes in relation to Oz, the themes tend to drive the scholarship. This collection of essays follows a different path, as it strives to follow Baum's archetypal characters as they've changed over time in order to examine what those changes mean in relation to Oz, American culture, and basic human truths.

This collection also strives to serve as a bridge between academia and fandom. Some of these essays (specifically Mark I. West's Dorothy, my Tin Woodman, and

1

Robert B. Luehrs's Wicked Witches) originated in the International Wizard of Oz Club's journal, *The Baum Bugle*. All of the contributors represent a cross section of Oz scholarship, and many are even members of the International Wizard of Oz Club (*http://ozclub. org/join-the-club/*). Of course, this means that, like Dorothy on her journey, *The Characters of Oz* has picked up many unique characters along the way, and each brings a unique viewpoint and voice to this collection. While every contributor was encouraged to consider how Oz has been adapted and readapted, and what those changes mean, contributors were not asked to follow a set formula or create something uniform. Like Baum's characters, every essay is different.

Of course, an astute reader is already critiquing my comment that Baum's characters are all different—Jack Pumpkinhead might be another version of the Scarecrow, Betsy Bobbin an alternate Dorothy, and Tik-Tok and the Tin Woodman often have words about which mechanical man is the better of the two. Like Baum's characters, certain themes, observations, and tropes come up again and again within this collection.

L. Frank Baum was something of a character himself (as his great-grandson, Robert Baum, illustrates for readers in our afterword). He lived his life in many settings—from his childhood home of Rose Lawn to his final stop in his California Ozcot home—and these various real-world settings all made their way into his writings. As Baum moved around the country, he tried on different hobbies and careers. As a young man, he wrote about chickens and stamp collecting, authored and acted in plays, and helped with his family's oil business. As an older man, he ran a shop (and created elaborate window displays), edited a newspaper, and, of course, wrote. He wrote under many names (Baum's great-granddaughter Gita Dorothy Morena lists several in her essay), many of which were female. Baum was fascinated with technology, and J.L. Bell, Paige Gray, and Robert B. Luehrs all note how that fascination influenced several of Baum's characters. Perhaps his major influence, though, was his mother-in-law, suffragist Matilda Gage. Essays by Angelica Shirley Carpenter, Paige Gray, Mary Lenard, Robert B. Luehrs, me, Gita Dorothy Morena, Shannon Murphy, Walter Squire, and Mark I. West all note Gage's influence on Baum's characters.

While it's easy to see Gage's imprint on Baum's fearless heroine (who might have been named after a deceased niece of Baum's, Dorothy Gage), readers can also see her in the nontraditional gender roles that Baum created for any number of his characters. This is discussed, sometimes sub-textually and often with a connection to the LGBTQ community, in Katharine Kittredge's essay on the Scarecrow, my essays on the Tin Woodman and the Winged Monkeys, Dee Michel and James Satter's essay on the Cowardly Lion, and Walter Squire's essay on Glinda. It is also played with, specifically as a contrast to the Angel of the House and other domestic female stereotypes, in Mary Lenard's and Shannon Murphy's essays on Ozma and Jinjur. Of course, Baum could also have been playing with any number of things when he created nontraditional gender roles for his characters. As J.L. Bell notes, Baum often liked to do something of a bait and switch with his adjectives. For example, characters Baum described as smart or clever, like Button Bright, are usually anything but smart. Baum's words are not always meant to be taken as they are defined in the dictionary.

There's something uniquely American about sub-textually teaching children to question what is being told to them by a seemingly reliable narrator. Of course, this is not the only American trait Baum worked into his novels. J.L. Bell, Paige Gray, Mary Lenard, and I all make connections between American people, politics, and literature from Baum's time within their essays.

Scarecrow at a typewriter (John R. Neill illustration from *The Scarecrow of Oz* [1915]).

While I've probably made these essays seem quite homogeneous, they are anything but!

A master of children's literature and myth, Mark I. West offers "Dorothy and the Heroine's Quest," which looks at how Baum's *Wonderful Wizard of Oz* sends Dorothy on a hero's journey very much in line with Joseph Campbell's monomyth, while any number of Oz adaptations do not offer her the same agency.

Katharine Kittredge, a professor of English at Ithaca College, offers "But First, There Was a Scarecrow…," which examines how the Scarecrow changes from a divine fool who is active within his own creation and evolution to something darker and far more dystopian as Oz evolves and modernizes from a children's text to something more adult.

My "Heart Over Head: Evolving Views on Male Emotional Intelligence and the Tin Woodman" examines Baum's Tin Woodman, as well as several modern adaptations of the character, through the lens of emotional intelligence in order to examine what readers can learn about men and emotions within our culture.

Dee Michel, author of *Friends of Dorothy*, and James Satter offer "The Proto-Sissy, the Sissy, and Macho Men: The Cowardly Lion in *The Wonderful Wizard of Oz*, the MGM *The Wizard of Oz*, and Dark Oz Stories," which looks at how Baum broke gender traditions with his Lion in ways that still feel relevant. It is worth noting that, while the authors' use of the term "sissy" might not seem politically correct to modern readers, it is both true to the use of the word in Baum's original text and to the primary author (Michel), who has used this term within his writings before (including a *Baum Bugle* article and his book *Friends of Dorothy*). The essay presented here is a continuation of past work that reflects years of scholarship rather than a correctness limited to one period of time.

Author and historian J.L. Bell's "A Good Man but a Bad Wizard? The Shifting Moral Character of the Wizard of Oz" not only questions the Wizard's goodness but also explores the connection between Baum's Wizard and P.T. Barnum and how subsequent adaptations do not share many of these connections.

Robert B. Luehrs brings his 46 years of teaching European intellectual history and the history of early modern Europe to "Witches, Wicked and Otherwise." This essay offers an in-depth look at the history of witchcraft, what Baum borrowed, and how subsequent adaptations distance themselves from Baum's vision.

I also offer a new take on past scholarly interpretations of Baum's Winged Monkeys in "Witch's Familiars or Winged Warriors? Liberating the Winged Monkeys," which traces how scholars have linked Baum's Monkeys to America's indigenous people, what has been left out of that reading, and what readers learn when they expand to adaptations of the Winged Monkeys.

Walter Squire, director of film studies at Marshall University, offers a fascinating compliment to Dee's gender observations in "Glinda and Gender Performativity," which explores how different Oz texts present Glinda's idealized femininity, including one text where Glinda is a man.

Mary Lenard, composition director for the Department of Literatures and Languages at the University of Wisconsin, takes a different approach to Baum's gender politics in "Ozma, Sorceresses and Suffrage: Women, Power, and Politics in L. Frank Baum's Land of Oz," which looks at the influence of L. Frank Baum's mother-in-law, Matilda Gage, on Oz's rightful ruler.

Paige Gray, professor of writing and liberal arts at Savannah College of Art and Design, explores American-ness in "A Living Thing: The Very American Invention of Jack Pumpkinhead," connecting Baum's pumpkin character to Nathaniel Hawthorne's "Feathertop" while exploring what this means for adaptations like Disney's *Return to Oz*.

Shannon Murphy's "Trading Knitting Needles for Pistols: The Feminist, Violent, and Sexual Evolution of General Jinjur" returns readers to Gage and her influence on Baum, while noting how Baum broke gender traditions with his women in ways that often feel more modern than even the most modern of adaptations.

Angelica Shirley Carpenter, a children's author and a past president of the International Wizard of Oz Club, offers a look at Baum's most-used villain in "The Nome King." While working on this essay, Angelica noted that many of the Nome adaptations get quite dark, and she prefers hers "sunny side up."

Gita Dorothy Morena, great-granddaughter of L. Frank Baum, offers not only an exploration of Baum's Patchwork Girl, but also an intimate look at some Baum family history in "Piecing Together the Patchwork Girl of Oz."

It is an honor and a privilege to bring these esteemed authors, and this collection of their essays, together. In tribute to that honor, this collection is being produced with the intention that all royalties from the sale of this book should go to the International Wizard of Oz Club in order to not only raise awareness about the club but also to encourage future academics to engage with the works of L. Frank Baum. I greatly appreciate the reader's contribution to this goal. Please, do not read passively. Find a way to make these characters, and the magic of Oz, your own.

Dorothy and the Heroine's Quest

Mark I. West

With the publication of *The Wonderful Wizard of Oz* in 1900, L. Frank Baum introduced a new type of heroine to American children's literature.[1] Throughout the nineteenth century, American children's books tended to divide along gender lines. Books for boy readers usually featured male characters who had far-away adventures, while books for girls focused on female characters who usually kept close to home. Often referred to as domestic fiction, girls' stories from this period tended to emphasize family life, but Baum broke with this tradition when he created Dorothy Gale. In a time when American children's authors seldom allowed their girl characters to venture away from home, let alone go off on adventures, Baum sent Dorothy on a bona fide quest. The truly innovative nature of Baum's portrayal of Dorothy becomes even more apparent when Baum's Dorothy is contrasted with the portrayals of Dorothy in some of the more famous retellings of her adventures. Baum's Dorothy has the traits of a questing heroine, but the same cannot be said of the more recent versions of the character.

Dorothy is one of the first girl characters in American children's literature to experience the type of heroic quest that Joseph Campbell analyzed in *The Hero with a Thousand Faces*, his 1948 landmark study of the questing hero in world mythologies. In this book, Campbell uses the term *monomyth* when referring to the narrative pattern often associated with quest stories. As outlined in Campbell's book, heroic quests that conform to the monomyth share the following narrative structure: a hero ventures forth from the world of common day into a region of supernatural wonder; fabulous forces are there encountered and a decisive victory is won; the hero comes back from this mysterious adventure with the power to bestow boons on his fellow man (Campbell 30).

The heroes in most of the narratives covered in Campbell's book are male, a point that Maria Tatar criticizes in her 2021 study titled *The Heroine with 1,001 Faces*. However, as Christine Mains argues in an article dealing with the female hero's quest, "it is certainly possible to use Campbell's monomyth as a critical framework for analyzing the quest of the female hero of fantasy" (Mains 23–35). Mains applies Campbell's framework to Patricia McKillip's fantasy fiction, but Campbell's concept of the monomyth can also be applied to Dorothy's adventures in Oz.

Campbell argues that an air of mystery often surrounds the origins of the archetypal hero. There are often questions relating to the identity of the hero's parents or the exact circumstances of the hero's birth. As Campbell explains, the hero typically experiences a difficult childhood: "The child of destiny has to face a long period of obscurity. This is a time of extreme danger, impediment, or disgrace. He is thrown inwards to his own depths or outward to the unknown; either way, what he touches is a darkness unexplored" (326).

Although not much information is provided about Dorothy's origins in the beginning of *The Wonderful Wizard of Oz*, the information that Baum does provide conforms to Campbell's observations about the birth and childhood of the archetypal questing hero. Baum makes it clear that Dorothy is an orphan, but he leaves unanswered all questions about Dorothy's parents or what happened to Dorothy before she began living with her uncle and aunt on their Kansas farm. Thus, there is a sense of mystery surrounding Dorothy's origins. Also, like Campbell's archetypal hero, Dorothy grows up in obscurity and experiences poverty and hardship.

For the questing hero, the period of obscurity is followed by what Campbell refers to as the "Call to Adventure." This call marks the beginning of the hero's quest:

> This first stage of the mythological journey ... signifies that destiny has summoned the hero and transferred his spiritual center of gravity from within the pale of his society to a zone unknown. This fateful region of both treasure and danger may be variously represented…, but it is always a place of strangely fluid and polymorphous beings, unimaginable torments, superhuman deeds, and impossible delight [58].

As Campbell explains, the call to adventure can come in a myriad of ways, and the hero's response to the call can vary widely. In some cases the hero makes a conscious decision to answer the call and deliberately embarks on the quest, but in other cases the hero may be simply "carried or sent abroad by some benign or malignant agent" (58).

In Dorothy's case, her call to adventure comes upon the winds of a storm. Early in the story, a cyclone descends upon the farm where Dorothy lives. She has the option of going down into the cellar before the cyclone hits the house, but decides not to seek safety until she rescues her dog Toto. She is in the process of taking Toto to the cellar when the cyclone tears the house off its foundation and sends it hurtling toward Oz. By risking her life in order to save Toto, Dorothy shows that she possesses the makings of a hero. As a result of her supernatural encounter with the cyclone, Dorothy leaves her common-day world and enters, what is for her, a completely unknown zone—the Land of Oz.

Campbell argues that in most heroic quest stories, the hero receives supernatural aid shortly after answering the call to adventure. As Campbell states, "the first encounter of the hero journey is with a protective figure who provides the adventurer with amulets against the dragon forces he is about to pass" (69). Usually, but not always, this protective figure is a female, and this figure represents a "benign, protecting power of destiny" (71).

Dorothy encounters such a protective figure shortly after she leaves the house and meets the Munchkins. A small, elderly woman approaches Dorothy and introduces herself as the Witch of the North. She presents to Dorothy the silver shoes that the Wicked Witch of the East had been wearing when she was killed by Dorothy's house landing on top of her. In addition to providing Dorothy with these magical shoes, the kind woman kisses Dorothy's forehead leaving a "round, shining mark" (Baum 27). As the story progresses, it becomes clear that this kiss carries protective powers. The Witch of the North also initiates the beginning of Dorothy's quest when she tells Dorothy, "You must go to the City of Emeralds" (27).

According to Campbell, after the questing hero receives aid from the protective figure, it is time for the hero to go "forward in his adventure" and cross the threshold

Dorothy saves Toto from falling out of the house and into the tornado (W.W. Denslow illustration from *The Wonderful Wizard of Oz* [1960 edition]).

beyond which is "darkness, the unknown, and danger" (77). As Campbell sees it, this point in the journey serves as the first real test for the hero and often functions as a point of no return in terms of the hero's quest.

Dorothy crosses her first threshold when she leaves the comparative safety of the Munchkins' farmlands. At this point in the story, the Scarecrow has already joined her on her quest, and together they follow the yellow brick road into a countryside that becomes increasingly desolate:

> There were no fences at all by the road side now, and the land was rough and untilled. Towards evening they came to a great forest, where the trees grew so big and close together that their branches met over the road of yellow brick. It was almost dark under the trees, for the branches shut out the daylight; but the travelers did not stop, and went on into the forest [48].

At the moment that Dorothy enters the forest, she fully commits to pursing her quest despite the sense of foreboding associated with this forest. For Dorothy, the decision to cross the forest's threshold amounts to a test of her courage and determination, and she clearly passes this test.

In many heroic quest stories, Campbell argues, the crossing of this first threshold is often followed by an event in which the hero has a brush with death and then is transformed or, in a metaphorical sense, reborn. In Campbell's words, "the hero ... is swallowed into the unknown, and would appear to have died." Campbell equates this experience to being inside the "belly of the whale" (90). By surviving this brush with death, the hero is better prepared to continue the quest without being overly daunted by the challenges that such quests always involve.

Dorothy has her brush with death shortly before she reaches the gates of the Emerald City. Dorothy, the Scarecrow, the Tin Woodman, and the Cowardly Lion come across a large "meadow of poppies" (93), and Dorothy is drawn to the flowers' beauty. However, she does not know that the flowers' scent is deadly. After the flowers put Dorothy to sleep, her companions become alarmed. The Lion is the first to realize that Dorothy's life is in jeopardy. He tells the others, "If we leave her here she will die. The smell of the flowers is killing us all" (94). By working together (and with a little help from the Queen of the Field Mice), they succeed in escaping the deadly poppies. Once Dorothy regains consciousness, she and her helpers are ready to meet the Wizard of Oz and face the difficult challenges that await them on the next stage of Dorothy's quest.

The next stage in the heroic quest is what Campbell calls "the road of trials." During this part of the adventure, the hero "must survive a succession of trials." As Campbell points out, this is a "favorite phase of the myth-adventure," and "it has produced a world literature of miraculous tests and ordeals" (97). For the successful hero, this stage culminates in a decisive victory over a formidable adversary.

For Dorothy, this stage of her quest begins shortly after she has her audience with the Wizard of Oz and asks him to send her back to Kansas. He tells her that before he will grant her wish, she must first "kill the Wicked Witch of the West" (128). She then assembles her helpers and sets out to defeat the Witch. She encounters a series of violent trials along the way, and as a result ends up becoming isolated from her companions. She ultimately has to face the Witch alone. The Witch constantly tries to gain possession of Dorothy's magical shoes. Dorothy, however, refuses to comply with the Witch's demands. At one point, the Witch manages to snatch one of the shoes, and this causes

Dorothy to rebel. She picks up a bucket of water and defiantly throws it at her captor, causing the Witch to melt and die. Dorothy then rescues her companions and together they return to the Emerald City.

As Baum makes clear, Dorothy's victory over the Witch is a key turning point in the story. Not only does she have more confidence after this event, but she also becomes a more forceful leader. This change is evident when she meets the Wizard for the second time. Rather than being intimidated by him as she had been during their first exchange, she now relates to him from a position of power. She demands of the Wizard, "You must keep your promises to us!" (183). In so doing she makes it clear that she is no longer "Dorothy, the Small and Meek" (127).

Campbell maintains that once the hero has achieved a final and decisive victory there is still one more step that many questing heroes must take before concluding their quest—a step he calls "the meeting with the Goddess." This meeting, he writes, is the "ultimate adventure," and it can only take place after "all the barriers and ogres have been overcome." Campbell states that when the adventurer is a male, this meeting with the Goddess results in a "mystical marriage" (109). However, he then goes on to argue that when the adventurer is a "maid," this meeting with the goddess can result in the adventurer finding a sense of "peace" in terms of her goals and desires (119).

Dorothy's meeting with the Goddess comes near the end of the book after she arrives in the country of the Quadlings. Dorothy requests an audience with the Good Witch Glinda, who rules over Quadling Country. One of Glinda's soldiers shows Dorothy "into a big room where the Witch Glinda sat upon a throne of rubies" (253). Dorothy tells Glinda about all of her adventures in Oz and then concludes by saying, "My greatest wish now is to get back to Kansas, for Aunt Em will surely think something dreadful has happened to me" (254). Glinda responds by informing Dorothy that the magical shoes that Dorothy has been wearing can take her back to Kansas. Glinda, however, also helps Dorothy resolve her lingering concerns related to the fates of her three famous traveling companions. It is only after these three characters are situated in their new homes with new roles that Dorothy is ready to click her heels and return to Kansas. Glinda not only provides Dorothy with the wherewithal to return to Kansas, but she does so in a way that is consistent with Dorothy's ongoing concern with the welfare of others. Dorothy returns to Kansas feeling at peace with her adventures in Oz and fully prepared for her return to Kansas.

For Campbell, the hero's return to the normative world is a crucial part of the heroic quest, but he notes that there is great variation in the details of the return. One of the longer chapters in *The Hero with a Thousand Faces* is titled "Return," and in this chapter Campbell discusses some of the more common variations of this aspect of the heroic quest story. In some cases the hero returns willingly and readily assumes the responsibilities of leadership, but in other cases, the hero is brought back to the normative world against his or her wishes.

Although the hero returns with new wisdom, this wisdom is not always recognized. The returning hero may eventually come to be seen as a sage or a saint, but this development may not occur the instant the hero returns. Campbell explains that in some tales the hero becomes a "master of two worlds." In such cases, the hero has the "freedom to pass back and forth across the world division" (229). Even though the details of the hero's return may vary widely, there is some common ground. The hero returns as a transformed and wiser person for having experienced the quest. The hero returns with the "power to bestow boons" (30) even if he or she often refrains from using this power. Finally, the hero's relationship with the people of the normative world is somehow different once the hero returns from the quest.

In Baum's *The Wonderful Wizard of Oz*, Dorothy's return to Kansas marks the end of the story, so it is difficult to apply Campbell's framework to this part of Dorothy's quest. Nonetheless, Baum went on to include Dorothy in later Oz books, and the role that Dorothy plays in these books suggests that Dorothy is in fact transformed by her initial adventures in Oz. In many ways, Dorothy is like the heroes describe by Campbell who become masters of two worlds. She repeatedly makes the transition between the normative world and the Land of Oz. In fact, in *Ozma of Oz*, Dorothy is recognized as one of the leaders of Oz and is crowned a princess. It is also clear that Dorothy has the power to bestow boons both in Oz and in the normative world. For example, in the *Emerald City of Oz*, Dorothy rescues her Uncle Henry and Aunt Em from financial disaster and moves them to a new home in Oz. Thus, Baum's Dorothy can be seen as fulfilling all of the criteria that Campbell associates with the archetype of the questing hero.

Since Dorothy made her public debut in 1900, her character has appeared in subsequent Oz stories created by people other than Baum. Some of the most notable examples include the MGM film *The Wizard of Oz* (1939), the Universal Pictures film *The Wiz* (1978), Gregory Maguire's novel *Wicked: The Life and Times of the Wicked Witch of the West* (1995), and the stage musical *Wicked* (2003), which is partially based on Maguire's novel. Dorothy's portrayal in these Oz tales varies considerably from Baum's version of Dorothy, and in each case her stature as a questing heroine is diminished.

The Dorothy in the MGM film is introduced in an elaborate frame story created by the scriptwriters. This frame story cleverly foreshadows several aspects of Dorothy's adventures in Oz, but it also serves to undermine Dorothy's heroic potential. The film introduces three farmhands who are later transformed into the Scarecrow, the Tin Woodman, and the Cowardly Lion. The farmhands are fully grown adults, and they are protective of Dorothy. This pattern is established in the opening scenes of the movie, and naturally the pattern persists when Dorothy meets the somewhat altered versions of these characters in Oz.

In both Baum's book and the MGM film, a cyclone transports Dorothy and Toto to Oz, but the film version of Dorothy does nothing that demonstrates heroic potential before the cyclone hits. In the movie, Dorothy is returning home, after having briefly run away, when the cyclone arrives. A piece of flying debris strikes her on the head and knocks her unconscious. She then dreams about being swept off to Oz. In this version, Dorothy is not risking her life to save Toto; she is simply in the wrong place at the wrong time. Moreover, her trip to Oz does not seem like the beginning of a quest because it is reduced to being a dream.

From the point when Dorothy's house lands on top of the Witch of the East to the point when Dorothy and her three companions enter the Emerald City, the film and the book are similar in terms of the role that Dorothy plays, but the film version deviates significantly from the book at the point when Dorothy meets the Wizard of Oz and asks to be sent back to Kansas. Unlike in the book, in which Dorothy goes alone to see the Wizard who then sends her on a quest to "kill the Wicked Witch of the West," in the film Dorothy and her companions go together to meet the Wizard who then assigns them the group task of bringing him "the broomstick of the Witch of the West." Thus, in the film,

Dorothy is not actually required to kill the Witch, nor is the responsibility of defeating the Witch assigned primarily to her. Although this version is a bit less daunting, it lessens the likelihood that Dorothy will emerge from the mission as a hero.

In the film, once Dorothy and her companions set out to find the Wicked Witch of the West, the girl is reduced to being a stereotypical damsel in distress. Shortly after they leave the Emerald City, Dorothy is separated from her companions. She and Toto are captured and brought to the Witch, who grabs Toto and threatens to drown him unless Dorothy gives her the magic slippers. Dorothy readily agrees to the deal, but when the Witch tries to take off the slippers, she receives a powerful shock. The Witch then says that the only way she can get the slippers is by killing Dorothy first, and she starts making plans to do so. At this point, Toto escapes and runs into the woods, where he finds the Scarecrow, the Tin Woodman, and the Cowardly Lion. These characters then set out to rescue Dorothy. Eventually they find Dorothy locked up in a little room in the castle. They break her out of the room and are in the process of sneaking out of the castle when the Witch discovers them. The Witch vows to destroy all of them one by one, starting with the Scarecrow. She sets the Scarecrow on fire, but Dorothy puts out the fire by pouring a conveniently placed bucket of water on the Scarecrow. Some of the water, however, splashes onto the Witch, and the Witch then melts. In other words, the film Dorothy never confronts the Witch. Although she ends up killing the Witch, it is by accident. Thus, while Baum's Dorothy emerges from her confrontation with the Witch as a victor, Dorothy in the film continues to see herself as a fairly helpless girl.

The conclusion of the film underscores Dorothy's non-heroic status. As soon as the Witch is pronounced dead and Dorothy is given the Witch's broomstick, the film jumps to the scene in which Dorothy and her companions present the broomstick to the Wizard. They soon learn that the Wizard is a humbug, and Dorothy is about to give up hope of returning to Kansas when Glinda suddenly appears. Glinda tells Dorothy that she had "always had the power to go back to Kansas," but she could not use this power until she learned a certain lesson. Dorothy is then asked what she has learned from her experiences in Oz, and Dorothy answers, "I think that it wasn't just enough just to want to see Uncle Henry and Auntie Em. It's that if I ever go looking for my heart's desire again, I won't look any further than my own backyard." Glinda nods approvingly and instructs Dorothy to click her heels together and thinks to herself, "There's no place like home." Dorothy then wakes up from her dream. The movie concludes with Dorothy exclaiming, "I'm not going to leave here ever, ever again, because I love you! And, oh, Auntie Em, there's no place like home!" Although poignant in its own way, this statement is hardly the speech of a heroine who has returned victorious from a life-changing experience.

When Campbell's framework is applied to Dorothy's adventures as portrayed in the MGM film, it is clear that her story cannot be seen as a true heroic quest. Because Dorothy's journey to Oz is presented as a dream, she really does not experience a sense of being called to adventure. Once she arrives in Oz, she survives the road of trials that Campbell associates with heroic quests, but these trials do not make her much stronger or more independent. Most importantly, she never has a decisive victory over a powerful adversary. As a consequence, she never becomes a leader or achieves a sense of self-reliance. What she carries away from her experiences in Oz is a sense of being chastened for having run away and a determination not to go on any more adventures.

Dorothy in the MGM film is a less forceful character than Baum's Dorothy, but the MGM Dorothy certainly has more gumption than the Dorothy character in the film *The*

Wiz. This Dorothy is a twenty-four-year-old kindergarten teacher who is so frightened and introverted that she cannot live on her own or even venture more than a few blocks away from the Harlem apartment where she resides with her uncle and aunt. After a Thanksgiving dinner, she gets lost in a snowstorm and is transported to an urban and rather seedy version of Oz. As Sydney Duncan points out in an article published in *Studies in Popular Culture*, this version of Dorothy comes across as a weak character from the beginning of the movie to the end:

> Dorothy is timid, weepy, and spends much of the movie shrieking in terror…. As a matter of fact, this Dorothy shows no aggression whatsoever; her dousing of the Wicked Witch of the West comes only at the Scarecrow's urging. She returns home seemingly having gained nothing in the way of confidence or sophistication…. This lost, needy adult who cannot cope with a world she does not understand stands in dramatic contrast to Baum's vital and vigorous child-hero [Duncan 60].

Dorothy is a minor character in Gregory Maguire's *Wicked: The Life and Times of the Wicked Witch of the West*, but she is a stronger character than Dorothy from *The Wiz*. Maguire's focus, of course, is on the Wicked Witch of the West, who is named Elphaba in this novel, but Maguire includes Dorothy in the opening scene of the book as well as in the book's conclusion. Maguire's Dorothy is a levelheaded and kind-hearted girl who finds herself caught up in events that she does not understand. However, because Maguire portrays Elphaba as a sympathetic character whose idealism is misunderstood, Dorothy's encounter with the Witch at the end of the novel is more tragic than heroic. The novel closes with Elphaba having something of a psychotic breakdown and with Dorothy trying to save her. Although Dorothy ends up causing the Witch's death, this scene cannot be described as a decisive victory for Dorothy. She emerges from this experience "more stunned than ever" (Maguire 405). Although Maguire does not elaborate on what happens to Dorothy after she returns to the Emerald City, he gives the impression that she will be scarred by her experiences in Oz. In fact, just before her final encounter with Elphaba, Dorothy screams, "Oh, will this nightmare never end" (402).

Dorothy's role in the musical *Wicked* is even smaller than her role in Maguire's novel. She is referred to several times in the concluding scenes of the musical, but she does not make her appearance until the end of the play, and even then, the audience sees her only as a silhouette. Unlike Maguire's Dorothy, the Dorothy in the musical is caught up in a hysterical mop scene. The crowd, with Dorothy in tow, storms Elphaba's castle, chanting, "Kill her! Kill the Witch!" Although it appears that Dorothy kills the Witch by dousing her in water, it is revealed at the very end of the play that Elphaba, with the help of her friend Glinda, has escaped unharmed. Thus, in the musical, Dorothy is not much more than a shadow puppet. She is controlled by the mob and manipulated by Elphaba and Glinda. She is reduced to a powerless figure. There is nothing heroic about her.

Of these various portrayals of Dorothy, only Baum's Dorothy can be described as a questing heroine. None of the other versions of Dorothy comes close to matching the archetypal hero described by Campbell. Moreover, of these different depictions of Dorothy, only Baum's version presents Dorothy as a powerful female. In creating Dorothy, Baum knowingly went against prevailing notions of femininity. Unlike many men of his period, Baum disagreed with the limitations society placed on females. He came to this position in part because of his close associations with the women's suffrage movement. His mother-in-law, Matilda Joslyn Gage, was one of the era's leading feminists. She lived with Baum for a number of years and encouraged him to question societal assumptions about gender roles (Carpenter 212).

This questioning spirit can be seen in many of Baum's books for children. In *The Wonderful Wizard of Oz*, he introduced a strong female protagonist. In some of his other children's books, he explored such topics as androgyny and matriarchal societies. He even wrote a number of books under various female pseudonyms, such as Edith Van Dyne and Laura Bancroft. In other words, Baum's decision to send Dorothy on a quest was not an isolated experiment but was instead an outgrowth of his questioning attitude toward societal gender roles. Like some other fantasy authors, Baum used his fiction to explore alternatives to the status quo. By portraying Dorothy as a questing heroine, he gave his readers a chance to imagine a world in which females are as empowered as their male counterparts and in which girls' faces are included among the thousand faces of the world's great heroes.

NOTE

1. This essay is a revision of my 2010 publication "Dorothy and the Heroine's Quest."

WORKS CITED

Baum, L. Frank. *The Wonderful Wizard of Oz*. George M. Hill, 1900.
Campbell, Joseph. *The Hero with a Thousand Faces*. Princeton University Press, 1968.
Carpenter, Angelica Shirley. *Born Criminal: Matilda Joslyn Gage, Radical Suffragist*. South Dakota Historical Society Press, 2018.
Duncan, Sydney. "Lost Girl: Diminishing Dorothy of Oz." *Studies in Popular Culture* 31.1 (2008): 55–67.
Maguire, Gregory. *Wicked: The Life and Times of the Wicked Witch of the West*. HarperCollins, 1995.
Mains, Christine. "Having It All: The Female Hero's Quest for Love and Power in Patricia McKillip's Riddle-Master Trilogy." *Extrapolation* 46.1 (2005): 23–35.
Tatar, Maria. *The Heroine with 1,001 Faces*. Liveright, 2021.

But First, There Was a Scarecrow…

KATHARINE KITTREDGE

Oz abounds with creatures whom we now recognize as "non-human persons" who gained life through a variety of processes ranging from wind-up mechanisms to magic dust. But before any of the others, there was the Scarecrow. In the early chapters of L. Frank Baum's *The Wonderful Wizard of Oz*, the Scarecrow gives us his origin story:

> I was only made the day before yesterday … when the farmer made my head, one of the first things he did was to paint my ears, so that I heard what was going on … he painted my right eye, and as soon as it was finished I found myself looking at him and at everything around me with a great deal of curiosity, for that was my first glimpse of the world [Baum vol. 1 28].

Although he is not an agent in his own creation, the Scarecrow is an active observer: "I had the fun of watching them make my body and my arms and legs; and when they fastened on my head, I felt very proud, for I thought I was just as good a man as anyone" (Baum vol. 1 29). What is more, he is an approving observer; like the God of Genesis, he looks upon his own creation and finds it good. The farmer who assembles the Scarecrow is presented as merely the mechanism that brings him into being, more conduit than creator. Although he may lack a brain, the Scarecrow already has a strong personality that manifests a positivity that will remain unwavering through many volumes produced over many decades.

When I think about the Scarecrow among the cavalcade of other created beings in the series, the question that comes most readily to my mind is "Why?" We see similar animated creatures—Jack Pumpkinhead and the Patchwork Girl—but both are brought to life through complicated magic. Every part of the Scarecrow achieves function as soon as it is given a humanoid shape or appearance. Is this a sign in the evolution of Oz? At the beginning, did Baum intend to populate his world with myriad objects-come-to-life, and simply find that such a landscape would be too cluttered to keep track of, let alone use as the setting for a story? These unexplained elements are part of the larger characteristic of the Oz books, identified by Perry Nodelman as part of Baum's "unliterary" "fecund and quick imagination," since he worked outside of any pre-existing "knowledge of literature and mythology" and with a verve that precluded careful craftsmanship (cited in Tuerk 9). In other words, it may not be productive to ask questions about Baum's larger schema or underlying philosophy, since it may not have existed. So we are left to piece together the nature of the Scarecrow in a fashion similar to his literary construction: used clothing, inexpert painting, and as much fresh straw as can be brought to hand.

Scarecrow in a cornfield (W.W. Denslow illustration from *The Wonderful Wizard of Oz* [1960 edition]).

It seems most likely that Baum created the Scarecrow before any of his other magical beings largely because it was a figure that he found personally compelling. Multiple sources testify to the power that the image of the scarecrow held for the young Baum. In the biography *To Please a Child*, we hear of how, as a child, Frank was fascinated by scarecrows, causing him to have a recurring nightmare "in which a scarecrow was chasing him. Happily, Frank always dashed away while the scarecrow waddled after him and finally collapsed into a pile of shapeless straw" (Baum and McFall 22). In a 1904 interview appearing in the *North American*, Baum says, "It was natural then, that my first character in this animated life series was the Scarecrow, on whom I have taken revenge for all the mystic feeling he once inspired" (quoted in Hearn 64). And, indeed, just nine chapters after bringing the Scarecrow to life, Baum subjects him to the fate of his dream nemesis when the Winged Monkeys "with their long fingers pulled all of the straw out of his clothes and head" (Baum vol. 1 104), carrying out the Witch's orders to "destroy" (Baum vol. 1 103) him.

As it turns out, the reports of the Scarecrow's destruction were exaggerated. Following the disposal of the Wicked Witch, his clothes are retrieved and "they were stuffed with nice clean straw; and behold! here was the Scarecrow, as good as ever, thanking them over and over again for saving him" (Baum vol. 1 114). In this iteration, it appears that the clothes take the place of a living being's corpus, while the straw contains all of the animating functions of internal organs. In spite of the crucial role played by the straw in his "life," the Scarecrow is almost cavalier in his willingness to be disassembled. He instructs the Tin Woodman to take the straw out of his body to hide Dorothy and the Lion from the attack of the Wicked Witch's bees, and once the straw is returned to his clothing "was as good as ever" (Baum vol. 1 101).

The Scarecrow's indifference to disassembly becomes even more pronounced after the Wizard gives him a separate head filled with "a measure of bran [...] a great many pins and needles [...] and stuffed the rest of the space with straw" (Baum vol. 1 138). Baum elaborates on the individual nature of the head in the next book, describing it as "a bag tied at the bottom" (Baum vol. 2 609). This means that his subsequent de-stuffing can be a source of humor, rather than a moment of peril, as when, in *The Marvelous Land of Oz*, the jackdaws bear away the straw that the Scarecrow has offered up to protect his companions, leaving him comically bemoaning that he is "ruined" and that he is glad to have "perished in so noble and unselfish a manner" (Baum vol. 1 340). In truth, the Scarecrow is easily reanimated with any available stuffing; in this case, he uses paper money stored by the Jackdaws in their nest. Although the other characters comment on his new composition, the Scarecrow himself dismisses their comments, reminding them that "my Brains are still composed of the same material. And these are the possessions that have always made me a person to be depended on in an emergency" (Baum vol. 2 342).

As the Scarecrow's identity becomes more based on the contents of his brain, rather than the physical elements that make up his body, we also see him take more control over the maintenance and (in some cases) reconstruction of his corporeal self. In book five, *The Road to Oz*, the Scarecrow travels back to Munchkin Land so that the "farmer who first made me" can repaint his face and restuff his body, leading him to declare, "Now I feel like myself again" (Baum vol. 2 352–353). By book six of the series, *The Emerald City of Oz*, the Scarecrow has created a life for himself which allows him to gain the status of his original creator, the farmer, as well as guarantee him the ability to maintain his body. He no longer lives as an adjunct to the ruler of the Emerald City, but has returned to an agrarian setting. The Tin Man reports that he "feels that he cannot be happy without a farm of his own, so Ozma gave him some land" (Baum vol. 2 598).

On his farm, the Scarecrow has many fields of corn but, perhaps most significantly, he also cultivates a field of oats, since he declares, "Oat-straw is, I have found, the best of all straws to re-stuff myself with when my interior gets musty or out of shape" (Baum vol. 2 609). He then goes on to describe how his servants touch up the paint on his face and "do the stuffing, under my direction," while his head remains intact (since it is), and so does his consciousness. The Scarecrow has evolved from watching a Munchkin farmer construct his body to *being* a farmer whose cornfields stretch in every direction and who employs servants to carry out his periodic reconstruction. He controls both the resources and means for his production.

In spite of his having taken complete control over his corporeal presence, the Scarecrow preserves the unique qualities that arose from his unusual creation. As he is described in *The Patchwork Girl of Oz,*

> The Scarecrow's face was very interesting, for it bore a comical and yet winning expression, although one eye was a bit larger than the other and the ears were not mates. The Munchkin farmer who had made the Scarecrow had neglected to sew him together with close stitches and therefore some of the straw with which he was stuffed tended to stick out between the seams [Baum vol. 3 134].

The Scarecrow, retired ruler of Oz, rich landowner, and master of a legion of servants has no reason to preserve the inadequacies of his initial construction. However, his unintimidating appearance, described as "comical yet winning," may ultimately be useful to him, since the Scarecrow has always been more interested in human connection than in power or competing in physical attractiveness. Later in this same chapter, the Scarecrow remarks that he is going to see an "old friend" Jinjur (the young woman who had led the army of girls who deposed him in book two) "who has promised to repaint my left ear. [...] Jinjur always fixes me when I get weather-worn" (Baum vol. 3 140). It isn't clear if Baum has simply forgotten the arrangements he detailed in the earlier books, or if he specifically wanted to make a show of how harmony reigns even among previous combatants.

Although the most traditional readings of the Scarecrow assume that he is "only a man stuffed with straw, an intellectual who only wants brains" (Beckwith 81), he is actually a consistently social being, who wants brains because "I do not want people to call me a fool" (Baum vol. 1 24), and he bewails the loneliness of his initial position in the field. The old crow urges him to find brains so that he will be "as good a man as any of them" (Baum vol. 1 30); in other words, the benefit of having brains is that they signal belonging. The Scarecrow's intense desire for connection and belonging are evident throughout the books, complementing the intense homosocial/likely homoerotic bond between him and the Tin Woodman which Tison Pugh has documented so persuasively (226–227). Others have focused on the Scarecrow's relationship with Dorothy, as when Osmond Beckwith remarks, "[Dorothy's] innocence is complemented and balanced by the innocence of the Scarecrow [an embodiment of Baum]." A love affair is indicated, and of course Dorothy does love the Scarecrow best of all, but after all he is only a man stuffed with straw (81). Beckwith sees the Scarecrow's lack of masculinity as the bar to their having a full sexual relationship (leaving aside Dorothy's status as a presexual, prepubescent, preadolescent). However, the larger factor is that, as Richard Tuerk has declared, the Oz books contain "the general precept that hints of explicit sexual attraction and activity do not enter Baum's fairyland" (Tuerk 197). In a world where sexual activity is missing, and friendship is the most valued of elements, the Scarecrow's loyalty and self-sacrifice make him the most beloved character.

The asexuality of the Scarecrow was emphasized to varying degrees in the trans-media embodiments of the character, partially through costuming, but also in the casting of androgynous-appearing actors. Fred Stone, the actor celebrated for his performance in the 1902 stage musical extravaganza "played the Scarecrow as a clown. He was madly active, constantly hanging from the scenery, turning somersaults, walking on his hands" (Mannix 5). The 1939 MGM film *The Wizard of Oz* gave us perhaps the most famous Scarecrow, Ray Bolger, who was described in his *New York Times* obituary as "five feet 10½ inches tall" and "so thin that in his solo performances in the spotlight he appeared much taller. His legs were so flexible he appeared to be disjointed—even disembodied—as he leapt into the air" (D19). Similarly, the 1978 film adaptation *The Wiz* featured a rail-thin teenaged Michael Jackson in a costume that made him more clown than sex symbol, especially in contrast to the nearly-nude and spectacularly muscled members of the dance corps gyrating around him. Physically, he could be said to resemble one of the next major stars to fill the role: Kermit the Frog, in the Muppets' *Wizard of Oz* released in 2005.

It is significant that the Muppets should cast Kermit as the Scarecrow given that he is the most universally beloved of the Muppets, and the one known for his gentle humor and tolerance. The Muppet's version of *The Wonderful Wizard of Oz* is, of all the recent film adaptations, the one that comes closest both to honoring the original text and to retaining the child-like wonder that Baum perpetuated in his early works. This may partially be due to the sunny but knowing personae of the Muppet creators and creations, but it can also be attributed to the fact that the primary audience for this film is the same as for Baum's work: children. Many of the twenty-first-century adaptations that are truest to Baum's work (and his initial vision of the Scarecrow) are for children; two of the best are the graphic novel versions of *The Wonderful Wizard of Oz* released by Marvel Comics and Puffin Books specifically for children. Eric Shanower's adaptation (with illustrations by Skottie Young) captures the whimsy of the original books. Working with a profusion of penny-candy colors and a constantly swirling perspective, the book features joyously goofy characters engaged in all of the familiar Oz adventures. The creators offer a Scarecrow that has some of the lankiness of the film actors who played the part topped by a large head that is touching in its asymmetry. In contrast, the manga-inspired adaptation by Michael Cavallero is a study in simplicity, with a jeans-and-sneakers-clad modern Dorothy and a floppy-bodied, minimally-featured Scarecrow rendered in black and white. Although it lacks the lushness of Shanower's edition, this version is painstakingly faithful to the original text and uses manga-developed tropes (especially the use of broken panels and enhanced action sequences) to bring additional drama to the story. The success of both of these very different texts—and their distribution by major child-oriented publishers—reminds us that there are new children born into the world every day, some of whom will still be imaginative and hopeful enough to delight in the creations of L. Frank Baum.

However, when we turn to the twenty-first-century texts that are intended for an older demographic, things take a significantly darker turn. One of the most widely studied adaptations is the Sci Fi Channel's 2007 "limited series" *Tin Man*. The story begins in twenty-first-century Kansas, where once again a young girl—"D.G. a twenty year-old part-time waitress and student—is whisked away to a magical land called 'The O.Z.'" (for "The Outer Zone") by means of a tornado. The O.Z. is a post–Baum world where the work done to establish a fairyland/Utopia in Baum's series has been undone. The hereditary rulers of the O.Z. have been corrupted when a wicked witch takes over the heir to the crown, the Princess Azkadellia, causing her to exile her royal parents and institute a cruel totalitarian rule over the O.Z. The witch/Azkadellia's ultimate goal is the destruction of the O.Z. through the corrupted use of the "Sunseeder" a device which was intended to bring enhanced agrarian riches to the land. D.G. is the lost younger princess, sent to Kansas for safe-keeping and now returned with the task of exorcizing the witch, reuniting her family and saving the O.Z.

Some of the most intelligent commentary on the series and its relationship to Baum's books has come from Kristen Noone who writes:

> Retelling *The Wizard of Oz* as a "SciFi" text, *Tin Man* already suggests its own hybrid nature: it is at once part of the fantasy tradition of its past, and yet stands in that science-fictional space of posited utopias, of gaps and hesitations, with a "sci-fi" name; it is also an adaptation, and thus shares an uneasy relationship with the text on which it is based. From the start, *Tin Man* creates a world of imaginary space that is not clearly one genre or another, but shifting, complex, and not precisely comfortable [95].

In this version of Oz, the part of the Scarecrow, called Glitch for most of the series, is once again played by an extremely slender man, the openly bisexual actor Alan Cumming who had most recently starred as a promiscuous gay man in the London revival of the antihomophobia-themed play *Bent*. Glitch looks and behaves in ways that are stereotypically coded as gay or gender queer. For example, when D.G. meets him in the Munchkin's cage/prison he is wearing visible make-up (eye shadow, mascara, brow pencil, and lipstick), and he speaks with a slight lisp, gesturing extensively with his hands and calling D.G. "doll" (Episode 1, 22:24) and "honey" (Episode 1, 22:55). He behaves in an effeminate fashion when faced with potential danger, brushing imaginary lint from the shoulders of the Tin Man's prison suit and giving a little shriek after breaking a bottle over an attacker's head. His hair is a mass of curls so matted that they appear almost like dreadlocks—a striking complement to his alabaster complexion. Glitch is contrasted with the hyper-masculine character Cain (the Tin Man character), whom he suggests needs therapy for his "issues with masculinity and what we call 'The Boy Scout Syndrome'" (Episode 2, 13:45–13:50). At one point they engage in pseudo-flirtation when, in the course of discussing attacking some opponents, Glitch asks Cain if he wants to "dance" (Episode 2, 23:18) and Cain replies "I'll lead, you follow" (Episode 2, 23:18–23:20) suggesting that in any intimate physical relationship he will be the "top" to Glitch's "bottom."[1]

At first, I felt confused by the extensive gay coding of the Scarecrow, but on reflection I believe that this is to prevent the possibility of D.G.'s developing a romantic relationship with him. Unlike Oz, the O.Z. is a place of very evident sexuality, with both male and female figures dressing in garb that approaches fetish ware, and female prostitutes highly visible in the grimy Central City that has replaced the capitol of Oz. It seems the only way that the creators of the series could prevent D.G., an attractive mature female, from having a sexual relationship with her male companions is by placing one of them in active mourning for his dead wife, making another a creature of a different species, and presenting the final character as a gay man. Within the limited series, there is no time for a romantic sub-plot, since all of the focus is on D.G.'s need to rediscover and rescue her biological family.

One of the first things we learn about Glitch is that part of his brain has been removed by Azkadellia's minions. Upon meeting him, D.G. remarks, "Your zipper is open" (Episode 1, 23:07–23:11), referring not to his fly, but to the large metal zipper running the length of his scalp. This potentially gaping hole is reminiscent of the visible stitching that Oz illustrators Denslow and Neill included in their depictions of the Scarecrow (through which straw was frequently visible), although their seams ran around the perimeter of his face, rather than bisecting the top of his head. In a similar vein, he wears a long, frayed coat with holes and threads sticking out (providing a sharp contrast to the slick leather clothing of most of the rest of the male cast), mimicking the Scarecrow's attire of discarded Munchkin clothing.

However, in other ways, Glitch's situation is a reversal of the arc of Baum's Scarecrow. The show slowly reveals that Glitch had been Ambrose—an inventor, a skilled martial artist, and the top advisor to the Queen of the O.Z. We are not shown the full range of inventions that Ambrose has produced, but the two that are featured are significant: (1) a device that records events and then projects them back as a looping holographic alternative reality and (2) the Sunseeder device that seeks to slow the movement of the O.Z.'s two suns so that the growing season is extended. The first invention aligns the Scarecrow with media creators like authors and filmmakers in his projection of a fictional mini-world within the larger fiction of the O.Z., although it is worth noting that his creation does not produce anything original, but rather simply repositions already-existing events. The second is more problematic because it shows the inventor usurping the Divine prerogative, since it was the God of Genesis who not only created Light, but decreed that there would be night and day. In seeking to disrupt the movement of the Sun, Ambrose joins the ranks of misguided men from Dr. Frankenstein to *Jurassic Park*'s John Hammond who transgress into the arena of the Divine, making scientific leaps with good intentions, but without the foresight to see how their creations could (inevitably) go wrong. Ambrose's holographic device becomes an instrument of torture and the Sunseeder is altered into a doomsday machine that will bring eternal darkness to the O.Z.—uses far different from Ambrose's initial conceptions of them, but logical uses for the mechanisms in the hands of those who mean harm to the O.Z. and its citizens. Ambrose "invents" by creating devices that disrupt/rearrange his world, thus making it vulnerable to corruption and destruction.

Although, in retrospect, Ambrose's creations proved nearly fatal to the O.Z., it should be noted that he does everything in his power to prevent them from being misapplied. Ambrose sacrifices his brain rather than tell the witch/Azkadellia the secret to the Sunseeder device. When he destroys the plans for the machine and refuses to reveal its mechanism, Azkadellia has half of his brain removed and then employs empaths to extract the information which will allow her to reconfigure it as a doomsday device. This operation reduces Ambrose to an inarticulate character called Glitch because his remaining brain is subject to malfunction, sending him into speech loops or discontinued thoughts and making him incapable of articulate expression. His lack of personal knowledge or history places him in a position similar to the newly-made Scarecrow who must establish human connections, and discover his nature and his identity, but for Glitch this requires him to gain access to a previous time, rather than embarking on a journey of adventure and self-discovery like his fictional predecessor.

In the final scene of the *Tin Man* series, Ambrose/Glitch is reunited with his lost brain (floating in a tank in Azkadellia's castle), and thus gains access to his previous identity and knowledge. However, the ending focuses on the destruction of the witch and the corrupted Sunseeder machine, celebrating the reunion of the royal family and the advent of their restoration as rulers of the O.Z. As Noone describes him, Glitch/Ambrose "thus occupies that shifting space, both human and monstrously changed from human, of the hybrid; he has helped to save the world, but he, and viewers, are left unsure of his place in it, as he cannot return to the place he once held" (99). Although this may be unsatisfying for the fans of *The Wonderful Wizard of Oz*, in which all three of Dorothy's companions ended as rulers of their own individualized kingdoms, readers of the Oz series know that it is in the Scarecrow's nature to move from one position to the next—scarecrow, king, advisor, farmer—caring more about the relationships that he makes than the rank that he holds. It is unclear how Ambrose will navigate his new position as a man with a divided brain, but it is to be hoped that, like his predecessor, he will learn how to take control of his unusual physical situation so that he will be able to make a place for himself in the world.

Another example of a "dark" Oz re-telling—and perhaps the most extensive re-visioning of the Scarecrow—can be found in Danielle Paige's 2014 Young Adult series known by its first book's title: *Dorothy Must Die*. The series follows the adventures of Amy Gumm, a twenty-first-century Kansan teenager whose trailer is whisked to Oz by a tornado. The world she finds is very different from the merry old land created by Baum. Dorothy Gale has become a powerful witch and has usurped the rightful ruler Ozma by mentally disabling her and reducing her to a child-like and incoherent state. Glinda the "good" witch enjoys enslaving and torturing the citizens of Oz, while strip-mining it for magic. As for Dorothy's companions, as Victoria Lynne Scholtz writes: "[they have] become twisted caricatures of themselves; after losing his cowardice, the Lion rules using fear; after receiving a brain, the Scarecrow's yearning for knowledge becomes a desire for omnipotence; after regaining a heart, the Tin Woodman becomes obsessed with earning Dorothy's love at any cost" (55–56). In the first two books of the series, Amy is tasked with undoing the work of *The Wonderful Wizard of Oz;* she must help the "wicked" witches regain their power, and confiscate the gifts of courage, heart, and brains from Dorothy's companions and then kill them as necessary precursors to destroying Dorothy and her evil empire.

The Scarecrow is presented with some vestiges of his traditional self and with additional infantilizing details. He is "a tall thin man dressed in a baby-blue-one-size-too-small suit. Beneath a small hat, bits of straw and yarn stuck out in every direction" (89). The real departure comes in the description of his face: "a skein of tightly pulled burlap with two unnervingly lifelike buttons sewn on in place of eyes. His lips were thin lines of embroidery stitched in pinkish-brown yarn underneath a painted red triangle for a nose" (89). The switch from painted features to those constructed of thread, buttons, and felt, subtly queers the Scarecrow by removing him from the purview of the male artist (the original Munchkin farmer) who constructed him as an outdoor "man" with an agrarian job to do and into a more feminine space. This new Scarecrow more closely resembles the Patchwork Girl of Baum's seventh Oz novel, crafted by the Magician's wife:

> Her eyes were two silver suspender-buttons ... [the wife] had cut a slit for the Patchwork Girl's mouth and sewn two rows of white pearls in it for teeth, using a strip of scarlet plush for a tongue ... one cheek was yellow, and the other red, her chin blue, her forehead purple, and the center, where her nose had been formed and padded, a bright yellow [Baum vol. 3 24].

Later, at a particularly revolting moment, Amy watches as the Scarecrow's "head lolled over to his shoulder and a little felt tongue I didn't even know he had dangled limply from his mouth" (268–269). The other, more repellent substitution is Paige's replacing the mix of vegetal and inorganic matter that the Wizard supplied for the

Scarecrow's brains with what is evidently a living mammalian brain.[2] Amy narrates: "I'd seen a monkey brain once in biology class. This was kind of like that, only pinker and goopier. The whole thing was suspended in red, gelatinous mush that I'd mistaken for blood" (268). This takes him out of the category of magically animated creature and places him in the more modern categories of transhuman or cyborg,[3] aligning him with the hybridity of the *Tin Man*'s reimagining of the character.

In the Oz books, the Scarecrow evolved from an interested observer of his creation into an active participant engineering his own maintenance and content. Through his adventures and repeated episodes of near dissolution, the Scarecrow comes to see the line between life and death as liminal for him, and potentially for other non-human persons. He alarms the mechanical man Tik-Tok by remarking, "Someday I'd like to take you apart and see how you are made." When Tik-Tok begs not to be disassembled, "for you could not put me together again, and my usefulness would be destroyed," the Scarecrow "kindly promised, 'I won't fool with your interior at all. For I am a poor mechanic and might mix you up'" (Baum vol. 1 465). The fact that the Scarecrow sees the potential destruction of another sentient being as a mechanical failure instead of a moral outrage is played for comedy in Baum's text, where the Scarecrow often plays the role of "the Divine Fool, a simpleton who makes good by his natural wits" (Hearn 69, n. 12), but the same disregard for the line between life and death and the sanctity of sentient life is the source of two sinister elements within Paige's narrative.

In *Dorothy Must Die*, the Scarecrow extends his self-care through the exploitation of other beings and goes beyond experimenting on himself to create new hybrid creatures to serve in the army that the Tin Woodman has created to enforce Dorothy's tyrannical rule. These beings include both human/machine hybrids like Melindra, the half-tin/half-human rebel girl, and humans who have been augmented with animal or machine parts. His activities resemble those of his literary predecessor, Dr. Frankenstein, and his creations, fueled by hatred for his violation, also seek to destroy him. Frankenstein made the mistake of creating a single, lonely being. Paige's Scarecrow errs in the opposite direction, maiming and reconstructing so many individuals that they become a force to marshal against him within the Anti-Dorothy resistance movement. He conducts his experiments/abominations in what Amy calls "The Scarecrow's House of Horrors," complete with "long metal tables set up with horrific instruments … a metal chair with restraints on the arms and legs" next to "a square, squat machine, with a bunch of circular dials and gauges on it."

> Along the wall was a huge shelf with big glass jars…. Many of them held what looked like brains floating in some kind of glowing green liquid … they were still alive … there were other body part, too, ears and hands and tiny little white wings. From baby [flying] monkeys? [354].

The motivating factor behind the Scarecrow's escalating violation of sentient life is his great fear of not being intelligent enough for the role he is expected to play in the maintenance of Dorothy's corrupt empire. Amy overhears him muttering to himself in despair as he struggles with a particularly complex experiment: "They will all laugh at me. Call me stupid." (343) it is implied that "they" will identify him for what he is: a created being with sham brains implanted by a bogus wizard.

The Scarecrow's fear of not being able to live up to the standards of high human intelligence also leads him to perform gruesome experiments on himself, unstitching the top of his head to reveal the brain beneath and then compelling a servant to inject his brain with a liquid he has distilled from multiple brains taken from humans and other intelligent beings. He claims this is "the price they [his victims] must pay to have the finest brain in all of Oz" (269). The Scarecrow has gone from being willing to give his life to preserve others to insisting that others give up their lives to preserve his reputation and privileged position. He is also violating the sacred mystery of his own creation—described but never explained throughout the series—by attempting to scientifically modify the knowledge that he gained through experience and study. The contempt shown for others' lives as well as his rejection of the knowledge he has gained through his own rich life makes this Scarecrow the adaptation that strays the furthest from Baum's own vision.

In an unprecedented, and mercifully underdeveloped subplot, it is also implied that this Scarecrow has some kind of sexually exploitative relationship, described as "creepy dalliances" (281) with a female servant. This seems partially included just to increase the "ick" factor of the character and to make us root for his downfall, but it is also symptomatic of the overtly sexual nature of much of this remaking of Oz. For example, Button Bright, the little lost boy of *The Road to Oz,* becomes the young man "Bright" described as "wiry but muscular at the same time ... wearing a pair of faded black skinny jeans with a loose tunic-like tank top that revealed his rail-thin physique. The best way to describe him was *pretty*" (*The Wicked* 186); he is the louche Royal Consort of Polychrome, whom Baum had presented as the pre-pubescent daughter of the Rainbow King. In what may be the most disturbing twist of all, the aged Wizard of Oz proposes to "marry" the mentally enfeebled Ozma; the wizard kisses her hand while lecherously intoning, "I can't wait to see what you blossom into" (*The Wicked* 288). Baum's original Dorothy was so young and innocent that even the word "virginal" seems too explicit to apply to her. Amy is a sexually aware twenty-first-century teenager whom Paige has involved in the tired Young Adult trope of love triangle with two hot boys: a beautifully muscled witch boy named Nox and an angsty green-eyed gardener named Pete (who is revealed to be gay in the second book). Pete and Nox largely fill the roles of Baum's Dorothy's travel companions, including educating her about the history of Oz and its current dangers. However, in this post–Katniss/Buffy retelling, Amy fights by the side of her companions, proving to be ultimately more lethal than either of them, and pausing mid-battle to enjoy a passionate kiss with Nox. Within this sexually charged hot house of implicit or impending YA sex, it is not surprising that Paige insists that even the Scarecrow must have a sexual inclination beyond the homosocial and companionate pleasures of his friendship with the Tin Man. It is not surprising, given her emphasis on his lack of respect for human life and autonomy, that his sexual tastes should run toward coercive and power-imbalanced exploitation.

There is little doubt that Danielle Paige knows her Oz lore, since much of her rewriting of the Scarecrow's character extends (or, one might say, "twists") characteristics that Baum had developed in the character over the course of numerous books. It is also significant that in his last scene the Scarecrow is, to some extent, returned to the character that Oz fans had come to love. In one of the final chapters, Amy comes upon him "lying on the steps [of the Emerald Palace] like a broken, discarded rag doll, his arms and legs splayed out in every direction.... [He] looked at me with his painted-on little eyes and gave a weak grimace" (272–273). His last act before Amy chokes the life out of him is to attempt to tell a joke. When he fails in his attempt to recall it, he is inconsolable: "I used to be very cleaver, you know! Everyone said so ... now look at me" (274). Even made into a monster of selfishness (and a worthy object of righteous violence), the Scarecrow remains a social being to the very end. The contrast between Paige's monstrous being and the original Scarecrow reminds us of one of the great and rare aspects of the world that Baum created: it is a place where power ennobles more often than it corrupts and where social anxiety and feelings of inadequacy bring out gentleness and kindness rather than a need to exploit and destroy those who are more vulnerable.

Although it is problematic to ascribe a master plan of character development to L. Frank Baum over the course of the Oz series, a close examination of the first non-human magical person in the series, the Scarecrow, shows that character gaining both self-knowledge and autonomy over the course of the series while still maintaining his essentially sociable and self-sacrificing nature. Subsequent retellings (primarily in the form of film versions from 1939 to 2006) have focused almost exclusively on the first book in the series, causing him to be presented as what Michael Patrick Hearn has described as a "Divine Fool, a simpleton," which facilitated his being used primarily for comic relief. Versions aimed at children largely preserve the magic of his spontaneous creation and subsequent joy in gaining mastery over himself and finding a place for himself in the world. In contrast, the various media adaptations aimed at an older audience, especially the Sci Fi channel's PG-rated limited series *Tin Man* and Danielle Paige's YA series *Dorothy Must Die*, transform his child-like wonder in the world and explorations of his own limitations into something much more problematic. Both texts feature dark, dystopic visions of Oz and present extensively reimagined versions of all the characters, including the Scarecrow. Although *Tin Man*'s Scarecrow figure retains his essentially positive nature, he also exhibits traits of queerness and hybridity that alienate him from the rest of the characters and make his place within the narrative and the imagined world problematic. This Scarecrow exercises the creativity that make him such a valuable part of Baum's world in ways that are scientifically positioned, but Creator-like in their scope. Instead of enhancing this created world, this character's creative energy threatens to literally destroy it. Paige's version of the Scarecrow also adds elements of hybridity to the character, and the author's choice to intensify a number of the Baum-created character's traits (his curiosity, liminal status as a living being, and sociability) to the point of pathology turn him into one of the most repellent antagonists in the text. This character also shows that creativity without respect for the limits of human life or the sanctity of living persons leads to the propagation of misery and will ultimately prove to be the character's undoing.

Considering these two texts together, one is led to conclude that today's media-saturated [young] adult audience is driven less by nostalgia for the simple messages of the original texts and more by a hunger for variety, embracing reimaginings that reflect the current pessimism about the state of the world, as well as an acknowledgment of the oppression and difficulties faced by those who are "othered," and the psychological effects that they experience from their "difference." The Scarecrow, a character that embodies much of Baum's creative verve and sense of humor is recast in these narratives as a threat to all forms of life, rather than as a miraculous and whimsical new form of life. This indicates that the world that Baum imagined in collaboration with his child audience at the beginning of the twentieth century, although it continues to be delightful to this generation's young and hopeful readers, also has been crafted as a character whose dark corners provide an area of exploration for older readers whose cynicism—earned or innate—makes them less suited for Baum's original messages.

NOTES

1. My reading is in contrast to Waterhouse-Watson's assertion that "the series is also heteronormative, as Azkadellia's sexual murders are exclusively heterosexual, and the only (implied) sexual relationships are between heterosexual couples who produce children, or the pimp de Milo, who travels with only female prostitutes" (182), although Waterhouse-Watson does affirm the queerness of Glitch's characterization.

2. There are some disparities in the final pages of the second volume; the Wizard produces "the Scarecrow's plush brains, which were glowing … blue" (286).

3. In her dissertation "Transfairytales: Transformation, Transgression, and Transhuman Studies in Twenty-first Century Fairy Tales" (Texas A&M; 2018), Victoria Lynne Scholz examines contemporary young adult literature, focusing on Marissa Meyer's *The Lunar Chronicles*, Danielle Paige's *Dorothy Must Die*, and Anna Sheehan's UniCorp series to consider their relationship to older source materials and the transhuman elements that have been incorporated into each text. For comments on Dorothy's companions, see especially 56–79.

WORKS CITED

Baum, Frank Joslyn, and Russell P. MacFall. *To Please a Child: A Biography of L. Frank Baum, Royal Historian of Oz*. Reilly & Lee Co., 1961.

Baum, L. Frank. *Oz: The Complete Collection*. Vols. 1–3. Alladin, 2013.

_____. *The Wizard of Oz: The Graphic Novel*. Adapted by Michael Cavallero. Puffin Graphics, 2005.

Beckwith, Osmond. "The Oddness of Oz." *Children's Literature* 5 (1976): 74–91.

Fowler, Glenn. "Ray Bolger, Scarecrow in 'Oz,' Dies." *New York Times* 16 January 1987, D1.

Hearn, Michael Patrick, ed. *The Annotated Wizard of Oz, Centennial Edition*. W.W. Norton, 2000.

Lumet, Sidney, dir. *The Wiz*. Universal Pictures and Motown Productions, 1978.

Mannix, Daniel P. "The Perfect Scarecrow, Part Two." *The Baum Bugle* (Autumn 1981): 2–11.

Noone, Kristin. "No Place Like the O.Z.: Heroes and Hybridity in Sci-Fi's *Tin Man*." *The Universe of Oz: Essays on Baum's Series and Its Progeny*, Kevin K. Durand and Mary K. Leigh, editors. McFarland, 2010. 94–106.

Paige, Danielle. *Dorothy Must Die*. HarperCollins, 2014.

_____. *The Wicked Will Rise*. HarperCollins, 2015.

Pugh, Tison. "'There lived in the Land of Oz two queerly made men': Queer Utopianism and Antisocial Eroticism in L. Frank Baum's Oz Series" *Marvels & Tales* 22, no. 2 (2008): 217–39.

Scholz, Victoria Lynne. *Transfairytales: Transformation, Transgression, and Transhuman Studies in Twenty-first Century Fairy Tales*. Texas A&M University, PhD dissertation, 2018.

Shanower, Eric. *The Wonderful Wizard of Oz*, Vols. 1–3. Adapted from the novel by L. Frank Baum. Marvel/Spotlight Books, 2014.

Thatcher, Kirk R., dir. *Muppets' Wizard of Oz*. Fox Television Studios, 2005.

Tuerk, Richard. *Oz in Perspective: Magic and Myth in the L. Frank Baum Books*. McFarland, 2007.

Willing, Nick, dir. *Tin Man*. RHI Entertainment and the Sci Fi Channel, 2007.

Heart Over Head

Evolving Views on Male Emotional Intelligence and the Tin Woodman

Dina Schiff Massachi

When L. Frank Baum created the Tin Woodman in 1900, he made a sensitive character who valued heart over head.[1] One hundred and twenty-three years and numerous adaptations later, is this still the Tin Woodman seen in American culture? Who is the modern Tin Man, and what does he reflect about American culture today? While it's easy to believe in society's forward progress, sometimes the metaphors hidden in our fairy tales reveal a different truth. When one focuses on a psychological principal, like emotional intelligence, and uses that lens to compare Baum's Tin Woodman to a far more modern Tin Man like the ones found in *Barnstormer in Oz* (1982), *Wicked* (1995), *The Muppets Wizard of Oz* (2005), *Tin Man* (2007), *Dorothy Must Die* (2014) and *Straight Outta Oz* (2016), a person can see how male emotional intelligence and expression, while embraced in some circles, is still limited in ways that existed more than a century ago. This also allows for another way to consider Baum as extremely forward thinking in regard to his views on gender.

Emotional intelligence was redefined in the psychological community in 1997 as "the ability to perceive accurately, appraise, and express emotion; the ability to access and/or generate feelings when they facilitate thought; the ability to understand emotion and emotional knowledge; and the ability to regulate emotions to promote emotional and intellectual growth" (Mayer and Salovey, 10). When discussing gender and emotional intelligence, things become tricky because stereotypes are intertwined with reality—women are sensitive, emotional, perhaps even hysterical (a word with a dark history, linked to the ancient Greek belief that the womb was the origin of all disease), while men are rational. Although this idea seems more ancient that Queen Lurline, the fairy queen who gave Oz its magic, there is some grounding in reality. Because of how men are typically socialized, psychologists have found that

> men […] avoid expressing their emotions. Male competitiveness, homophobia, avoiding vulnerability and openness, and the lack of appropriate role models have all been highlighted as obstacles that prevent men from expressing themselves emotionally. Boys therefore specialize in minimizing any emotions linked to vulnerability, guilt, fear and pain [Sánchez-Núñez, Fernández-Berrocal, Montañés, Latorre 460].

Baum's Tin Woodman, and all of the various characterizations of Tin Man post–Baum, is linked to emotion because of his "missing" heart. The Tin Woodman has been read

Shining Tin Woodman (W.W. Denslow illustration from *The Wonderful Wizard of Oz* [1960 edition]).

as emotional, homosexual, and, among other things, representational of a Civil War amputee—interpretations that practically beg for an examination of gender and emotional intelligence.

Baum's Dorothy meets the Tin Woodman in the fifth chapter of *The Wonderful Wizard of Oz*. Scarecrow is just commenting to Dorothy on how inconvenient flesh must be when the two stumble on a man made entirely of tin who has "been groaning for more than a year" (55) and has a "sad voice" (55). Within the first moments of introduction, Baum's Tin Woodman seems to be weak, sad and emotionally vulnerable—the opposite of traditional masculine stereotypes. Of course, anyone who knows about the author would not be surprised that a man who took on female pen names, and worked in the suffrage movement, had some rather nontraditional views on gender. In spite of the less masculine attributes the Tin Woodman is initially prescribed, he quickly proves both useful and capable of traditional male roles when using his axe to remove obstacles blocking the path of his companions. His backstory includes a tale of a fiancée left behind—his axe, enchanted by a wicked witch, caused him to self-mutilate until he was entirely made of tin, and thus heartless and unable to love. This backstory seems to support traditional male gender roles. Tin Woodman was to marry a "pretty Munchkin girl" (59) in a very heterosexual fashion, and his transformation "recalls underlying questions about what happens to the amputee Civil War veteran's sense of self once his body has been merged with prosthetic limbs" (Loncraine 176).

If the Tin Woodman's transformation reflects the experiences of a war veteran, it may make sense to read his weak, sad, and emotionally vulnerable state as symptoms of post-traumatic stress disorder (PTSD). However, it is worth noting a few things about a PTSD reading of the Tin Woodman. First, not every adaptation borrows the backstory that Baum created; without that backstory, the trauma often disappears. Second, and more important, PTSD is not a universal experience, but experienced in a way that might reflect the person's time, culture, and society. As Michelle Balaev notes in her article "Trends in Literary Trauma Theory," "the 'unspeakability' of trauma claimed by so many literary critics today can be understood less as an epistemological conundrum or neurobiological fact, but more as an outcome of cultural values and ideologies" (157). Like gender stereotypes, PTSD reflects cultural values and ideologies, so understanding the Tin Woodman through an emotional intelligence lens can complement a trauma reading. Finally, while one can speculate that Baum may have been reflecting the veteran experience of his day within his Woodman character, it is clear that Baum pushed against the gender stereotypes of his time. This is why it is not surprising that Baum does not keep his Tin Woodman on a traditional male continuum. Shortly after Baum offers a backstory with a heterosexual relationship and an axe that removes obstacles, he adds an interlude where the Tin Woodman cries "tears of sorrow and regret" (71) over a beetle that he steps on, changing his alignment from the male side of the binary to the emotionally intelligent, if "oversensitive," female side.

Baum's Tin Woodman seems to exist in a sort of androgynous, or simultaneously male and female, emotional intelligence. He is in touch with his feelings, and is relatively unafraid to cry (though he fears the consequences of those actions: rusting), but he is also able to set his emotions aside and kill any creatures that attack his friends. This deviance from gender standards seems revolutionary, but is unsurprising when one considers Baum's history with gender. Baum wrote his "Our Landlady" column for his Dakota newspaper as a female and published several books under the female pen names

Edith van Dyne and Laura Bancroft. Baum also created what can be read as the first transgender character in American children's literature in his second Oz novel—the character Ozma, the rightful ruler of Oz, who was born a girl, transformed into a boy and then transformed back into a girl. Baum continues to explore what androgynous emotional intelligence might look like as his novels evolve past *The Wonderful Wizard of Oz* and the Tin Woodman becomes even more emotionally complex.

In Baum's second novel, *The Marvelous Land of Oz*, the Tin Woodman describes his heart as "somewhat large and warmer than most people possess" (129). Now that he has obtained a heart, he is even more emotionally aware. This emotional awareness is especially important when placed in context with the Scarecrow's trajectory within this second Oz story. Scarecrow, left by the Wizard to rule the Emerald City in the first novel, finds himself usurped when General Jinjur and her all-female army capture and take over Oz. Ozma, the rightful (by birth) ruler of Oz, is eventually restored to the throne at the end of the novel. With this restoration comes the question "What is to become of the Scarecrow?" (286). Scarecrow explains, in a quote often highlighted for its homosocial intimacy, that he "shall return with his friend the Tin Woodman, [....] [They] have decided never to be parted in the future" (286). Baum did not create many romantic relationships in Oz, but he did create many loving friendships. In *The Utopia of Oz*, S.J. Sackett examines the Scarecrow and Tin Woodman and hypothesizes that Baum used them to unite "the intellect and the emotion[al] in a harmonious relationship" (287). Together this "queerly made" (Baum, *LWS*, 135) pair represent emotional intelligence.

While Baum likely meant queer as a synonym for strange or odd, again I must draw attention to the homosocial intimacy attributed to the Scarecrow/Tin Man pairing. Tison Pugh points out that "if any couple stages the beauty of a long-term romantic relationship in Oz, it is the Scarecrow and the Tin Woodman—for no male-female friendships receive as much detailed attention and unqualified praise throughout the series" (64). It is almost as if readers don't know how to equate the traditionally male realm of rational thought and the traditionally female realm of emotional thought depicted in a harmonious relationship that isn't sexualized.

Of course, it is also worth noting that Baum had very little interest in sexualizing harmonious Ozian relationships. Consider, for instance, *The Tin Woodman of Oz*—a novel in which the central quest is to find the Tin Woodman's lost Munchkin love, Nimmie Amee. Once the Tin Woodman and Captain Fyter, another fiancé of Nimmie Amee who was turned to tin, find the Munchkin woman, they learn she married Chopfyt, a man created from a mixture of the human parts that remained from the tin men's transformations. Nimmie Amee tells her tin suitors that "there are times when I have to chide [Chopfyt]" (244), but she will not marry either tin man because Chopfyt "is now trained to draw the water and carry in the wood and hoe the cabbages and weed the flower-beds and dust the furniture and perform many tasks of a like character. A new husband would have to be scolded—and gently chided—until he learns my ways" (245). Here Baum depicts marriage, the pinnacle of a sexualized relationship depicted as harmonious, as a form of subjugation and imprisonment. While the Tin Woodman can be read as homosexual, this reading likely speaks more to our culture's views on an emotionally intelligent male than to the author's intent.

Cultural views and stereotypes all play a part in how we process, internalize, view, create, and recreate emotional intelligence, so it is important to take a moment to acknowledge a bit about the Tin Woodman's sexual orientation as depicted in the

1939 MGM film and in MoTown's *The Wiz*. In the 1939 film, the Tin Man is introduced with his solo, "If I Only Had a Heart." The song opens with "And yet I'm torn apart. Just because I'm presumin' that I could be kind-a-human/If I only had a heart" (Hearn, *Wizard of Oz Screenplay*, 74). MGM's Tin Man is torn apart because he is not human and therefore is incapable of feeling. While he believes he should be on his mettle—he should show strength and cope well with difficulties in a traditionally masculine way—he would prefer tenderness, sentimentality, and a life of emotional intelligence.

While this Tin Man's song seems to line up beautifully with a trauma reading, MGM's Tin Man may never have been human. This Tin Man isn't given the same backstory of a lost love; he merely rusted. These omissions from Baum's tale remove any logic from a trauma reading and create character gaps that, along the way, some have tried to explain. Season 9 of *Mad TV* includes a wonderful Oz parody that explores some of these gaps. In it, their Dorothy calls Tin Man "tinsel toes," implying, in a derogatory way, that he is gay. Whether one agrees with this particular reading of the character or not, it is worth discussing how MGM's Tin Man fits within American gay male culture, especially because it seems impossible to discuss male emotional intelligence without mention of sexual orientation, which certainly comments on how our culture views emotionally intelligent men.

In his essay "My Beautiful Wickedness: The Wizard of Oz as Lesbian Fantasy," Alexander Doty notes his attraction to MGM's Tin Man, stating that "the Tin Man might stand in for my girlfriend's older brother, and subsequent crushes on older boys: an emotionally and physically solid male who needed to find a heart so he could romantically express himself to me" (49). For Doty, the Tin Man, once whole and with a heart, is the ideal man. Where mainstream culture may have celebrated a war hero, macho, wealthy, Clark Gable/Rhett Butler type for a number of years, other cultures see value in a more androgynous, emotionally aware man. Dee Michel noted in his *Baum Bugle* article "Not in Kansas Anymore: The Appeal of Oz for Gay Males" that MGM's Wizard of Oz has a special place in the gay subculture. It appears consistently on lists of favorite gay movies, is frequently used or alluded to within the gay subculture, and has become part of the stereotype of gay men (31). Michel identifies un-macho males and acceptance of diversity as two main reasons that Oz holds appeal for gay males. This is worth highlighting because it relates back to larger issues of cultural views, stereotypes, and how men display their emotions.

While it is easy to pair Baum's Oz and the MGM version as depicting cultural views from a Caucasian perspective, these views can be expanded when one considers *The Wiz*, a 1979 film adaptation based on the Broadway show of the same name. *The Wiz* provides the opportunity to discuss a Tin Man of a different color and all of the cultural baggage that comes with that racial shift.

In his essay "The Black Interior, Reparations and African American Masculinity in *The Wiz,*" Jesse Scott highlights the Tin Man's position under Teenie. Scott relates the Tin Man's position beneath his wife to the matriarchal family structures discussed in the 1965 report that Daniel Patrick Moynihan gave to President Lyndon B. Johnson. Scott notes that the Tin Man desires mobility and knowledge along with the ability to be vulnerable, stating that "Tinman [*sic*] identifies the historical stereotyping of African American men as predatory, brutal, mentally inferior and hyper sexual beasts—inhuman—as the injury that leaves him in a state of disrepair" (75). In the second verse of "What Would I Do If I Could Feel," one of two solos the Tin Man sings in *The Wiz*, Tin

Man asks, "If I could reach inside of me/And to know how it feels to say/I like what I see" (45:18–45:32). *The Wiz* offers a Tin Man detached from his emotions because he does not like what society has caused him to become. The Tin Man depicted in *The Wiz* represses any emotional intelligence in order to survive the circumstances life has handed him—a common theme with the character when one considers the possibility of a trauma read. As the Tin Man in *The Wiz* learns to evolve past his state of disrepair, he learns the value of his emotions. His tears even save his friends when they are trapped by the Poppy Girls, demonstrating the value of his strong emotions.

Baum's Tin Woodman operates within an androgynous emotional intelligence, MGM's Tin Man is linked to gay culture because of his emotional intelligence, and MoTown's Tin Man shows how society can force men to detach from their emotions, as well as the benefits that can come from repairing this emotional rift. What about younger, more modern Tin Men?

While 1982's *Barnstormer in Oz* is not the most recent, it does provide readers with a unique take on Oz, primarily because the author, Philip Jose Farmer, was already famous for his *World of Tiers* and *Riverworld* series before he penned his way down the Yellow Brick Road. Farmer, known for adult science fiction and fantasy that use sexual and religious themes, creates an Oz that acts as a very adult sequel to Baum's first Oz novel. In Farmer's Oz, Dorothy never returns to Oz, instead she has a son who, as an adult, accidentally flies his plane into Oz where he meets several familiar characters, impregnates a Munchkin, and falls in love with Glinda. Farmer clearly makes many changes to the story we are all familiar with. How does his Tin Man fit into our exploration of male emotional intelligence?

Farmer's Tin Man is introduced when Hank, Dorothy's son, is sent to bring the Scarecrow and Tin Man to Glinda. Readers are quickly told that Nicholas the Chopper—Farmer's Tin Man—did not resemble the tin men that Baum's illustrators, Denslow and Neill, depict. He looks less like a tin creation and more like a man who happens to be tin instead of flesh. He is compared to "a knight's suit of armor" and is described as being naked and having "sex organs" (91). This nakedness aligns him with Scott's observation about a "hyper sexual beast" (75). Farmer's Tin Man is visibly male. He is simultaneously dehumanized through his nakedness and elevated by the comparison to a knight, which aligns him with a traditional defender/protector role.

Like Baum's Tin Woodman, Farmer's Nicholas the Chopper is ready to defend his friends with his axe. Mere pages after his introduction, Nicholas the Chopper splatters the windshield of Hank's plane with the blood of several hawks. But, unlike Baum's Tin Woodman, there is no sorrow, regret, or tears for the animals whose lives Nicholas the Chopper cuts short. This lack of regret makes sense when one considers that Nicholas the Chopper has a slightly different origin story in Farmer's tale. The backstory readers are likely familiar with—a love story with a young woman, a witch placing a curse on his axe—are all mentioned with the line "That's what I told your mother" (110), implying that this is at least part fabrication. In Farmer's story, "Glinda [came to Nicholas] with an offer. She transferred [his] persona to the tin body [because] she wanted [him] to accompany Dorothy to the land of Oz. [He'd become] Dorothy's advisor and protector" (115). Farmer's Glinda is an all-powerful and quite manipulative force. His Tin Man is an agent of that force. Like a medieval knight, Farmer's Tin Man exists to serve, protect, and quest. He is not a round character with motivations of his own and, therefore, is incapable of emotional intelligence.

This flattened version of the Tin Man seems popular with modern interpretations of Oz. One such flattened interpretation is included in Gregory Maguire's 1995 novel *Wicked*—a revisionist Oz adaptation intended for adults. *Wicked* focuses on Elphaba, The Wicked Witch of the West. As one can imagine from an adult tale centered around the primary villain of the 1939 Oz film, this novel revamps Oz politically, socially, and ethically. While one can compare Maguire's Oz to the Civil Rights movement, or any other point in time marked by racism and discrimination, readers do not see all of the Oz characters they know and love fully fleshed out. Take, for example, the Tin Woodman. Maguire devotes less than two pages to a woodcutter that Nessarose, Elphaba's sister, is asked to "do something about" (313). Nessarose agrees to enchant an axe to cut off this unnamed woodcutter's arm, but the conversation quickly turns to the ethics behind the trading of anthropomorphic Animals, rather than the man. Later, the Tin Woodman is mentioned as "hollow, a tiktok cipher or an eviscerated human under a spell" (389), but he is never fleshed out as a character. Like Farmer's Nicholas Chopper, Maguire's Tin Man is not a round character with motivations of his own, and, therefore, is incapable of emotional intelligence.

Stephen Schwartz built on Maguire's *Wicked* and turned it into a stage musical that premiered in 2003. In Schwartz's version, the Tin Woodman is morphed with Maguire's Boq, a friend of both Maguire's and Schwartz's Elphaba from her time in school. Schwartz makes Boq a failed love interest for Elphaba's sister. When Boq confesses his love for Glinda, Nessarose attempts to cast a spell from Elphaba's spell book, but mispronounces it, causing Boq's heart to rapidly shrink. In order to save his life, Elphaba turns Boq into a tin man. Boq is angered by this transformation, and becomes part of the witch hunt for Elphaba that occurs toward the end of the musical. While this version of the Tin Woodman seems rounder than Maguire's, it is at the cost of flattening out Boq. Maguire's Boq narrates a whole section of the novel, has developed friendships, and even marries. When Boq and the Tin Woodman merge into one character, Boq loses his roundness; instead his whole story revolves around a love triangle. Boq, as the Tin Woodman, is unable to accept the rejection of Glinda and, in turn, leads Nessarose on in order to impress Glinda. Where Maguire's Boq demonstrates moments of emotional intelligence more in line with a Baum character, Schwartz's Tin Man is neither intelligent about his own emotions, nor careful with the emotions of others.

Farmer and Maguire, examples of Eighties and Nineties Oz adaptations, flatten the character of the Tin Man. Schwartz offers a millennial Tin Man with an example that recalls some of Scott's verbiage when he described the Tin Man in the *Wiz*. While race is no longer an obvious factor, the millennial Tin Man, as shown in *Wicked*, is predatory and brutal in his hunt for Elphaba, mentally inferior in his inability to read the cues of the women he loves and is loved by, and primarily concerned with his own sexual interests—namely his crush on Glinda. The shift we see with Schwartz's millennial Tin Man continues into other, twenty-first century, Oz adaptations, which makes this pattern particularly intriguing and notable, especially when discussing male emotional intelligence.

In 2005 the Muppets Studio, Touchstone Television, and Fox Television Studios produced *The Muppets Wizard of Oz*. This project went into production right after Disney bought the rights to The Muppets, a point worth noting because one does not tend to associate Disney with hyper sexual beasts. However, viewers see this exact depiction when examining the Tin Man, or in this case the Tin Thing. *The Muppets Wizard of Oz* follows Baum's novel closer than the 1939 film. Dorothy's shoes are silver as in the original book, there are four witches, the four friends have to make it past the Kalidahs (although the Muppets makes them into critics instead of beasts) and other such details missing from the 1939 film.

Despite these similarities to Baum's Oz story, though, *The Muppets Wizard of Oz* takes many liberties with the material in order to seem funny or modern. One such modernization is found in the name change to Tin Thing, a research assistant who was transformed into a computerized being by the Wicked Witch because he wanted time off to marry his beloved. While this transformation may seem like a logical modernization, it is played for laughs in ways that simultaneously dehumanize the character and sexualize him. Consider, for instance, the initial meeting of Dorothy, Toto, Scarecrow, and the Tin Thing. The Tin Thing needs to reconstruct his body before the group can head off to see the Wizard. Toto, played by Pepe the Prawn (who not only speaks, but also uses his voice to provide the bulk of the comic relief), questions the Tin Thing about his metal body. He touches him and is then disgusted when he learns he was manipulating the Tin Things nipples. While this particular hyper-sexualization might be overlooked, the point is driven home when the four friends each separately make their requests to the Wizard. The Tin Thing, like Baum's Tin Woodman, initially sees the Wizard as a fairy. This fairy, who is wearing far less clothing than the one depicted by Denslow, transforms into the Tin Thing's left-behind fiancé in an attempt to both taunt and seduce the Tin Thing into agreeing to kill the witch. Played again for laughs, the fiancé, who is a chicken, is described as having a "big beak" and "huge floppy wings" (49:58–50:60), attributes which are listed as the fairy wizard slowly changes appearance and the Tin Thing stutters and stares, obviously attracted to the aforementioned attributes. It is worth highlighting that this is a family-friendly, children's adaptation of Oz, yet this Tin Man is also sexualized and dehumanized. It is impossible to discuss how a character is "regulat[ing their] emotions to promote emotional and intellectual growth" (Mayer and Salovey, 10), as an emotionally intelligent person is defined as doing, when that character is dehumanized in this manner.

When one considers time period and producer of text, it is particularly fascinating to observe how some family-friendly tin men (like the Tin Thing) operate counter to expectations, and some tin men, like Cain from the 2007 Sci Fi channel's miniseries titled *Tin Man*, operate in a manner that is the opposite of what one would expect from that particular depiction because of how it differs from other popular texts of the time. On the surface Cain seems a perfect exploration of how men are taught to suppress their emotional intelligence. Sci Fi channel's *Tin Man* miniseries modernizes the Oz story by making many changes to Baum's tale. Dorothy is a waitress transported to an alternate world called the Outer Zone; Scarecrow, called "Glitch" here, is a former advisor to the queen who has been lobotomized; and Cain, the tin man of the story, is titled such for the tin star he wore when he was a lawman. Azkadellia, the Wicked Witch of this story, has taken over the O-Z, corrupting it. Cain, a sort of heroic western sheriff, was tortured because he remained true to his ideals. He was forced into a tin suit and made to watch a recording of his family being beaten and taken from him. As one would expect of a tortured western hero, Cain is played as a man's man. He minimizes "any emotions linked to vulnerability, guilt, fear and pain" (Sánchez-Núñez, Fernández-Berrocal, Montañés, Latorre 460), exactly in the manner psychologists have found that men are typically socialized to do.

While Cain seems to fit the mold of a man taught to suppress his emotional intelligence, Sci Fi's *Tin Man* distinguishes itself from other popular Oz versions of the time by returning to the notion that the Scarecrow character is meant to balance the Tin Man character in a union of "the intellect and the emotion[al] in a harmonious relationship" (Sackett 287). Consider the scene thirteen minutes into the second episode of the miniseries, in which Glitch sits with Cain as he awakens from a near-death experience and the two talk. Glitch names Cain's emotional shortcomings, challenging him to seek therapy and become more emotionally intelligent. Where most post–*Wiz* Tin Men embrace the emotional shortcomings the character can demonstrate, this incarnation forces the viewer to question the mental and emotional wellbeing of a character forced to enact stereotypical gender traits. Interestingly enough, Cain not only learns to evolve past his prescribed role but, when he finally reconnects with his son, he helps the younger man let go of his violent revenge plans and, instead, embrace something healthier and more emotionally intelligent.

It would be nice to view Cain as the incarnation that marks a return to Baum's emotionally intelligent Tin Man, but Danielle Paige's *Dorothy Must Die*, published in 2014, returns us to a predatory, brutal, mentally inferior, hyper-sexual beast depiction much like the Tin Men mentioned in other twenty-first-century adaptations. Danielle Paige's Oz, like the Oz shown in the Sci Fi adaptation, is darker and has a bit of a punk-goth feel. *Dorothy Must Die* centers around Amy Gumm, a high schooler who hates her Kansas trailer park life. When Amy is transported to Oz, she finds it to be a dystopian world in environmental peril from a dictator Dorothy who mines the land for magic. While Amy finds travel companions that one could parallel to the original Oz friends, Dorothy's Scarecrow, Tin Man, and Lion all exist as nightmare versions of the characters Baum created. Paige's nightmarish Tin Man is described as "a machine that had been cobbled together out of spare parts. His face was pinched and mean. His oversize jaw jutted out from the rest of his face in a nasty underbite, revealing a mess of little blades where his teeth should have been" (78). As one can see from this description, this Tin Woodman is predatory and brutal from his first introduction.

It is difficult to imagine how basic emotion can come from a character with blades for teeth, but, about mid-novel readers learn that this Tin Woodman became a monster because of love. Via a magic mirror, Amy and Dorothy overhear a conversation between the Wizard and the Tin Woodman where the Wizard asks the Tin Woodman, "Why don't you just tell her how you feel?" The Tin Woodman responds, "I couldn't possibly. I—Everything I do, I do for *her*. And still, she will never love me the way I love her" (290). The "her" discussed in these quotes is Dorothy, who does not return the Tin Woodman's affection. Paige's Tin Woodman not only recalls a predatory, mentally inferior, hyper-sexual beast Tin Woodman—after all, he has knives in his fingers and can't pick up on the social cues of rejection—he also avoids vulnerability and openness when he states he couldn't possibly tell Dorothy how he feels, which is a clear rejection of emotional intelligence. Even though readers are offered insight into the motivations of Paige's Tin Woodman, he does not evolve as a character. When, in the end of the novel, Amy defeats the Tin Woodman, Amy comments that slicing "diagonally across his chest was as simple as popping the top on a can of soda. […] he was only made of tin" (450). Since he is only tin, Paige's Tin Woodman recalls the static nature of Farmer's and Maguire's Tin Men, leaving him incapable of emotional intelligence. Further, he echoes Scott's mentally inferior, hyper-sexual beast depiction found in *The Wiz,* the musical

Wicked, and *The Muppets Wizard of Oz*—all of which play with male stereotypes that limit the characters emotionally.

Thankfully, Todrick Hall returns audiences to Baum's emotionally intelligent Tin Man in the truest sense of any modern depiction. Hall, an *American Idol* alum and YouTube star, uses the familiar touch-points of Oz and Dorothy's journey in his 2017 visual album *Straight Outta Oz* as a backdrop for the tale of his journey from growing up in Plainview, Texas, to trying to make it in "Oz Angeles." He manages to morph into every character and include obvious Oz references ("Thank you for Flying Monkey Airlines" [28.00–28.03]) and less obvious Oz references (the entirety of Hall's "Expensive" recalls the "Green, Red, Gold" Emerald City sequence in *The Wiz*). The album also has numerous celebrity appearances and modern topical issues (like police brutality and race relations) seamlessly woven in without distracting from the journey or the Oz themes. While Hall's use of the Tin Woodman demonstrates male emotional intelligence coupled with traumatic heartbreak, one cannot discuss male emotional intelligence in *Straight Outta Oz* without first discussing the song "Over the Rainbow."

Hall opens "Over the Rainbow" with "Little boys don't cry [...] /Little boys are tough/They do stuff that little girls don't try" (7:06–7:16), which illustrates the findings about boys minimizing emotions linked to vulnerability. Little boys do not cry because they are taught, as Hall's father instructs him in the vignette before the song, that crying is a weak female action. This theme echoes as the song moves into a religious allegory, equating "over the rainbow" with heaven. Here Hall presents the idea that "there's somewhere over the rainbow/And if you change the way you love/Then maybe you can go" (7:52–8:13). In these lyrics Hall's father suggests that his son can go to heaven if he changes the way he loves from loving boys to loving girls. These lyrics bring us full circle to the discussion of the sexual orientation of the Tin Woodman and Scarecrow as, yet again, feeling and acting on emotion in a way that falls within the traditionally female sphere is linked with sexual orientation. This point is driven home when, the audience is visually presented with a young Todrick Hall wearing sparkly red high heels as the lyrics mention bricks of gold. Young Hall does not differentiate between the male and female spheres, and that is part of the change his father desires.

The theme of an outsider finding self-acceptance via Oz, especially as it relates to sexual orientation, is discussed by Alexander Doty in "My Beautiful Wickedness" and by Dee Michel in his *Baum Bugle* article "Not in Kansas Anymore: The Appeal of Oz for Gay Males." Michel notes that "being gay seems to facilitate an appreciation of Oz" (33) and he attributes this appeal to four themes that can be found within Baum's Oz series. Like Doty, Michel explores the image of sissies. As Michel states, "Dorothy's three male companions are all gentle, loving, and silly. In addition to the dandyism of the Tin Woodman and the sissy-ness of the Lion, the MGM Scarecrow slips and slides and sings[....] these three are not exactly Han Solo or John Wayne material" (34). Michel believes that this lack of macho behavior is part of what makes Oz resonate with gay boys and men. Michel also notes how "many kids who grow up gay have an acute sense of being different" and "diversity is valued in the Oz of both the books and the movie" (34). Oz becomes a safe space to be who you really are, especially if you don't fit the societal mold. This point is furthered when Michel notes how many gay men have "strong feelings about home: wanting to leave for someplace better, but also wanting to be accepted and return to where they grew up" (35). Like Dorothy, there seems to be a quest to find a place where one belongs. When we layer Dee Michel's observations with the adaptations explored in this essay, and the concept of emotional intelligence, an interesting conclusion begins to form. The Tin Men with the most emotional intelligence seem to be androgynous, like Baum's Tin Woodman, or depicted as homosexual, like some have read MGM's Tin Man. This further highlights how showing emotions that are traditionally in the female sphere, when you're male, continue to have additional social implications.

In the case of Todrick Hall, the additional implications linked to his willingness to cry, sing, wear pink, and so on, are true. Even though he, at one point, had a girlfriend, he learns he prefers men when he meets Gareth. Their biracial, same-sex relationship is depicted in the song "Color," a clever bit of wordplay on both race and the new way Hall sees the world. He leaves Gareth to seek fame and, as *Straight Outta Oz* audiences learn in "If I Had a Heart," Gareth moves on to another man. Hall depicts the universal experience of losing a first love with emotional rawness. His repeated claim, if he "had a heart, it would still bleed/It would still be beatin' for [Garath], feenin' for [Garath]" (33.24–33.35) suggests that he is trying to distance himself from his emotions and become "heartless." This notion is furthered by the images of Hall visiting an unnamed wizard or magician who proceeds to remove his grey, unbeating heart in a manner that recalls the 1914 silent film *His Majesty, the Scarecrow of Oz,* as Hall's heart is pulled from his chest in the same manner that Gloria's heart was in the 1914 film. The great irony of this claim of heartlessness is that while the song depicts Hall as avoiding vulnerability and openness, which is the opposite of showing emotional intelligence, the fact that he is able to capture and express the emotional pain of this time in his life suggests "the ability to perceive accurately, appraise, and express emotion" (Mayer and Salovey, 10), the very definition of emotional intelligence. Todrick Hall, as depicted in his visual album, is an amalgamation of Oz characters and displays the very combination of intelligence and emotion that Baum depicts in the friendship between the Scarecrow and the Tin Woodman.

L. Frank Baum defined the untraditional male in both his life and his characters. Dorothy is often noted for subverting the gender expectations of her time, but Baum's Tin Woodman, much like Baum himself, also subverts those expectations. While this is not always true for the modern Tin Man, Todrick Hall captures our current, conflicting cultural view on emotionally intelligent males in his Tin Woodman and other Oz characters into which he morphs throughout his visual album *Straight Outta Oz.* The very fact that Hall takes on different guises and characters relates directly to Baum's various careers and personas. What is highlighted in these parallels and in the deviance from these parallels in other modern works like *Barnstormer in Oz* (1982), *Tin Man* (2007), and *Dorothy Must Die* (2014) is the circular progress we, as a society, tend toward when it comes to certain social issues.

L. Frank Baum created Tin Woodman with something of an androgynous emotional intelligence. The character was able to emotionally connect to situations (and cry) the way a woman is typically depicted while also using his axe to solve problems in a macho-like way. While androgyny seems remarkably apt for a children's character made of metal (and thus, not living), adaptations of Baum's work do not seem to have the same comfort level with characters traveling back and forth from typical gender norms. Instead, scholars and critics tend to read the MGM Tin Man as gay and the MoTown Tin Man as forced to detach from his emotions (while also being animal-like with a predatory nature). Whether in an effort to offer something new to audiences or a further comment on the emotional range offered to men, examples from the 1980s and 1990s examined in this essay flatten the Tin Woodman until he is incapable of emotions because he is not round enough as a character. Stephen Schwartz echoes Maguire's flattened Tin Woodman while merging him with Boq, creating a character that returns to the sort of Tin Man so wrapped up in his own emotions that he cannot think of others. And while Schwartz's Tin Man is not the sort of Tin Man a woman would want to leave alone with her drink at a bar, *The Muppets Wizard of Oz* takes this one step further when they overtly sexualize their Tin Thing. Danielle Paige echoes this history when she creates a brutal, detached Tin Woodman with a stalker-like crush on Dorothy. Only Sci Fi's and Todrick Hall's incarnations of the Tin Man offer modern versions that offer any amount of emotional range, but this range is still connected to sexuality. Sci Fi's version is depicted as heterosexual and thus has to learn emotional range, beginning as a typical macho man with a journey and character arc aimed towards emotional intelligence. Todrick Hall's Tin Man is the opposite, depicted as a homosexual man who is fully emotionally aware and trying to avoid the pain caused by losing his love. While there seems to be some limited progress in how emotional intelligence is depicted in these tin characters, overall the lesson seems to be that manly men do not show feeling. Only an androgynous character in a child's book is allowed to be that round and fully developed. Male emotional intelligence and expression, while embraced in some circles, is still limited in ways that existed a hundred-and-twenty-something years ago, eighty-something years ago, twenty-something years ago, and today.

NOTE

1. This essay is a revision of my 2018 publication "Metal Malleable Male: The Tin Creations of L. Frank Baum and Todrick Hall."

WORKS CITED

Balaev, Michelle. "Trends in Literary Trauma Theory." *Mosaic* (Winnipeg) 41, no. 2 (2008): 149–66.
Baum, L. Frank. *Little Wizard Stories of Oz*. Books of Wonder, 1994.
_____. *The Marvelous Land of Oz*. Dover, 1969.
_____. *The Tin Woodman of Oz*. Ballantine, 1981.
_____. *The Wonderful Wizard of Oz*. HarperCollins, 1987.
Doty, Alexander. "'My Beautiful Wickedness': The Wizard of Oz as Lesbian Fantasy." *Flaming Classics: Queering the Film Canon*. Routledge, 2000.
Farmer, Philip José. *A Barnstormer in Oz: or, A Rationalization and Extrapolation of the Split-Level Continuum*. Berkley Books, 1983.
Fleming, Victor, dir. *The Wizard of Oz*. MGM, 1939.
Hall, Todrick. *Straight Outta Oz*. YouTube, 12 March 2017, www.youtube.com/watch?v=4mUSwHhJ6zA.
Langley, Noel, Florence Ryerson, and Edgar Allan Woolf. *The Wizard of Oz: The Screenplay*. Michael Patrick Hearn, editor. Delta/Dell, 1989.
Loncraine, Rebecca. *The Real Wizard of Oz: The Life and Times of L. Frank Baum*. Gotham Books, 2009.
Lumet, Sidney, dir. *The Wiz*. Universal Pictures and Motown Productions, 1978.
MAD TV. Season 9, episode 19.
Maguire, Gregory. *Wicked: The Life and Times of the Wicked Witch of the West*. Regan Books, 1995.
Mayer, J.D., and P. Salovey. "What Is Emotional Intelligence?" *Emotional Development and Emotional Intelligence: Implications for Educators*. Basic Books, 1997. 3–32.
Paige, Danielle. *Dorothy Must Die*. HarperCollins, 2014.
Pugh, Tison. "John R. Neill: Illustrator (and Author) of L. Frank Baum's Queer Oz." *Marvels & Tales* 29, no. 1 (2015): 64–86.
Sackett, S.J. "The Utopia of Oz." *The Georgia Review* 14, no. 3 (1960): 275–91.

Sanchez-Nunez, M. Trinidad et al. "Does Emotional Intelligence Depend on Gender? The Socialization of Emotional Competencies in Men and Women and Its Implications." *Electronic Journal of Research in Educational Psychology* 6, no. 2 (2008): 455–74.

Schwartz, Stephen. *Wicked*. 2003.

Thatcher, Kirk R., dir. *Muppets' Wizard of Oz*. Fox Television Studios, 2005.

Willing, Nick, dir. *Tin Man*. RHI Entertainment and the Sci Fi Channel, 2007.

The Proto-Sissy, the Sissy, and Macho Men

The Cowardly Lion in The Wonderful Wizard of Oz, the MGM The Wizard of Oz, and Dark Oz Stories

Dee Michel and James Satter

In both L. Frank Baum's *The Wonderful Wizard of Oz* and the MGM *The Wizard of Oz*, the Cowardly Lion wants to gain courage. Bravery is a traditional male quality in American culture and the Lion's lack of this traditionally male characteristic makes him an unusual role model for boys reading Baum's original book and seeing the 1939 film. The Lion is a coward no more in several recent Oz texts, but a violent Lion betrays Baum's vision of a nontraditional masculinity. This is a loss for the LGBTQ community in particular and our culture as a whole.

L. Frank Baum created the Cowardly Lion in his *The Wonderful Wizard of Oz* in 1900, but the Lion's most famous incarnation is likely Bert Lahr's rendition in the 1939 MGM classic *The Wizard of Oz*. Versions of the Lion or characters based on him also appear in many more recent Oz stories with darker content. Before examining the Cowardly Lion's various incarnations in these works, and why he is no longer cowardly in the darker works, it would be useful to look at what lions are and what they represent.

Symbolism of the Lion

Lions are physical creatures; they are wild animals par excellence. They prey on animals of different sizes and often eat "any meat they can find" (*Britannica*). Unlike other cats, male lions have manes, which visually sets them apart from their female counterparts. Lions appear in art, architecture, and literature as symbols. An example of architectural guarding lions is Patience and Fortitude, "world-renowned" marble lions who sit in front of the 42nd Street branch of the New York Public Library. In the film version of *The Wiz*, the Cowardly Lion first appears from inside Patience, the one to the south (New York Public Library). While the specific symbolism of the lion may vary from culture to culture, some general qualities are seen across cultures, both historically and in the present.

The lion's masculine power is associated with the sun, as opposed to the lioness's relationship to the moon (Bruce-Mitford 28–29; 61). Lions have symbolized strength for thousands of years ("Lions" *Wikipedia*). The King of Beasts is associated with both courage and wisdom in Buddhism (Tressider 125), with Buddha himself described as "a lion among men" in part due to his courage (Tressider 125). Richard I of England was called "Lion-heart" due to his bravery (Brewer 554), and in the Harry Potter series the lion is the symbol of Gryffindor, the Hogwarts house associated with bravery. Lions are used to symbolize protection and guardianship on buildings, thrones, and entrances, especially in China and Japan (Bruce-Mitford 61; Tressider 124).

The lion has been considered the "king of beasts" in many cultures and eras (Bruce-Mitford 61; 114). Because of this kingship, the royal beast is used in heraldry (Bruce-Mitford 61) and seen on the royal emblems of both Scotland and England (Tressider 125; Brewer 554), and During the nineteenth century the British Lion was a symbol of imperial power (Tressider 125). The lion is part of the Churchill family emblem (*Britannica*) and is the family symbol of the Lannisters in George Martin's *A Song of Fire and Ice* series (better known as *Game of Thrones* in its television version). In the world of animation, the young cub Simba is reckless in his youth, but matures into a responsible king in Disney's *The Lion King*.

Despite this powerful image, the strength of the Lion can take on negative connotations when used to signify royal power, dominion, and military victory. The lion in the wild can symbolize the "great and terrible in nature" and negative aspects of power, such as "cruelty, devouring ferocity, and death," are also associated with the large feline (Tressider 123). When seen at the feet of crusaders and martyrs, lions symbolize death in Christian mythology (Brewer), while Greek mythology sees lions as the guardians of the dead (Tressider 124).

The flip side of ferocity is meekness, and several classic stories tell of a wild lion who is helped by a human and then becomes a tame companion to the helper. Some examples of tame

Crying Cowardly Lion (W.W. Denslow illustration from *The Wonderful Wizard of Oz* [1960 edition]).

lions are found in Aesop's "Androcles and the Lion," as well as in the stories of St. Jerome and St. Gerasimus (Brewer 554; Bruce-Mitford 112). The real-life Elsa the Lioness, Who appears in Joy Adamson's *Born Free*, its sequels, and film incarnations, demonstrates the appeal of a domesticated lion even in the real world. Following this "gentle lion" theme, astrological lions ("Leos") are warm, loyal, generous, and friendly, and "want to be the center of attention. They are characterized to have a powerful personality with a touch of the dramatic" (Bruce-Mitford 112).

The above six qualities—physicality, strength/bravery, royalty, ferocity/death/sacrifice, domesticity/loyalty, and drama—play out in different ways in Baum's original Cowardly Lion, the MGM Cowardly Lion, and in the various analogs of the Lion in relatively recent dark Oz works. However, all six attributes may not be associated with each version of the Lion.

The Proto-Sissy

The Cowardly Lion makes a memorable entrance in Baum's *Wonderful Wizard of Oz*:

> Just as he spoke there came from the forest a terrible roar, and the next moment a great Lion bounded into the road....
>
> Little Toto, now that he had an enemy to face, ran barking toward the Lion, and the great beast had opened his mouth to bite the dog, when Dorothy, fearing Toto would be killed, and heedless of danger, rushed forward and slapped the Lion upon his nose as hard as she could, while she cried out:
>
> "Don't you dare to bite Toto! You ought to be ashamed of yourself, a big beast like you, to bite a poor little dog!"
>
> "I didn't bite him," said the Lion, as he rubbed his nose with his paw where Dorothy had hit it.
>
> "No, but you tried to," she retorted. "You are nothing but a big coward."
>
> "I know it," said the Lion, hanging his head in shame. "I've always known it. But how can I help it?"
>
> "I don't know, I'm sure. To think of your striking a stuffed man, like the poor Scarecrow!"...
>
> "What makes you a coward?" asked Dorothy, looking at the great beast in wonder, for he was as big as a small horse.
>
> "It's a mystery," replied the Lion. "I suppose I was born that way...."
>
> "But that isn't right. The King of Beasts shouldn't be a coward," said the Scarecrow.
>
> "I know it," returned the Lion, wiping a tear from his eye with the tip of his tail. "It is my great sorrow, and makes my life very unhappy. But whenever there is danger, my heart begins to beat fast."...
>
> "Then, if you don't mind, I'll go with you," said the Lion, "for my life is simply unbearable without a bit of courage" [46–50].

Two things are notable about this passage. It is surprising how much of this dialogue made it into the MGM film, and this character is the opposite of the courageous king and powerful killer, resembling perhaps the tame companion archetype.

The Lion is "flesh and blood" like Dorothy and Toto (Baum 30). All three need to eat and sleep, and as biological creatures they succumb to the sleeping power of the poppies, while the Scarecrow and Tin Woodman are unaffected by the magic. The Lion symbolizes the physical, the Scarecrow represents the intellectual, and the Tin Woodman stands for the emotional. All three of Dorothy's companions are incomplete non-traditional males. Osmond Beckwith goes so far as to describe them as eunuchs (77). The Scarecrow and the Tin Woodman physiologically lack a brain and heart, and hope to get actual organs, but no body part is clearly associated with courage, so the Lion hopes that the Wizard might cure him of what might be considered a psychological state or character flaw. The Lion's lack of bravery is more a part of his character than the lacks of Dorothy's other two companions. In the chapter after the Lion in introduced, Baum first refers to him as the "Cowardly Lion," drawing attention to the courage that he seeks from the Wizard (55). In contrast, Dorothy's other companions are not called the Dim-Witted Scarecrow or the Heartless Tin Woodman. At the end of Baum's novel, the Wizard gives Dorothy's three companions more or less what they want. In subsequent Oz books by Baum and others, the Scarecrow is wise, the Tin Woodman is kind-hearted, and the Lion is brave. For example, he is courageous when he offers to jump over a ditch with the others on his back, he faces the monstrous and ferocious Kalidahs with a loud roar (despite trembling), and he swims against the current in a large river. Nevertheless, he is still called the "Cowardly Lion."

The Lion resembles Dorothy in terms of aspirations. Dorothy wants to return home to Kansas and, although the Lion asks for nerve, he is seeking courage so he can return to his perceived natural role as king of the forest. Being king of the forest would also be a position of leadership. Various species in Baum's book also use royal titles, such as King Crow and Queen of the Field Mice, but only the Lion earns the honor of King of the Beasts. When other forest animals hold a meeting to discuss a danger in their midst—a spider with a body the size of an elephant—only the post–Wizard Lion is brave enough to face the creature. Attacking at night, the Lion pounces on the giant spider and beheads it.

The Lion would pose the greatest threat to Dorothy were he ferocious rather than cowardly, with his size making him more intimidating than Dorothy's other companions. Baum shows his readers this intimidation when the travelers enter the Emerald City, and a woman is taken aback by the large lion until Dorothy assures her that the lion is not only tame but also a coward. The lion reveals something of a defense mechanism, describing how he roars to keep others away. This bluster is a false front, trying to get other animals to believe he is something he is not.

While Baum's original Lion is not as flamboyant as the MGM Lion, he is meek and domestic. Within two pages, the Lion says he is "terribly afraid" (Baum 56, 57). Like most of us, the Cowardly Lion shows both bravery and cowardice and can get discouraged easily. As the characters' quest continues, the Scarecrow and Tin Woodman worry that they will never get their brain and heart. The Lion, however, is more defeatist, saying, "I haven't the courage to keep tramping forever, without getting anywhere at all" (134). Baum's Cowardly Lion turns the symbolism of the lion on its head. Although he is brave on occasion, he thinks he is a coward. He is strong, but rarely fights. He is not the King of Beasts, but wants to be.

The Sissy

Bert Lahr, with the help of the MGM screenwriters, takes Baum's Cowardly Lion a bit further. How far? One might say "over the top." He is "one of filmdom's professional sissies" (Tyler 341) and "the cinema's best-loved nelly character" (Smith 60). The writer of *The Zen of Oz* even urges the Lion to come out of the closet as gay (Green 84). When Dorothy and her companions encounter the Lion in the scary forest, he appears to be tough. Like a schoolyard bully, he challenges the travelers to a fight. "Hah, put 'em up, put 'em up. Which one of ya first? I'll fight ya both together if ya want." Then he teases them and calls them names. He taunts the Tin Woodman: "How long can ya stay fresh in that can? Come on! Get up and fight, ya shiverin' junkyard." And to the Scarecrow, "Put ya hands up, ya lopsided bag of hay!" But as soon as Dorothy slaps him, he starts to sob. "Well, ya didn't have to go and hit me, did ya? Is my nose bleedin'?" Then the Lion sings to his new friends about how he feels: "/When you're born to be a sissy/Without the vim and verve." He actually calls himself a sissy! This is unusual for any character, in a book or movie, directed at kids or adults. Soon after, the Lion sings, "I'm afraid there's no denyin' /I'm just a dandy-lion/" (Langley 79–80).

As a child, film scholar Alexander Doty found the Lion embarrassing and worse. He writes:

> Then there was that Cowardly Lion who was teaching me self-hatred. From between the ages of about five and fifteen, I was actually far less disturbed by the Witched Witch than I was by the Cowardly Lion. When he sang about how miserable he was to be a "sissy," I cringed. Because I was a sissy, too…. At this stage "sissy" seemed to be a gender thing. It meant being like a girl, liking what they liked…. While watching *The Wizard of Oz* each year, my gender and sexuality turmoil reached its peak when Dorothy and the Cowardly Lion emerged from their Emerald City beauty treatments with nearly identical perms and hair bows. And then this ultra-sissified lion dared to sing "If I Were the [*sic*] King of the Forest"! I would sit in front of the television set paralyzed: my desire for and identification with Dorothy battling my loathing for and identification with the Cowardly Lion [49].

The Lion's cowardice is evident throughout the film. He is only a bit fierce at the beginning before Dorothy slaps him, and his lack of courage makes him meek, domestic, and loyal. He is the most reluctant of the travelers. For example, when the group first encounters the visage of Oz, with his booming voice and pyrotechnics, the Lion flees down the hall and jumps out the window. Later, in the forest, as the group approaches the Witch's castle, the Lion is unnerved by the sight of owls and suggests they heed the advice of a sign that prompts them to turn back. He does go into the witch's castle, but reluctantly, saying, "Talk me out of it" (Langley 112). Only through the encouragement of the others does the Lion continue on the quest.

When the four travelers emerge from their makeovers at the Wash and Brush Up Company in the Emerald City, the Lion has a blue ribbon in his hair, similar to Dorothy's red one, and his hair has been elaborately curled. When Dorothy and her companions are told they can't see the Wizard, the Lion complains in a campy Mae West voice, "Aw shucks, and I had a permanent just for the occasion" (Langley 94). Here the Lion seems to acknowledge his sissiness and plays on it. Ray Bolger's Scarecrow and Jack Haley's Tin Woodman are effeminate or non-macho, but by declaring himself a sissy and acting effeminately, Lahr's Cowardly Lion opens himself up to being seen as gay. The MGM Cowardly Lion is memorable both for the sissy character the many screenwriters created and Lahr's embodiment of it. The mostly gay audience at the Castro Theatre in San Francisco has cheered the "sissy warrior" of the Lion (Davis 4). This jives with Doty's feelings changing from embarrassment to embracing once he came out and discovered aspects of gay culture. As he says, "Somewhere in my twenties, I became aware of butches and of camp, which fed into my developing 'gay' appreciation of *The Wizard of Oz*.... I found him fabulously outrageous. King of the Forest? He was more like a drag queen who just didn't give a fuck. Because of this, he seemed to have a bravery the narrative insisted he lacked" (50).

"Drama queen" is another expression that applies to the Lion. "If I Were the King of the Forest" provides the character with more screen time, as he was the last of the trio to join Dorothy. In the song, the Lion makes one large dramatic gesture after another. Being the center of attention is an attribute of the astrological lion. In fact, Lahr's performance is so hammy, so over the top, that he draws attention in every scene he is in. In addition, his campiness and flamboyance demonstrate how silly masculinity is; it is something created by society, not an innate quality.

But ultimately the Lion's wish is not only about courage, but about gender and desire. "It's been in me so long, I just have to tell you how I feel...." This empathic connection made with the audience is over gender: the Lion wants to lose his weakness and be a "[real, male] lion, not a [sissy, effeminate] mou-ess" (Davis 5). After furiously failing to meet his own and others' demands to be a man or butch it up or, at the very least, *fake it*, the Cowardly Lion is made aware of both the significance and constructedness of masculinity itself by taking the journey to Oz.

While the Lion's main goal is to get courage, he also wants to take his rightful place as a King. "If I Were King of the Forest" expresses this secondary goal to be a leader. Although the Wizard recognizes the Lion's courage, the Lion's secondary aspiration for leadership is only partially fulfilled at the end of the film. The Lion is the only one of Dorothy's companions who has shown an interest in leadership, but the Wizard places all three equally in charge of Oz. The Wizard's decision tells us that the three characters will make the strongest decisions when they work together, but the Lion has not become King of the Forest or king of anywhere.

Dark Oz Stories

Baum's original book and the MGM movie are perhaps the most well-known of the traditional Oz stories. They were created for children, although adults enjoy reading the book and seeing the film as well. Within this early tradition, Ruth Plumly Thompson depicts the lion in *The Cowardly Lion of Oz* as gradually coming to accept his own bouts of cowardice as a sign of virtue. Another more recent genre of Oz story might be called "dark Oz." Works in this genre are written for adolescents and adults, and often have more sex and violence than is usually found in the lighter Oz stories created for children. Early examples of dark Oz stories include the 1976 Australian movie *Twentieth Century Oz* and Philip Jose Farmer's 1982 novel, *A Barnstormer in Oz*. However, more current portrayals of the Lion appear in two dark Oz comics series, *Oz Squad* and Caliber's *Oz*, as well as the television series, *Tin Man* and *Emerald City*.

Oz Squad is a ten-issue comic book series written by Steve Ahlquist from 1991 to 1996. In addition, Ahlquist created two special issues in 1995, published a complete annotated collection of the series in 2008–09, and a novel in 2001. While additional information and occasional stories related to the original series began appearing online in 2011, we will examine the Lion in the core of *Oz Squad*, the ten issues that tell a more or less continuous story. Interestingly, despite the title of the series, the term "Oz Squad" is not used in the text itself. What had been Dorothy and her companions in earlier versions of Oz stories are now the main members of Gale Force, a unit within the CIA "in charge of Earth/Oz relations" (issue #7, inside cover). Dorothy seems to be the head of the unit. She has grown up, has short hair, and often wears a low-cut tank top. Nick Chopper is the Tin Woodman with a special double opening at his eyes, like the X-Men's Cyclops, from which he can shoot energy. Nick also has various weapons inside him that can be activated when needed. The Scarecrow looks like John R. Neill's drawings of Scarecrow, and as the series begins he is very depressed. It is unclear what his superpowers are. Mr. Lion, without the descriptor of cowardly, appears as a human like Dorothy, with shoulder-length shaggy hair and often wears a jacket and tie, but he can turn into a wild animal when needed. Lion's ability to be alternately human and a ferocious animal contrasts with the always-human Dorothy and Scarecrow and Nick Chopper, who are both always their unique non-human selves.

In his human form Mr. Lion might accompany Dorothy on Earth to negotiate with bad guys. As part of the assault on Rebecca the East Witch's castle in issue #2, Mr. Lion brings along the unnamed Hungry Tiger, also a human, who morphs to fight a Kalidah protecting the castle. Turning into a lion seems to destroy Mr. Lion's shirt and jacket, for he is always bare-chested when he returns to his human form after a fight. No details of how or why he can do this are given. He seems to be able to let out his inner savage animal at will. Except for one incident when his strength is needed to escape an exploding taxi, his transformation always happens in fight scenes, where he becomes a lean, mean fighting machine. Mr. Lion is taunted once by a Kalidah for being a coward, but all four main members of Gale Force are ferocious fighters and seem to be equally strong and brave. Depicting fight scenes seems to be the raison d'être of the series: using guns, swords, fists, and claws.

The vaudeville lineage of the MGM Lion appears when the *Oz Squad* Lion says that the ice cream Dorothy and Ozma are eating on Earth is an "animal by-product." When Dorothy asks him how he feels about that, his reply is "Hey, cows are for eating" (issue #10, p. 31). As the unnamed official greeter of Tik Tok at an airport in Kansas, Mr. Lion is the first person seen in issue #1. Readers learn who he is on the second page, when Tik Tok calls him "my friend Lion" (2). Soon after, a police officer sees his CIA identification and calls him "Mr. Lion" (4). Thus, Mr. Lion seems important at the beginning of the series, as someone who deals with Earth authorities. Even so, he only appears in six of the ten issues of *Oz Squad* and, where he does show up, his role is minor and his character is never developed. Nick Chopper has issue #9 devoted to his origin, and an unaccompanied time-travelling Scarecrow visits Leonardo DaVinci for the whole of issue #6, but Lion never appears in more than a few panels at a time. How does he feel about his Clark Kent/Superman transformations from regular guy in a suit to super-masculine animal with muscles for days? Is he the traditional strong and silent type? How does he feel about having to always get new shirts? Being a stereotypically traditional male, he does not express his feelings.

Oz Squad was not the only dark Oz comic created during the 1990s. Plotted by Ralph Griffith and scripted by Stuart Kerr, twenty issues of *Oz* were published by Caliber Comics from 1994 to 1996. Arrow Comics took over in 1997, calling it *Dark Oz* for five issues, and in 1998–99 came out with nine issues of *The Land of Oz,* which were "more orthodox" ("Oz [comics]"). Caliber also issued two mini-series and five special prequel issues outside the main narrative sequence, and here we will focus on the Lion as presented in the twenty issues and five prequels. One female and two male college-age friends are transported to an Oz that is ten years after Dorothy was there in the original story. Scarecrow, Tin Woodsman, and Lion are evil kings, enchanted by the Nome King, who despotically rules in the Emerald City. The two college-age males figure out how to change the evil kings back to good guys. Other familiar Oz characters, including a more violent Tik-Tok, Hungry Tiger, Jack Pumpkinhead, Woggle-bug, General Jinjur, Amber Ombi, the Gump, the Sawhorse, and a Hammerhead, are cast as the Freedom Fighters—underground rebels planning to get rid of the Nome King and put Ozma back on the throne. At the end of fifteen issues, Ozma is back on the throne, but due to ten years of the oppression of the Nome King, Oz is not as merry is it used to be. There are many fight scenes which have little or no dialog.

A 1995 prequel special issue titled "Lion" and issue #5 both feature the evil Lion. The Scarecrow and Tin Woodman each have two issues as well, but in the larger story the Lion is not given as much action as the Tin Woodsman or Scarecrow. The Lion in this *Oz* is a talking animal who walks upright and wears a loincloth. He is "one of the most powerful creatures in all of Oz" (issue #14, p. 19). Once free from the enchantment of being evil, he defeats an equally powerful Winged Monkey because he "now rules his own heart and has the strength of his passions" (issue #14, p. 19). In an extra-textual comment in issue #1, the authors say, "Few in Oz would dare to call this King of the Forest a coward!" (38), but his cowardly roots appear when he occasionally advises caution or is more doubtful than his two companions. This is as close as this Lion comes to being meek or domestic, and is a very nice touch. The Lion's royalty is stressed in his prequel special. During his fight with the Hungry Tiger he says, "The crown of the King of the Jungle. No longer a fancy plaything, a mere symbol. For now I am a true king with all of the power that goes with such a crown. Do I not look regal, Tiger?" (10).

In Baum's Oz, difference is not just tolerated, but celebrated. Dorothy's companions and others are literally celebrities. In both of these comic series, when the Lion is no longer cowardly, he loses his uniqueness. The Scarecrow is still made of straw, and the Tin Man, or Woodsman, is still made of tin. Whether they are evil or fighting for good, the reader/viewer still knows who they are, but the newly reconstituted Lion just looks like any old ferocious lion. Being cowardly is a behavior and a psychological trait; the former Cowardly Lion's identity is erased when he becomes simply a fighter. The Lion, the Scarecrow, and the Tin Woodsman all act the same. Their characters are hardly differentiated. They are just drawn differently.

Two twenty-first-century television shows also offer a darker vision of the Land of Oz, the Sci Fi channel miniseries *Tin Man* (2007) and the NBC television series *Emerald City* (2015). The Cowardly Lion as such does not appear in either show, but there is an analogous character in each. *Tin Man* is a miniseries broadcast in three 90-minute segments on the Sci Fi channel in 2007. It became Sci Fi's "most-watched program" (Castro). The Oz of *Tin Man* is called "The O.Z." or "Outer Zone." Much of the land is desolate, presumably due to totalitarian methods of the evil sorceress Azkadellia ("Poppies" *Oz Wiki*). Her tight-fitting outfits allow for "unnecessary shots of her heaving bosom" (civilservant). The look of the O.Z. is high steam-punk, with cars and guns, nefarious machines, and lots of gears. There are drugs and debauchery in abundance, and a *Star Wars*–like "resistance" opposing Azkadellia. The "Dorothy" character is D.G., played by Zooey Deschanel. She was born Ozian royalty, but sent to Kansas to be protected from her evil older sister, Azkadellia. The story of *Tin Man* is DG's quest to recover memories of her past, find her real family, and use her "light" to stop her sister from creating permanent "darkness."

Early in her quest, D.G. befriends Glitch, a former advisor to her mother the queen, half of whose brain was taken by the evil sister (he locks his skull with a zipper). D.G.'s next companion is Cain, who was formerly a sheriff with a tin badge working for the Wizard (called here "The Mystic Man"). D.G. meets her third companion when she encourages Cain to free something caught in a cocoon. It is Raw, analogous to the Cowardly Lion. He is a hybrid human/lion "Viewer." (This is never stated explicitly in the miniseries, but online material always refers to him using this term ["Raw" *Oz Wiki*].) By touching another creature, he can create images of what the other creature has experienced. He also heals with his touch. He seems to shun the spotlight, and is not happy about being forced to produce empathic images.

Raw speaks like Tarzan and looks like the missing link or Bigfoot. His beard is tied to create a tail, and he also has a knot or ribbon in his tail, perhaps nods to the Lion's ribbon in the MGM film. He sports black leather fingerless motorcycle gloves with spiky chrome studs, but his hands are often folded in submissiveness. Raw exhibits no particular strength, and is often seen trembling or hunched in a meek, frightened posture. He is a sensitive and loyal companion who eschews drama. By the end of the series, and after a pep talk from D.G., he is ferocious enough to kill Azkadellia's chief mad scientist. Unlike most versions of the Lion, Raw is not unique, but seems to be part of a race or tribe of similar creatures ("Raw" *Reference Wiki*). Azkadellia has imprisoned at least two other lion-like beings with the same ability to sense and project other people's feelings and experiences. Fully grown Lylo is Azkadellia's main source of information, and Kalm is a youngster. The spotlight is on Raw much less than Glitch (the Scarecrow equivalent) or Cain (the Tin Woodman analog), but Raw's gift of being an empath—being more sensitive to others' feelings than the stereotypical male of any culture—allows him to become the most interesting and relatable of the dark Oz Lions.

Unlike *Tin Man*, which had a fixed length, *Emerald City* was written to be an ongoing series. Nevertheless, it was cancelled after a ten-episode first season. While Dorothy gets back to Kansas in the last episode, there is a cliff-hanger setting up Dorothy's second trip to Oz. Like the O.Z., the Oz of *Emerald City* is full of sex, drugs, and violence. The Wizard has come to power by first defeating the Beast Forever, a creature that shows up periodically in various elemental forms. This Wizard then has the current rulers, Samuel and Katherine Pastoria, slashed to pieces by Eamonn, the head of his Guard. The Witch of the West runs a brothel and keeps herself and her charges feeling good with poppies. While there is no explicit sex, heterosexual couples are seen the night before and the morning after. As in Baum's second Oz novel, *The Marvelous Land of Oz*, the orphan boy Tip is really the female Ozma, the heir to the throne of Oz. In this version, once Tip is Ozma, she gets in touch with her true powers and leads a band of witches against the Wizard.

The character that brings to mind the Cowardly Lion is Eamonn, the Wizard's right-hand man, head of the Wizard's Guard. The members of the Guard wear faceted armor, usually with helmets, but Eamonn frequently does not wear his helmet. This allows viewers to see his beard and shoulder-length, mane-like dark hair, making him a human who appears vaguely lion-like. He first appears when the Wizard charges him to lead a group of guardsmen to discover what came from the rip in the sky. A flashback scene shows viewers that Eamonn was wearing a lion outfit when he killed Ozma's parents. The outfit is primarily a head with front paws projecting from the wearer's shoulders, with a lion-colored cape attached in back. In the final episode of the series, when Tip/Ozma arrives at the Emerald City, Eamonn appears on the royal staircase wearing the lion outfit. He kneels before Ozma, and puts down his sword to accept her judgment. When Ozma asks why he killed her parents, he replies, "To save myself" (10:04–10:06). He says he spared Ozma because she reminded him of his daughter, and he saw himself the way she would see him: "a murderer, a coward" (10:34–10:39). Still kneeling, he gives Ozma the crown. As punishment, Ozma takes away his family without killing them by removing their memories. She then strips Eamonn of his land and title and condemns him to wander Oz "as the beast you truly are" (13:29–13:32). Eamonn is last seen walking along a road made of yellow bricks in the lion suit. He looks up to see the shadow of a flying Beast Forever and croaks out a roar (episode 10). The head of the Wizard's Guard is a human, not an animal, but he takes on the appearance of a lion with his outfit. His strength is shown when he slashes the King and Queen of Oz to bits, as is his association with royalty. He is also the one to return the crown of Oz to Ozma and he briefly runs the Emerald City when the Wizard sets off to Ev.

Eamonn is a ferocious warrior, but he also has a good heart. At the behest of the Wizard, he orders young girls in the Emerald City to be rounded up because they might be witches. But one citizen pleads with him, and he relents and lets the girls be quarantined in their homes. In addition, Eamonn's acknowledgment of being a coward while kneeling at the feet of Ozma is a sacrifice of sorts. He is seen as being domestic with his family, the members of which he cares about greatly.

Loyalty seems to be Eamonn's most prominent quality. He is a steadfast protector and advisor to the Wizard. He is a loyal officer, good at following orders. When the Wizard departs to Ev to get an army's worth of guns, Eamonn says he should be with the Wizard. But the Wizard counters by leaving Eamonn to run the Emerald City in his place. Eamonn is "weirdly underdeveloped" (Burt) and, given his importance in the plot, it is bizarre that there is no explanation of why he wears the lion outfit. Perhaps the writers had more planned for him in the second season that never happened.

While the Lions or their equivalents in the four dark stories are not the Cowardly Lion we know and love, they are not uniformly macho.

- In *Oz Squad*, Lion is fierce when a lion, but also makes jokes. As a human, he is a government operative, asserting his authority.
- While the Caliber Lion is a vicious fighter both when evil and when good, he is also more cautious than the Tin Man or the Scarecrow. He also exhibits remnants of his vaudeville/Lahr origins: "I knew we shouldn't trust a Nome. But would anyone listen to me? Nooo!" (Caliber issue zero.)
- *Tin Man*'s Raw is an empath, and only manages to be brutal at the very end of the story after a pep talk from DG, the Dorothy figure.
- Eamonn in *Emerald City* is a violent soldier, but he is a human with feelings. He wants to protect his family, and he listens to a friend and refrains from one bad deed.

Bring Back the Sissy—or—Who Wants to Be a Macho Man?

The Lions of the dark Oz stories differ greatly from their counterparts in the MGM film and Baum's original story. What does this mean for readers and viewers today?

Most writing on Oz describes the texts of Oz stories and does not talk about what readers and viewers get from the stories, except perhaps anecdotally (Davis, Doty). As part of Dee Michel's research into why gay boys and gay men love *The Wizard of Oz*, he asked respondents about their favorite characters and also those with whom they identified (9). This research showed that the Lion's sissyness resonates with some gay fans (20). They identify with him more than any other character except Dorothy, and he is gay Oz fans' fourth most popular character, after Dorothy, the Scarecrow, and the Wicked Witch of the West. Fans say they identified with the Lion when they were younger because they themselves were considered "sissies" as kids and found solace in him (109).

What is so marvelous about Baum's Cowardly Lion and Bert Lahr's rendition in the MGM film is what a stereotypical sissy he is. While all three of Dorothy's companions in the *Wonderful Wizard* and the MGM film model nontraditional male behavior, it is the Lion who is the most anti-masculine. The Cowardly Lion is a role model for young gay boys and non-macho heterosexuals, precisely because he is cowardly. When he loses his cowardice, he loses what makes him special. If the Lions in dark Oz stories are not relished by gender atypical boys, who appreciates them? Presumably the target audience of these comics, like that of most comics: straight male teenagers.

The dark Oz comics depict a strong and brutal Lion, with violence apparently his raison d'être. The dark television series present more nuanced characters who are not notable for being either strong or violent, but the Oz the characters inhabit is similar to that of the dark comics. "Sex, drugs and, rock and roll" was the straight boy's mantra in the 1960s and 1970s ("Sex"). Rock and roll is replaced here by fighting, but *Twentieth Century Oz* had a rock score, with Dorothy as a groupie. *Emerald City* and *Tin Man* add sex and drugs to the violence, and Oz becomes a stereotypical teenage heterosexual boy's sexual fantasy.

My guess is that the creators of all four dark Oz works consciously tried to reach the science fiction target audience, but they could also be embodying their own fantasies. A third possibility is that the creators of the lions in *Oz Squad*, the Caliber *Oz*, and *Emerald City* are reacting specifically against the namby pamby Cowardly Lion created by Baum and MGM. A violent Lion betrays Baum's vision of a nontraditional masculinity. This is a loss for the LGBTQ community in particular and our culture as a whole. But luckily for gender atypical youngsters, the newer versions have not replaced the older. Baum's *The Wonderful Wizard of Oz* and the MGM film *The Wizard of Oz* are still readily available to all who seek them, with images of a sissy Lion in abundance. And in those classic versions, as well as in dozens of other later incarnations of Oz in all media, the Cowardly Lion is still a coward.

WORKS CITED

Adamson, Joy. *Born Free*. Pantheon Books, 1960.
Ahlquist, Steve. *The Complete Annotated Oz Squad*. Tumbletap, 2009.
_____. *Oz Squad*. #1–3, Brave New Words, 1991. #4–10, Patchwork Press, 1994–1996.
_____. *Oz Squad: March of the Tin Soldiers*. Smashwords, 2011.
_____. *Oz-Squad.com*, https://www.oz-squad.com/, accessed 24 September 2021.
Allers, Roger, and Rob Minkoff, dirs. *The Lion King*. Walt Disney Pictures, 1994.
Baum, L. Frank. *The New Wizard of Oz*. Movie ed., Bobbs-Merrill, 1939.
Beckwith, Osmond. "The Oddness of Oz." *Children's Literature* 5 (1976): 74–91.
Brewer, E. Cobham. "Lion." *Brewer's Dictionary of Phrase and Fable*. Revised by John Freeman, rev. ed. Harper and Row, 1963. 553–55.

Britannica. "Lion." *Britannica.com*, https://www.britannica.com/animal/lion, accessed 15 September 2021.

Bruce-Mitford, Miranda. *The Illustrated Book of Signs & Symbols*. DK Publishing, 1996.

Burt, Kayti. "*Emerald City* Episode 10 Review: No Place Like Home." *Den of Geek*, 4 March 2017, https://www.denofgeek.com/tv/emerald-city-episode-10-review-no-place-like-home/, accessed 16 September 2021.

Castro, Adam-Troy. "Sci-Fi Sets the Record Straight on *Tin Man* TV Series." *SyFy Wire*, 14 December 2012, https://www.syfy.com/syfywire/sci_fi_sets_the_record_straight_on_tin_man_tv_series, accessed 15 September 2021.

civilservant. "Re: No Place Like the O.Z." *Clothesmonaut*, 16 April 2009, https://clothesmonaut.wordpress.com/tag/azkadellia/, accessed 30 October 2021.

"Cultural Depictions of Lions." *Wikipedia*, https://en.wikipedia.org/wiki/Cultural_depictions_of_lions, accessed 15 September 2021.

Davis, Reid. "What WOZ: Lost Objects, Repeat Viewings, and the Sissy Warrior." *Film Quarterly* 55, no. 2 (Winter 2001–02): 2–13.

Doty, Alexander. "'My Beautiful Wickedness': *The Wizard of Oz* as Lesbian Fantasy." *Flaming Classics: Queering the Film Canon*. Routledge, 2000.

Farmer, Philip Jose. *A Barnstormer in Oz, or, A Rationalization and Extrapolation of the Split-Level Continuum*. Phantasia Press, 1982.

Fleming, Victor, dir. *The Wizard of Oz* MGM, 1939.

Green, Joey. *The Zen of Oz: Ten Spiritual Lessons from Over the Rainbow*. Renaissance Books, 1998.

Griffith, Ralph. *Oz*. Caliber Comics, 1994–1996.

Hartwell, David. "Running Away from the Real World." *Age of Wonders: Exploring the World of Science Fiction*. McGraw-Hill, 1984. 61–73.

Karp, Andrew. "Utopian Tension in L. Frank Baum's Oz." *Utopian Studies* 9, no. 2 (1998): 103–21.

Langley, Noel, Florence Ryerson, and Edgar Allan Woolf. *The Wizard of Oz: The Screenplay*. Michael Patrick Hearn, editor. Delta/Dell, 1989.

"The Library Lions." *New York Public Library*, https://www.nypl.org/help/about-nypl/library-lions, accessed 16 September 2021.

Löfvén, Chris, dir. *Twentieth Century Oz* (originally called *Oz* and also called *Oz—A Rock 'n' Roll Road Movie*). Greater Union, 1976.

Lumet, Sidney, dir. *The Wiz*. Universal Pictures and Motown Productions, 1978.

Martin, George. *A Song of Fire and Ice*. Bantam, 1996.

Michel, Dee. *Friends of Dorothy: Why Gay Boys and Gay Men Love* The Wizard of Oz. Dark Ink Press, 2018.

"Oz (comics)." *Wikipedia*, https://en.wikipedia.org/wiki/Oz_(comics), accessed 15 September 2021.

"Poppies." *Oz Wiki*, https://oz.fandom.com/wiki/Poppies#Tinman, accessed 15 September 2021.

"Raw." *Oz Wiki*, https://oz.fandom.com/wiki/Raw, accessed 7 October 2021

"Raw." *Reference Wiki*, https://referencewiki.bookwormlibrary.us/index.php?title=Raw, accessed 16 September 2021.

"Sex Drugs and Rock and Roll." *A Journal of Musical Things*, https://www.ajournalofmusicalthings.com/-phrase-sex-drugs-rocknroll-actually-come/, accessed 20 September 2021.

Singh, Tarsem, dir. *Emerald City*. National Broadcasting Company (NBC), 2016–2017.

Skoble, Aeon J. "Superhero Revisionism in Watchmen and the Dark Knight Returns." *Superheroes and Philosophy: Truth Justice, and the Socratic Way*, Tom Morris and Matt Morris, editors. Open Court, 2005. 21–41.

Smith, Richard. "Daring to Dream: On the Centenary of the Birth of Yip Harburg." *Gay Times* (London) 211 (April 1996): 60–61.

Thompson, Ruth Plumly. *The Cowardly Lion of Oz*. Reilly & Lee, 1923.

Tresidder, Jack. "Lion." *Dictionary of Symbols*. Chronicle Books, 1997. 123–125.

Tyler, Parker. *Screening the Sexes: Homosexuality in the Movies*. Da Capo Press, 1993.

Willing, Nick, dir. *Tin Man*. RHI Entertainment and the Sci Fi Channel, 2007

Wolf, Stacy. "'Defying Gravity': Queer Conventions in the Musical *Wicked*." *Theatre Journal* 60, no. 1 (March 2008): 1–21.

A Good Man but a Bad Wizard?

The Shifting Moral Character of the Wizard of Oz

J.L. Bell

In the second chapter of *The Wonderful Wizard of Oz*, the Good Witch of the North advises Dorothy to walk to the Emerald City and ask "Oz, the Great Wizard" to send her home. The first question the little girl asks about Oz is "Is he a good man?" The witch can reply only "He is a good Wizard. Whether he is a man or not I cannot tell, for I have never seen him" (27). The Good Witch is not sure the Wizard is a man, good or bad, but she is sure he is a wizard. As it turns out, Oz is *not* a wizard—and the question of whether he is a good man hangs in the air. This early exchange about the Wizard's moral standing begins a dialogue that runs through L. Frank Baum's book, subsequent books, and early adaptations of the Oz books into other media.

As Dorothy nears the Emerald City, having gathered the Scarecrow, Tin Woodman, and Cowardly Lion along the way, the information she hears about the Wizard becomes more mysterious and threatening. A man living outside the city tells her that Oz "can take on any form he wishes"—bird, elephant, cat, or brownie—"But who the real Oz is, when he is in his own form, no living person can tell" (113). At the city walls the Guardian of the Gates assures Dorothy that the Wizard "rules the Emerald City wisely and well," but "if you come on an idle or foolish errand to bother the wise reflections of the Great Wizard, he might be angry and destroy you all in an instant" (116). Both of those men refer to the Wizard using the term "terrible," as do his servants (126).

Dorothy's meeting with the Wizard bear out those descriptions of a powerful, frightening shape-shifter. "I am Oz, the Great and Terrible," he announces from his throne, in the form of a giant head with no body (127). He appears to each of the other petitioners in a different shape—a lovely winged lady; a giant beast with five eyes, ten limbs, and thick, woolly hair; and a hot ball of fire. These forms seem designed to confound Dorothy's companions by presenting each of them with someone, or something, he cannot connect with (Hearn 194; Tuerk 38). Oz offers all four visitors a fearsome bargain: he will grant their wishes if they kill the Wicked Witch of the West for him. Forestalling the question of whether a good person would ask a little girl to kill, the Wizard tells Dorothy, "Remember that the Witch is Wicked—tremendously Wicked—and ought to be killed" (129).

To everyone's surprise, Dorothy does kill the Wicked Witch. When she brings her companions back to the Emerald City, however, the Wizard does not immediately fulfill his side of the bargain. Pressured into letting the group into his throne room, he

Dorothy goes before the Wizard of Oz to ask for help (W.W. Denslow illustration from *The Wonderful Wizard of Oz* [1960 edition]).

manifests as nothing but "a solemn Voice," and the "stillness of the empty room was more dreadful than any of the forms they had seen Oz take." Dorothy and her friends ask Oz to carry out his promise to them. He replies, "What promise?" This angers the visitors. In the brouhaha, Dorothy's dog Toto knocks over a screen and reveals "a little old man, with a bald head and a wrinkled face, who seemed to be as much surprised as they were" (182–83).

Oz, the great and powerful shapeshifter, thus turns out to be a small man speaking "in a trembling voice" and begging Dorothy and her friends not to reveal his secret. "I have been making believe," he admits; "I'm supposed to be a Great Wizard." The Scarecrow declares Oz to be a "humbug," and the man agrees with that term, "rubbing his hands together as if it pleased him" (184). The Wizard explains how he worked at an American circus, was carried away to Oz in an errant balloon, and seized on the natives' belief that he was a wizard to have them build the Emerald City. He concludes his story by declaring that he cannot keep any of the promises he made to Dorothy and her friends. That prompts this exchange: "'I think you are a very bad man,' said Dorothy. 'Oh, no, my dear; I'm really a very good man, but I'm a very bad Wizard, I must admit'" (189). Oz's claim thus presents a moral paradox for readers. The Wizard is an admitted liar on a grand scale. He cannot keep his side of a deal he designed. He sent a little girl and her companions into dreadful danger from which they barely escaped, and there may be other misdeeds in his past. Nonetheless, he claims, "I'm really a very good man." Is that possible?

Having come clean to Dorothy and her companions, the Wizard tries to remain honest with them. He tells the Scarecrow, "You don't need [brains]." Spelling out one of the book's morals, he assures the Lion, "You have plenty of courage." He advises the Tin Woodman, "I think you are wrong to want a heart. It makes most people unhappy." All three immediately reject his advice (189–90), so with a sigh the Wizard agrees to go back to his humbuggery. The title of the chapter that follows highlights the paradox of the character Baum created: "The Magic Art of the Great Humbug."

By using the term "humbug," and showing his character embracing it, Baum linked Oz to the legendary showman P.T. Barnum, who had died just nine years earlier. Baum knew that American popular culture linked Barnum with fooling the public. In an 1890 newspaper column about unscrupulous shopkeepers, he wrote, "Barnum was right when he declared the American people liked to be deceived. At least they make no effort to defend themselves. The merchants are less to blame than their customers, for the cry is not so much for genuine worth as for something pretty and attractive at a good cost" (Koupal 114).

According to Barnum, his humbuggery was about more than parting fools from their money. Like Oz, he was pleased to be called a humbug. In 1855, the year before Baum was born, Barnum proudly declared in his autobiography, "The titles of 'humbug' and the 'prince of humbugs'' were first applied to me by myself" ("Life" 225). He distinguished between his form of enticing the public and frauds of the sort he exposed ten years later in *The Humbugs of the World*. His humbuggery was harmless, Barnum insisted, because his New York City museum gave visitors plenty of value for their money. As he explained:

> my permanent collection of curiosities is, without doubt, abundantly worth the uniform charge of admission to all the entertainments of the establishment, and I can therefore afford to be accused of "humbug" when I add such transient novelties as increase its attractions. If I

have exhibited a questionable dead mermaid in my Museum, it should not be overlooked that I have also exhibited cameleopards, a rhinoceros, grisly [*sic*] bears, orang-outangs [*sic*], great serpents, etc., about which there could be no mistake because they were alive; and I should hope that a little "clap-trap" occasionally, in the way of transparencies, flags, exaggerated pictures, and puffing advertisements, might find an offset in a wilderness of wonderful, instructive, and amusing realities ["Life" 225].

More privately, in an 1845 letter to C.D. Stuart, Barnum wrote:

humbugging [is] particularly requisite for our line of business, for as the Lord does not work miracles now-a-days—and as the people are determined to see miracles wrought & are willing to pay for them too—of course it is our duty as well as pleasure & profit to perform said miracles, or rather pretend to do so which is quite as well provided the thing is managed adroitly. Let "humbug" then be the motto, but do not confound that charming and valuable science with the stupid catch-penny impositions of the day, which bear the stamp of falsehood upon their brow, & make each victim exclaim, "curse the rascal[—]he has cheated me." … A genuine humbug consists in making a man feel that he has got the worth of his money [Saint-Pierre].

Barnum wrote about humbuggery in the middle of the nineteenth century when his primary business was his New York museum. In 1871 he lent his celebrated name to a traveling circus. That fall, the Barnum show visited Syracuse, New York, near the teen-aged Baum's home, shortly after an aeronaut made a balloon ascension in the same city (Loncraine 52–53). Ten years later Barnum negotiated a merger of his circus with James A. Bailey's similar show, so Baum's readers knew of the Barnum & Bailey Circus. In *Dorothy and the Wizard in Oz*, Baum cemented Oz's link to Barnum by having him work for "Bailum and Barney's Great Consolidated Shows" (44).

We see Barnum's style of humbugging in how the Wizard serves the Scarecrow, Tin Woodman, and Cowardly Lion. Those characters are all "determined to *see* miracles wrought," even after the little man has assured them that no miracles are necessary. So Oz pretends to supply what they want from a wizard, with enough style and art to make each feel they have gotten value for all their effort. Baum thus offers his readers an unspoken lesson, acknowledging that sometimes we need symbolic outside reassurance of our internal qualities.

Oz cannot gently fool Dorothy the same way, however. She does not want, or need, any better internal qualities. She wants to be in a different place, and the only way the Wizard can think to transport her home is in a hot-air balloon—which we already know from his previous journey is a chancy proposition. Baum also makes clear that Oz has reasons of his own for leaving the Emerald City: "If I should go out of this Palace my people would soon discover I am not a Wizard, and then they would be vexed with me for having deceived them" (205). Still, the balloon seems to be Dorothy's only way home, so she dutifully sets about helping Oz sew the canopy.

But then the balloon sails away without Dorothy and Toto. It is clear that Oz did not want to leave them behind, but still he has failed to fulfill his promise to carry her home. His good intentions are not enough. Baum himself raises the question of the Wizard's moral standing as Dorothy and her companions set off to ask Glinda the Good Witch for help:

"Oz was not such a bad Wizard, after all," said the Tin Woodman, as he felt his heart rattling around in his breast.

"He knew how to give me brains, and very good brains, too," said the Scarecrow.

"If Oz had taken a dose of the same courage he gave me," added the Lion, "he would have been a brave man."

Dorothy said nothing. Oz had not kept the promise he made her, but he had done his best, so she forgave him. As he said, he was a good man, even if he was a bad Wizard [220].

Dorothy thus silently disagrees with the other characters' conviction that Oz was not "a bad Wizard, after all." Their new self-identities require them to believe in his ability to confer a heart, brains, and courage, though they might recognize his flaws, such as not being "a brave man." Dorothy, on the other hand, cannot overlook the Wizard's failure to carry her back home, so in her mind she still decides "he was a bad Wizard."

At the same time, Dorothy agrees with the Wizard's insistence that "he was a good man." He had not "kept his promise," but she believes that "he had done his best." Dorothy thus evaluates Oz's morality by his intentions, not his deceptive methods or insufficient results. With the book's heroine reaching this conclusion, it would be hard for readers to disagree. And yet questions do float over the character of the Wizard. He has proved unreliable for Dorothy, provided sham assets to her companions, and left the people of the Emerald City as deceived as ever. Are these the actions of a truly good man?[1]

The next time L. Frank Baum presented the Wizard of Oz to an audience, the story pointed to a different conclusion. Baum was part of the team of dramatists who created the 1902 stage extravaganza *The Wizard of Oz*, based on his novel—but only loosely.

Baum's original script for a comic opera cut down the part of the Cowardly Lion and cut out the quest to kill the Wicked Witch of the West, but otherwise stayed close to his book. Again, Dorothy and her companions travel to the Emerald City to ask favors from the Wizard. Taking various forms, he refuses to help them, but then Dorothy reveals that man to be a fake. He sings a song titled "When You Want to Fool the Public," echoing Barnum. Oz provides the Scarecrow and Tin Woodman with symbolic brains and heart, advises Dorothy to visit Glinda for a way home, and departs in a balloon. This character thus avoids some of the worst failings of the Wizard in the book.

Theatrical producer Fred Hamlin thought Baum's script was not entertaining enough and brought in director Julian Mitchell to rework it, producing a more loosely plotted extravaganza. Mitchell added several subplots, including a love story for an adolescent Dorothy. Most important, he constructed a major storyline about the attempts of the rightful ruler of Oz, Pastoria, to wrest his crown back from the usurping Wizard. The goal of these changes appears to have been to please adult theater-goers. A promotional booklet for the show's Chicago premiere declared that, even though *The Wizard of Oz* was based on a children's fairy tale, "it will be sufficiently spicy and alluring to engross a sophisticated Chicago audience, ... play-goers of all ages and all degrees of intellect" (Swartz 61).

One result was to make the character of the Wizard into an out-and-out villain. As in the book, the circus performer became ruler of Oz after landing in a balloon. However, the stage Wizard actively seized the throne by fooling Pastoria into entering the basket of his balloon and cutting the ropes, sending the king back to America. The first performance even suggested the Wizard was holding Pastoria's beloved daughter, Princess Weenietotts, as a hostage in his court. (That detail was cut after one performance to shorten the run time.)

Baum's book held out the possibility that the Wizard was a genuine magician until Dorothy's return to the Emerald City. In contrast, even before the Wizard appears on stage in the extravaganza, another character denounces him as a fake. His magic consists of familiar vaudeville tricks, such as having an assistant step into a large basket, running it through with swords, and then letting the assistant out unscathed. While the Wizard provides the Scarecrow and Tin Woodman with fake brains and heart, he offers no help for Dorothy, not even a balloon ride. As Mark Evan Swartz wrote in *Oz Before the Rainbow*, Baum's book presented the Wizard as charming and "still essentially beneficent," but in Mitchell's extravaganza "he is not particularly likable" (52).

After Pastoria overthrows the Wizard, the chorus sings a song Baum wrote with the composer Paul Tietjens called "The Wizard Is No Longer King," all about putting the fraudster in jail. In the uproar, however, the Wizard escapes in his balloon. The chorus still sings, "Rejoice for the Wizard is no longer king!" Swartz notes, "The people of Oz are happy to be rid of him" (52). In sum, the Wizard character that people saw on stage was not just a bad wizard but a bad man.

The Wizard was the show's title character, and the actor who played that role, John Slavin, originally had top billing. A dialect comedian with a fine singing voice, Slavin was assigned the already popular song "Mr. Dooley," about an Irishman, and "Wee Highland Mon," about Scotland. However, at the very first performance it became clear that David Montgomery and Fred Stone as the Tin Woodman and the Scarecrow had danced away with the show. "I guess I haven't got the goods this time. They hardly knew I was there," Slavin told the *Chicago Evening Post*. He changed the character's makeup and talked about trying different accents, but got to the root of the problem when he said, "If there is a man in this town who will 'write up' that part for me and make something out of it I'll pay him $200" (Swartz 87). The problem was that this Wizard had little audience appeal. Slavin left the show after only a few weeks. A comedian named Bobby Gaylor took over the role and played it for more humor as a stereotypical stage Irishman. Later another Irish comedian, James K. Wesley, would replace Gaylor.

In January 1903, *The Wizard of Oz* opened on Broadway. All extravaganzas of the period could evolve from month to month, with songs or performers being replaced to keep audiences coming back, so the New York audiences saw quite a different show from what had premiered in Chicago. In particular, the Wizard's first number was now "On a Pay Night Evening," linking him with the working man (or, to be exact, with a set of chorus girls carrying pickaxes and dinner pails). The revelation of the Wizard's fakery became the climax of the second act. Most important, this version of the show kept the Wizard in the third act as a convict in striped clothing, weighed down by a ball and chain. Pastoria, king once more, sentences him to clean the streets, underscoring how this Wizard is a villain to be punished.

The *Wizard of Oz* stage show was a huge hit in New York, running straight from January to October even though theaters usually shut down in summer. Fred Hamlin then sent two productions on the road, playing in cities large and small and occasionally returning to New York. In 1906 Montgomery and Stone left the show, and later that year Hamlin sold the rights to another theatrical firm, but *The Wizard of Oz* continued to tour with new actors and musical numbers until 1909. The producers then made the play available for stock and amateur companies, leading to regular local performances through the 1910s. Thus, in the first two decades of the twentieth century, the stage play was as influential as Baum's books in defining Oz and its major characters for the public, especially adults. That audience knew the Wizard as a comical villain, not a sympathetic good man with good intentions who happens to be a bad wizard.

In 1904, as the extravaganza toured the country and made him rich, Baum wrote his first sequel to *The Wonderful Wizard of Oz*. Titled *The Marvelous Land of Oz* but subtitled *Being an account of the further adventures of the Scarecrow and Tin Woodman...*, the book featured pictures of Montgomery and Stone in their fairyland costumes. Baum drew a lot of his inspiration from the stage show. The characterizations, the humor, the interlocking storylines, the political overlay, the armies of young female soldiers in ranks like a chorus line—all show the influence of Mitchell's extravaganza. That play featured King Pastoria as a major character, with a very brief appearance of his daughter. Baum adopted the idea of Pastoria as a past king of Oz with a lost daughter and built his dénouement around that.

The Wizard himself never appears in *The Marvelous Land of Oz*, but the memory of him as ruler of the Emerald City hovers over the story. Early on, the young hero Tip explains to his recently animated creation Jack Pumpkinhead that the Emerald City "was built by a mighty and wonderful Wizard named Oz" (35). Soon, however, Tip summarizes the preceding story this way:

> Dorothy went to the Emerald City to ask the Wizard to send her back to Kansas; and the Scarecrow and the Tin Woodman went with her. But the Wizard couldn't send her back, because he wasn't so much of a Wizard as he might have been. And then they got angry at the Wizard, and threatened to expose him; so the Wizard made a big balloon and escaped in it, and no one has ever seen him since [36–37].

In Baum's previous book, the Wizard floats away in his balloon before he means to; only in the stage play does he use it to "escape." There is no hint in *The Wonderful Wizard of Oz* that Dorothy and her companions reveal Oz's lies to the people of the Emerald City, but he is publicly exposed in the play—and evidently also before *The Marvelous Land of Oz*.

Throughout this second book, the Scarecrow and Tin Woodman praise the Wizard for giving them their brains and heart. When a new character, the Woggle-bug, announces, "I have been informed that the Wonderful Wizard of Oz was nothing more than a humbug!" the straw and tin men are affronted. The Scarecrow insists, "he was a very great Wizard, I assure you. It is true he was guilty of some slight impostures..." (241–42). One of Baum's strengths as an author was giving all of the characters he created their own say, and of course the Scarecrow and Tin Woodman still want to believe in Oz's magic even though the whole world has heard the same information as the Woggle-bug.

Still, the Wizard's political actions are troubling. Toward the end of the book Glinda asks the Scarecrow how he came to the throne of the Emerald City.

> "I got it from the Wizard of Oz, and by the choice of the people," returned the Scarecrow, uneasy at such questioning.
> "And where did the Wizard get it?" she continued gravely.
> "I am told he took it from Pastoria, the former King," said the Scarecrow, becoming confused under the intent look of the Sorceress [240].

That was not part of the story the little man told in the previous book, but it is part of the stage play, and it presents Oz's rule in a different light.

Glinda goes on to reveal that the late king Pastoria had a daughter named Ozma, and that "the Wizard of Oz, when he stole the throne from Ozma's father, hid the girl in some secret place; and by means of a magical trick with which I am not familiar he also managed to prevent her being discovered" (241). This book thus reveals Oz as not simply a usurper but a kidnapper. Finally, Glinda says, "We know that the Wizard taught … many of his tricks of magic" to Mombi the witch, the main villain of this novel (244). Rather than being an antagonist to all the wicked witches, the Wizard was an ally.

After an armed march on the Emerald City, Glinda succeeds in capturing Mombi and forcing her to confess her bargain with Oz: "The Wizard brought to me the girl Ozma, who was then no more than a baby, and begged me to conceal the child.… He taught me all the magical tricks he knew. Some were good tricks, and some were only frauds; but I have remained faithful to my promise" (269–70). Thus, in his eagerness to follow on the success of the stage extravaganza, Baum ended his second Oz book telling readers that the Wizard was a so-so wizard but undoubtedly a bad man.

Baum did not leave the Wizard in that sorry moral state, however. In 1906 he agreed to write new Oz novels which showed Dorothy making more trips to the Emerald City. The second of those adventures, *Dorothy and the Wizard in Oz*, brought back the Wizard as well. In his foreword Baum wrote: "There were many requests from my little correspondents for 'more about the Wizard.' It seems the jolly old fellow made hosts of friends in the first Oz book, in spite of the fact that he frankly acknowledged himself 'a humbug.' … You will find him in these pages, just the same humbug Wizard as before" (9). While reinforcing the idea of humbuggery, Baum made no mention of the more villainous things he had depicted the Wizard doing since his first appearance.

Indeed, the Wizard enters the novel just as he exited *The Wonderful Wizard of Oz*, in a runaway balloon. Dorothy recognizes him immediately, and he confirms by ironically reciting his old line, "I am Oz, the Great and Terrible" (41). There are only slight hints of the stage show's influence. Baum originally wrote that the Wizard's "head was long and entirely bald" (41); illustrator W.W. Denslow drew him with no hair, and also of Dorothy's height. Illustrator John R. Neill appears to have modeled his Wizard after the comedians who played the character on the New York stage, adult-sized and with a fringe of dark hair around his head. That also gave Oz a resemblance to Harry Kellar, who retired from touring theaters as "the Dean of American Magicians" in 1908, just as *Dorothy and the Wizard in Oz* was published (Brown; Hearn 260).

The most important trait of the Wizard remains, however, that he is a humbug. Even he admits, "In the strict sense of the word I am not a Wizard, but only a humbug." Dorothy agrees: "The Wizard of Oz has always been a humbug" (62). Where once the little girl introduced herself to the Wizard as "small and meek," after her first adventure Baum's books consistently emphasize her assertiveness, as in this exchange after a character asks the Wizard, "Do you ever make mistakes?"

"Never!" declared the Wizard, boldly.

"Oh, Oz!" said Dorothy, "you made a lot of mistakes when you were in the marvelous Land of Oz."

"Nonsense!" said the little man, turning red—although just then a ray of violet sunlight was on his round face [42].

Just what those mistakes were, however, Baum never addresses in this book.

The Wizard plays a major role in *Dorothy and the Wizard in Oz*, even more than in Baum's first novel. He joins Dorothy's young cousin Zeb and his horse as her protectors, and she is lucky to have him. The adventures in this book take place in dimly lit caverns among mostly hostile people. There is a great deal of talk about some characters eating others. Oz proves to be a problem-solver, savvy about the people they meet and technologically resourceful. He can turn a pin into a fishhook or ordinary lanterns into an impressive show of "magic."

Just as important, Oz is ruthless in protecting himself and his young friends. He carries a sword and pistols. Forced into a duel with a rival magician, he cuts the sorcerer in two. He lures ignorant people into flames, stabs a bear through the heart, and sets fire to a wooden country and its wooden populace. The Wizard thus not only saves Dorothy, but he also saves Baum from having to depict the little girl committing such murderous violence.

In Chapter 14 of *Dorothy and the Wizard in Oz*, the Wizard returns to the Emerald City. He has expressed interest in seeing the people of Oz again but worries, "I wonder if they would treat me nicely." Dorothy assures him, "They are still proud of their former Wizard, and often speak of you kindly" (161). Indeed, Oz soon meets some of the people who waited on him in *The Wonderful Wizard of Oz*, leading to this exchange:

> "I assure you, my good people, that I do not wish to rule the Emerald City," he added, earnestly.
>
> "In that case you are very welcome!" cried all the servants, and it pleased the Wizard to note the respect with which the royal retainers bowed before him. His fame had not been forgotten in the Land of Oz, by any means [168].

This Wizard is clearly not the usurper portrayed on stage.

Then Dorothy introduces Oz to her friend Ozma, the rightful ruler of Oz—and, according to *The Marvelous Land of Oz*, the Wizard's kidnap victim. They have a long conversation about his past, starting from his childhood:

> "I must tell you that I was born in Omaha, and my father, who was a politician, named me Oscar Zoroaster Phadrig Isaac Norman Henkle Emmannuel Ambroise Diggs, Diggs being the last name because he could think of no more to go before it. Taken altogether, it was a dreadfully long name to weigh down a poor innocent child, and one of the hardest lessons I ever learned was to remember my own name. When I grew up I just called myself O. Z., because the other initials were P-I-N-H-E-A-D; and that spelled 'pinhead,' which was a reflection on my intelligence" [172].

The Wizard repeats his story about accidentally coming to Oz and then nearly as accidentally making himself the founder and ruler of the Emerald City—tacitly following his father into the field of government. Baum hints that the elder Mr. Diggs was a bit of a windbag, and that the callings of politician and humbug circus performer might not be that far apart.

Ozma responds to the Wizard's story by describing the early history of Oz and how her family lost the throne:

> Once upon a time four Witches leagued together to depose the king and rule the four parts of the kingdom themselves; so when the Ruler, my grandfather, was hunting one day, one Wicked Witch named Mombi stole him and carried him away, keeping him a close prisoner. […] Mombi was still my grandfather's jailor, and afterward my father's jailor. When I was born she transformed me into a boy, hoping that no one would ever recognize me and know that I was the rightful Princess of the Land of Oz. But I escaped from her and am now the Ruler of my people [174–75].

This version contains not a word about the Wizard's complicity in Ozma's kidnapping and transformation.[2] And with that erasure, Baum turned his Wizard back into a good man.

Princess Ozma offers the elderly Oz a job for life: "You shall be the Official Wizard of my kingdom, and be treated with every respect and consideration." Dorothy once again notes, "He's only a humbug Wizard, though," to which Ozma replies, "And that is the safest kind of a Wizard to have" (175–76). In this book's final section, Oz tries to save Dorothy the heartache of losing her kitten with another of his non-magical tricks. Though this scheme does not work, Baum once again shows the Wizard using his sly deceptions for the greater good, and for Dorothy's particular benefit.

Obviously Baum liked the character of Oz the Wizard enough to bring him back into the Oz books, back to the Emerald City, and back into Dorothy's good graces. It is hard not to see this decision as rooted in the novelist's affinity with the character (see Hearn 269). Baum himself was a showman—a professional actor, playwright, and theatrical producer in his early years. He never discarded that ambition, going back to writing for the stage while he found success as a novelist, and even exploring the new medium of cinema with the Oz Film Manufacturing Company.

Baum was also, of course, a storyteller, best known for impossible tales of magical adventures. Every fiction author is in some sense a liar, telling readers about events that never happened to people who never lived. Baum went further into humbuggery, however. He wrote books for different audiences using seven pen names. Both in print and in conversation, he teased people by quoting fictitious Bible verses. Baum's nephew Henry B. Brewster recalled, "Mr. Baum always liked to tell wild stories, with a perfectly straight face, and earnestly, as though he really believed them himself.... There was nothing wrong, but he did love to 'fairytale,' or as you might say, tell 'white lies'" (Hearn xciv).

Much like Barnum, Baum used newspapers to spread word of his entertainment enterprises. He told stories in publicity interviews that are, to say the least, hard to corroborate. In 1905, for instance, he informed a reporter that he had bought Pedloe Island off the coast of California to make it into an amusement park called "The Land of Oz." Though this news story came with the name and photograph of a little girl who was supposed to preside in the park ("A Real Princess"), there was no such island and no other trace of this elaborate plan has surfaced. Having published his own weekly newspaper in Aberdeen, South Dakota, worked as a journalist in Chicago, and edited the trade magazine *The Show Window*, Baum knew the value of entertaining copy. If his tall tales prompted people to pick up his books or attend his shows and they were entertained, by Barnum's rule that was merely harmless humbugging.

The Wizard, having returned to the city he built years before, might have faded off into retirement. Instead, Baum concocted a new dimension to the character over his next two books. The little old man starts to take lessons in real magic from Glinda the Good. At the end of *The Road to Oz*, the Wizard entertains a crowd by making giant soap balloons, large enough to carry people away. In *The Emerald City of Oz*, readers learn that he has invented pills of concentrated learning, then see him turning handkerchiefs into fully furnished tents. "You were always a good man," Dorothy assures him, "even when you were a bad wizard." And her Aunt Em adds, "He's a good wizard now" (244).

When Baum restarted his Oz series in 1913, he presented the Wizard as one of the most powerful magicians in Oz, and possibly the most dynamic. All of Baum's *Little Wizard Stories of Oz* refer to his powers. Most notably, in the story "Little Dorothy and Toto," when the girl and her dog are captured by a magic-working giant named Crinklink, he turns out to be the Wizard in disguise, having devised the scheme to teach

Dorothy a lesson about wandering too far. In *The Patchwork Girl of Oz*, published later that same year, Baum brings the Wizard on at the end to magically solve the problem that has frustrated the young hero. The author could have used Glinda or Ozma with her Magic Belt in this role, but instead the scene confirms Oz's astonishing new level of power.

Making the Wizard a real magician instead of an ordinary old man allowed Baum to continue to use him as a major character. But what kept him interesting? Baum built most of his best characters around contradictions. Ozma looks and plays like a young girl, but she is a dedicated monarch and, later books say, a powerful fairy. The Scarecrow and the Patchwork Girls are literally dummies made of cloth, straw, and cotton, yet they are among the most intelligent people in Oz. The Tin Woodman is metallic but warm-hearted. The Shaggy Man is a hobo proud of his ragged appearance. Jack Pumpkinhead is a tall man with the mind of a child. Tik-Tok the robot is utterly unreliable and liable to run down at any moment. Even Dorothy is a paradox, a simple little girl who spends most of the first books in the series deposing one ruler after another like Napoleon sweeping through Europe.

Resolving those paradoxes, Baum came to understand, rendered the characters far less interesting. *The Wonderful Wizard of Oz* settled the contradiction inherent in the personality of the Cowardly Lion by dosing him with courage, leaving him as a stereotypically brave lion ruling the forest. That character was no longer as compelling, and he had no role in the next book. When Baum brought the Lion back in *Ozma of Oz*, the first thing the character says is to assure Dorothy and readers that he's "as cowardly as ever" (107). Furthermore, the Lion is accompanied by another contradictory creature, the Hungry Tiger, whose tender conscience holds back his ravenous appetite.

When the true nature of the Wizard is finally revealed in *The Wonderful Wizard of Oz*, the character fits that pattern of paradox. Oz is believed to be a powerful magician but is actually a humbug, a good man but a bad wizard. When the character returns in *Dorothy and the Wizard of Oz*, it is entertaining to watch him muster his mechanical resources to fool fairyland audiences into believing that he is doing magic. That pleasure goes away when the Wizard can simply wave his wand over a marble statue and bring it back to life.

Baum nonetheless managed to preserve some of the Wizard's contradictory nature in the second half of his series. Having been a wizard who is really a humbug, the character becomes a humbug who is really a wizard. Baum repeatedly reminds readers that Oz had to learn his craft, unlike the fairy Ozma, and is not nearly as powerful as his teacher, Glinda. Unlike them and other natives of Oz, he is mortal. He is also an older male in a subordinate position to younger (or at least younger-looking) females. In Baum's time, as still to an extent in ours, that is a paradoxical state.

Another notable element of the Wizard's magic is how he incorporates some of the technology of our Great Outside World, just as he did when he used his skills as a balloonist and ventriloquist to convince the people of the Emerald City that he could do magic. In contrast to Ozma's magic belt and fairy wand, the Wizard's magic often consists of physical hardware: handkerchiefs, pincers, and shears. In *Tik-Tok of Oz*, the Wizard has invented a set of magical mobile telephones. Baum often equated the technological advances he had witnessed in America, such as the electric light, with the fairyland magic he imagined. Conversely, it was common for the American press to refer to famous inventors such as Thomas Edison and Nikola Tesla as "wizards."[3]

When Baum used Oz as a major character in his later plots, he usually made sure the man's magic is unavailable or not quite up to the job. In *The Lost Princess of Oz*, the Wizard's black bag of tools has been stolen, and he has only his American ingenuity to help find the thief while protecting Dorothy and her friends. In *The Magic of Oz*, the Wizard's bag is once again stolen at a crucial moment, and he is transformed into a fox. In both that book and *Glinda of Oz*, the Wizard finds his magic ineffective against the powerful spells governing islands. Thus, even when Oz is no longer a "bad wizard," Baum's plots rest on him being a stymied one.

Satisfied with how he characterized the Wizard in his later Oz novels, Baum extended that portrayal into the movies he oversaw as head of the Oz Film Manufacturing Company. The Wizard appears as a supporting character in both *The Patchwork Girl of Oz* and *His Majesty, the Scarecrow of Oz*, released somewhat deceptively as *The New Wizard of Oz*. The character is clearly based on how Baum's books depict the Wizard. Played in the two movies by Todd Wright and J. Charles Haydon, respectively, he was designed to look like Neill's illustrations, with a fringe of hair, large top hat, and frock coat. He is a reliable ally to Ozma and her friends. Most important, he can work actual magic (with the help of cinematic special effects). In sum, he is both a good man and a good wizard.

In contrast, the adaptations of *The Wonderful Wizard of Oz* not made by Baum present the Wizard as morally ambivalent at best, showing the influence of the 1902 stage extravaganza. In 1910, the Selig Polyscope Company released a short film titled *The Wizard of Oz* which portrays the Wizard as a puppet ruler, under "the Power of Momba the Witch"—an amalgamation of Mombi and the Wicked Witch of the West (03:10). In his first scene, this Wizard announces that he wants to escape from the witch's control and return to Omaha. Eventually he floats away in his balloon, leaving Dorothy behind.[4] While not as bad as some versions of the character, this Wizard is out for no one but himself.

The Wizard also appears morally split in Larry Semon's 1925 movie *The Wizard of Oz*, its screenplay credited to Semon, his gag writer Leon Lee, and Baum's son Frank Joslyn Baum, using the pseudonym "L. Frank Baum, Jr." Like the stage show, its storylines emphasize love and political intrigue. Indeed, this adaptation completely jettisons the original story's quests for brains, heart, courage, and a return to Kansas in favor of a new tale about securing Dorothy on the throne of Oz with a boyfriend who can protect her.

In Semon's movie the Wizard, played by fifty-three-year-old comedian Charlie Murray, is the first character that audience members might recognize from any earlier version of the story.[5] In this telling, however, the Wizard is not on the throne of Oz. Instead, that country is under the rule of a usurping prime minister named Krewel and his evil advisors. An intertitle immediately tells viewers that the Wizard is a fake: "just a medicine-show hokum huckster, but he fitted in nicely as the Prime Minister's 'yes-man.'" His job, the dialogue reveals, is to "distract" the people of Oz with spectacle. The Wizard does this with a trick involving a large basket, reminiscent of the stage extravaganza.[6] In short, this supposed "great Wizard of black art" starts out as not only a bad wizard but one of several bad men (05:00–09:30).

Later, however, the 1925 movie shows the Wizard helping the heroes, potentially becoming a good guy. When Dorothy and her companions—in this version, her uncle Henry and three farmhands—are blown to Oz by a storm, the prime minister orders the Wizard to transform the men. Instead, he whispers to the farmhand played by Semon,

"I'm just a fake—I couldn't change a quarter" (47:40). Semon puts on a scarecrow costume and gives the Wizard a wink. The Wizard then takes credit for turning that man into a scarecrow, and for turning another farmhand played by Oliver Hardy into a tin man. The prime minister arrests the three farmhands and the Wizard together, but when the action resumes the Wizard is once again part of the prime minister's court. He then helps two of the captive farmhands escape from a dungeon before disappearing from the movie entirely. It is impossible to derive a coherent storyline from this movie, but the action does depend on the Wizard being morally ambiguous.

When the MGM studio adapted *The Wonderful Wizard of Oz* into a musical, its producers and screenwriters thus had a choice of how to portray the Wizard. Had he stumbled into holding the throne of the Emerald City, or had he usurped the crown from the rightful ruler? Did he treat Dorothy and her companions cold-heartedly, or was he simply trying to survive? The moviemakers chose to follow Baum's original course in presenting the Wizard as a well-intentioned humbug rather than a dangerous fraud.

The studio's most important step was to cast Frank Morgan as the Wizard, as well as four other related roles. Morgan was a popular character actor in his late forties known for portraying, as Leslie Hallowell wrote, "endearing if slightly fuddled" older men (445). He could support big stars like Shirley Temple in *Dimples* and even carry small pictures. Simply by showing audiences Frank Morgan, the studio assured them that the Wizard was a good-hearted man.

Furthermore, the movie prepares its audience for the revelation that the Wizard is a humbug through Dorothy's encounter with his Kansas counterpart, the threadbare traveling magician Professor Marvel, also played by Morgan. Early in the film Dorothy meets the professor while running away from home. Toto steals a sausage, and the man forgives him—an immediate signal of kindness. The professor offers to tell the girl's fortune. The audience quickly sees that he is a fake, peeking through Dorothy's belongings for clues about her life while she keeps her eyes closed. Professor Marvel even lies to the girl about her aunt's health. Yet it is also clear that he does all that for her own good, to send her back home.

With that groundwork laid, the MGM movie could closely follow Baum's story as Dorothy and her companions confront the Wizard after killing the Wicked Witch. As in the book, the Wizard maintains a fearsome face as he refuses to cooperate, the heroes get angry, and Toto ends up revealing a man behind a curtain. And once again the Wizard lays out the contradictions in his character while declaring his fundamental goodness:

WIZARD: I'm a humbug.
DOROTHY: Oh, you're a very bad man!
WIZARD: Oh, no, my dear, I—I'm a very good man—I'm just a very bad Wizard [Langley et al. 122].

NOTES

1. While this essay finds that Baum left the Wizard's moral status up in the air at the end of *The Wonderful Wizard of Oz*, see Richard Tuerk's "The Wonderful Wizard of Oz: The Wizard Himself" for a negative judgment. After comparing the character to a traditional Trickster and a Jungian clown, Tuerk concludes that "Baum depicts the Wizard as a bad Wizard" and also "a bad man who, in spite of themselves, readers find appealing" (Tuerk 35–44).

2. The lack of any confrontation between Ozma and the Wizard over her kidnapping, so clearly established in an earlier Oz book, led Hugh Pendexter III to write the fanfiction story "Oz and the Three Witches"

in 1977. It describes a longer, more frank discussion among Ozma, the Wizard, and Glinda about what exactly the balloonist did to survive his first years in Oz.

3. In *Finding Oz*, Evan I. Schwartz declares that "the four faces of the Wizard" were Edison, Barnum, the oil magnate John D. Rockefeller, and the Hindu monk Swami Vivekananda (228). However, the book offers only the most tenuous support for that assertion, such as newspaper articles Schwartz credits to Baum with no evidence that he actually wrote them or even read them, and public events that Baum may or may not have attended. Edison, Barnum, and Rockefeller were household names in Baum's America, so it is no surprise that he mentioned each man in his writings—as did many other authors. The link from the Wizard's "humbug" to Barnum seems clear. Baum never equated the Wizard and Edison so closely, but he did like to equate modern inventions and magic. The influence of Rockefeller on Oz is hard to discern, and there is no indication Baum had any opinions on Vivekananda.

4. Or does he? Dorothy does not appear in the surviving movie's final scene, a dance by the Scarecrow and Tin Woodman, so perhaps they did succeed in lifting her into the basket of the Wizard's balloon in a lost part of the previous scene. On the other hand, descriptions of Selig Polyscope's subsequent Oz films, which are now lost, indicate they showed both Dorothy and the Wizard living in Oz as friends, so maybe he never left (*Moving Picture World* 571, 848).

5. Like most of the actors who had portrayed the Wizard on stage, Murray was known for playing Irish characters, as in his 1926 movie *The Cohens and Kellys*. There is nothing notably ethnic about this performance, however.

6. Both the Selig Polyscope and Semon movies undercut their statements that the Wizard is a humbug by depicting his supposed magic through jump cuts, which are impossible in the real world, rather than revealing his fakery or suggesting it with a glimpse of backstage machinery. Even when their stories depended on the Wizard being a fraud, the filmmakers could not resist giving audiences the thrill of movie magic.

Works Cited

Barnum, P.T. *The Humbugs of the World.* James Camden Hotten, 1866.
_____. *The Life of P.T. Barnum.* Redfield, 1855.
Baum, L. Frank. *Dorothy and the Wizard in Oz.* Reilly & Britton, 1908.
_____. *The Emerald City of Oz.* Reilly & Britton, 1910.
_____. *Glinda of Oz.* Reilly & Lee, 1920.
_____. *The Little Wizard Stories of Oz.* Reilly & Britton, 1913.
_____. *The Lost Princess of Oz.* Reilly & Britton, 1917.
_____. *The Magic of Oz.* Reilly & Lee, 1919.
_____. *The Marvelous Land of Oz.* Reilly & Britton, 1904.
_____. *Ozma of Oz.* Reilly & Britton, 1907.
_____. *The Patchwork Girl of Oz.* Reilly & Britton, 1913.
_____. *The Road to Oz.* Reilly & Britton, 1909.
_____. *Tik-Tok of Oz.* Reilly & Britton, 1914.
_____. *The Wonderful Wizard of Oz.* Geo. M. Hill Co., 1900.
Bell, J.L. "Dorothy the Conqueror." *The Baum Bugle* 49, no. 1 (Spring 2005): 13–17.
Brown, Sonia B. "Was This the Wizard Who Was the Wizard of Oz?" *The Baum Bugle* 28, no. 1 (Spring 1984): 5–7.
Fleming, Victor, dir. *The Wizard of Oz.* MGM, 1939.
Hallowell, Leslie. *Halliwell's Filmgoer's Companion*, 8th ed. Charles Scribner's Sons, 1984.
Harmetz, Aljean. *The Making of "The Wizard of Oz."* Alfred A. Knopf, 1977.
Hearn, Michael Patrick, ed. *The Annotated Wizard of Oz, Centennial Edition.* W.W. Norton, 2000.
Koupal, Nancy Tystad, ed. *Baum's Road to Oz: The Dakota Years.* South Dakota Historical Society Press, 2000.
Langley, Noel, Florence Ryerson, and Edgar Allan Woolf. *The Wizard of Oz* (screenplay). Faber & Faber, 1989.
Loncraine, Rebecca. *The Real Wizard of Oz: The Life and Times and L. Frank Baum.* Gotham Books, 2009.
MacDonald, J. Farrell, dir. *His Majesty, the Scarecrow of Oz.* Oz Film Manufacturing Company, 1914.
_____, dir. *The Patchwork Girl of Oz.* Oz Film Manufacturing Company, 1914.
The Moving Picture World 6 (January–June 1910).
Pendexter, Hugh, III. "Oz and the Three Witches." *Oz-Story* 6: 60–75.
"A Real Princess of Oz." *Courier* (Evansville, Indiana), 3 August 1905, p. 4.
Riley, Michael O. *Oz and Beyond: The Fantasy World of L. Frank Baum.* University Press of Kansas, 1997.
Rogers, Katharine M. *L. Frank Baum: Creator of Oz.* St. Martin's, 2002.
Saint-Pierre, Adrienne. "Barnum on 'Humbugging & Puffing,'" *The Barnum Museum*, 5 June 2020, https://barnum-museum.org/humbugging-and-puffing/, accessed 30 October 2021.

Schwartz, Evan I. *Finding Oz: How L. Frank Baum Discovered the Great American Story*. Houghton Mifflin Harcourt, 2009.

Semon, Larry, dir. *The Wizard of Oz*. Chadwick, 1925.

Swartz, Mark Evan. *Oz Before the Rainbow: L. Frank Baum's* The Wonderful Wizard of Oz *on Stage and Screen to 1939*. Johns Hopkins University Press, 2000.

Tuerk, Richard. *Oz in Perspective: Magic and Myth in the L. Frank Baum Books*. McFarland, 2007.

Turner, Otis, dir. *The Wonderful Wizard of Oz*. Selig Polyscope Co., 1910.

Witches, Wicked and Otherwise

ROBERT B. LUEHRS

The Land of Oz, according to its creator and chronicler, L. Frank Baum, provides a home for a number of witches with various temperaments and powers.[1] The state of Kansas, according to one of its young citizens, Dorothy Gale, has no witches at all. In *The Wonderful Wizard of Oz* the grandmotherly Good Witch of the North explains to Dorothy the cause of this phenomenon: "In the civilized countries I believe there are no witches left; nor wizards, nor sorceresses, nor magicians. But, you see, the Land of Oz has never been civilized, for we are cut off from all the rest of the world. Therefore we still have witches and wizards amongst us" (24). Because Kansas belongs to civilization, it is dismal and gray; nobody and nothing magical exists there.

The Good Witch of the North also tells Dorothy that there were only four witches in Oz, now reduced to three since the little girl's house fell on one of them, pulverizing the hag to dust. Such is not exactly the case, however, even in the Good Witch's own territory, the domain of the Gillikins in the north. There the Good Witch has outlawed the practice of witchcraft by anyone other than herself; yet, her malevolent predecessor as ruler, Mombi, continues to cast spells, brew potions, and indulge in the black arts. Baum's last Oz book, *Glinda of Oz*, features a half dozen Gillikin women who practice magic. It would seem not every witch necessarily identifies as a witch. Mombi, for instance, refers to herself as a "Sorceress" or a "Wizardess" (Baum, *Land* 2). Nonetheless, these spell weavers qualify as witches, and there are many of them.

Oz shares in a venerable and sometimes disquieting cultural heritage that reaches back at least to the Neolithic era, a legacy which speaks of witches and their craft. This western tradition concerning witchcraft was transmitted to Baum through his general knowledge of fairy tales, legends, folklore, and superstition. He was interested in spiritualism and mysticism, with he and his wife even joining the Theosophical Society of Helena Petrovna Blavatsky and Henry Steel Olcott in 1892.[2] Baum praised the occultism found in the novels of H. Rider Haggard and Edward Bulwer-Lytton in his newspaper, *The Aberdeen Saturday Pioneer*. He found inspiration in the ideas of his remarkable mother-in-law and fellow Theosophist, Matilda Joslyn Gage, suffragist and historian, who argued that accused witches were often women of superior intellect and ability. Baum referred to Gage as "in the first rank amongst the thinkers of our age" (*Pioneer*, June 28, 1890, 4).[3] Above all, Baum's depiction of witches in his Oz books came from his own imagination, original characters who do not always reflect the "historical" images of their kind. These workers of magic sometimes exhibit most curious qualities.

The basic assumption of magic is the existence of hidden relationships among all

Dorothy melts the Wicked Witch of the West with a bucket of water (W.W. Denslow illustration from *The Wonderful Wizard of Oz* [1960 edition]).

things. The material and spiritual realms, animate and inanimate objects, the seen and unseen are all linked by invisible chains of sympathy and mutual influence. Thus a pin thrust into a wax doll harms an enemy, a rabbit's foot brings good fortune, a horoscope deciphers celestial messages about human destiny, and mistletoe acts both as an antidote for every known poison and as an aphrodisiac. If a witch or other conjurer knows the proper ceremonies, utters the correct incantations, and perhaps calls upon the right gods or demons, that individual will control and command the hidden forces of the cosmos.

Magic, in other words, can be seen as a sort of arcane science, based on the "natural" principles which bind the universe together. These principles can be discovered by any individual with the wit and perseverance to secure the knowledge; that, in turn, can be manipulated to bring about specific results. Such has been the customary interpretation of magic in western civilization, and such was the view of the early Theosophists and of Baum. In *The Patchwork Girl of Oz,* the Shaggy Man sings of "Ozland…. Where magic is a science" (140), while in *Tik-Tok of Oz* he speaks of all nature being magical (161–62). One of the three Adepts in *Glinda of Oz* refers to magic as "secret arts we have gleaned from nature" (244). Matilda Gage, in her book *Woman, Church & State*, remarked:

> "Magic" whether brought about by the aid of spirits or simply through an understanding of secret natural laws, is of two kinds, "white" and "black," according as its intent and consequences are evil or good, and in this respect does not differ from the use made of the well known laws of nature, which are ever of good or evil character, in the hands of good or evil persons [236].

Like science, magic is neither benevolent nor pernicious in itself. Everything depends on who is using it and for what purposes. The terms "white" and "black" magic, which Gage employed, are of relatively recent coinage; the more historically accurate distinction is between High Magic and Low Magic, the magic of the wizard and that of the witch.

The wizard, the adept of High Magic, is invariably male. He is primarily a scholar and a philosopher seeking understanding of the universe in order to better himself spiritually and intellectually. Although he may attempt to coerce supernatural beings to serve him, he is more likely to be concerned with natural or Hermetic magic, such as alchemy or astrology.[4] The wizard might be feared but is generally respected. Authorities rarely bother him and often accord him considerable prestige because of his wisdom. The extent to which the Wizard of Oz exemplifies these qualities, especially in Baum's s early books, most assuredly is debatable.

According to the traditional view, the witch with her Low Magic is of quite a different sort. The witch is customarily female, and her skill is a perversion of the wizard's art. It is homespun, utilitarian, materialistic, frequently harmful, and most certainly not scholarly. The witch is commonly described as a broomstick-riding crone in league with terrible, uncanny beings. She enjoys injuring her neighbors and harming their property. She is antisocial, disagreeable, quarrelsome, irascible, and often physically deformed, traits many of Baum's wicked witches share.

This image of the witch took millennia to evolve. Its origins lie especially in Greco-Roman antiquity, where the environment was permeated with magic and otherworldly influences. In those civilizations the purveyors of magic offered defense against supernatural menaces, cursed enemies, sold love potions, devised remedies for all diseases, found lost objects, made predictions, and conversed with both gods and ghosts. These were the services of Low Magic. While the ancients deemed such services necessary, they considered the magicians who made them possible as suspicious, untrustworthy, and frightening individuals.

Particularly dangerous were female magicians, the witches. The literature and folklore of the ancient Greeks and Romans associated witches with night, the netherworld, and appalling deities such as three-faced Hecate, lunar queen of the dead and patroness of enchantments. Witches were accused of maiming livestock, spreading disease, destroying crops, stirring up storms, provoking lust, hindering love, and being sexually aggressive. They were said to have the ability to turn people into animals. For example, in Homer's *Odyssey* Circe transforms Ulysses' men into swine with a potion and a wand. Witches were also said to shapeshift. For example, the Roman night witch or *striga* flew after sunset in bird form and preyed on unattended children, devouring their entrails. Classical witches foretold the future and summoned the dead, forcing them to disclose secrets. There were some exceptions, but for the most part to the ancient Greeks and Romans witches were the opposite of decent women. Women were supposed to be caring mothers and respectful wives, not career-minded viragoes with powers surpassing those of men.

The reputation of sorceresses and enchantresses was no better among the ancient German tribes. The sagas picture witches as healers but also as disquieting women who debilitated the enemies of their clients and avenged slights by a magic that involved charms, ceremonies, the manipulation of objects, and spoken or written formulas. At night, so said the legends, they might ride out mounted on flying animals in the company of a motley array of goddesses, monsters, and specters. Careening through the skies, they would revel and cause devastation. Germanic witches, like their sisters in Mediterranean areas, were considered useful but ominous.

The blend of tales from the ancients became the basis for the image of the wicked witch in medieval and modern times. Baum drew heavily on this concept as he created his own versions of this creature. He did, however, reject the most notable and enduring contribution of the Middle Ages to the concept of witchcraft: the idea, propounded by the Church, that a witch secured her magical powers through an infamous pact with Satan, whereby he performed unspeakable acts through her and she, in turn, rendered him unwavering loyalty. Witchcraft, theologians argued, was actually devil-worship, and its devotees would periodically gather in secret conclave, in a "sabbat," to blaspheme Christian rites, give homage to their infernal master, receive instructions about crimes they were expected to commit, and wallow in orgies. Church leaders believed witchcraft to be such a menace that from the fifteenth through the seventeenth centuries they launched major campaigns to exterminate it. Courts sentenced hundreds of thousands of supposed witches to death. The majority of the executed were women, said by theologians to be easier marks for the Devil's blandishments than were men.

Baum did not accept the existence of the Devil.[5] Those in Oz who hurt others through magic do so because of flawed personalities and nasty temperaments and not because they have sold their souls to the Prince of Darkness. As Matilda Gage alleged, magic is knowledge and skill which can be used for all sorts of purposes, good ones as well as bad. Witches in Oz are not necessarily wicked—some are neutral, not seeking to harm or to help anyone else, while others are actually completely benevolent—a situation medieval Christianity held to be impossible.

Some of Baum's wicked witches come close to having the standard attributes, without the demonic alliance, of course. He created a trinity of outstanding malefactors: the Wicked Witch of the West in the first Oz book, Blinkie in *The Scarecrow of Oz*, and Mombi in *The Marvelous Land of Oz*. Less traditional, but still recognizably members of the sinister sisterhood, are another three: Rora Flathead, who spends most of her time in *Glinda of Oz* as a Golden Pig; the vain, arrogant ruler of the Skeezers in the same book, Coo-ee-oh, a self-proclaimed Krumbic Witch with a library of tomes written in blood and a pantry of pickled toads, snails, and lizards; and the Wicked Witch of the East, whose nefarious exploits are glimpsed in the Oz series.

Of all the Ozian necromancers, the ones most clearly indebted to tradition are the Wicked Witch of the West, Blinkie, and Mombi. All three have the requisite appearance and personality. They are all very old. Blinkie and Mombi are scrawny, while only Mombi still has both eyes. Each is solitary, irascible, sharp-tongued, tyrannical, and mercenary. Blinkie and Mombi cook noxious brews, while all conjure with theatrical gestures and incomprehensible incantations, precisely the sort of thing expected of a model witch. Every one of them reflects individually Baum's ingenious use of some of the peculiarities associated with witches as usually conceived.

The Wicked Witch of the West is afraid of both the dark and water. Her fear of darkness is ironic, for that is where real witches are supposed to feel most comfortable. However, she comes by her concern about water honestly. Historically water has been associated with healing, cleansing, purity, and holiness—all anathema to the wicked. Water blessed by a priest is supposed to drive off evil spirits and protect against bewitchment, while popular belief has said that witches and other demonic beings cannot cross running water. Witches are even unable to shed tears, at least according to the great witch-hunter's manual, the *Malleus Maleficarum* (*Hammer of Witches*), published in 1486. Still, no European witch was ever recorded to have been melted by water, the fate of the Wicked Witch of the West. The normal procedure for dispatching witches was to hang them or burn them at the stake, as King Krewl of Jinxland threatens to do to Blinkie in *The Scarecrow of Oz*.

The wolves, crows, and bees the Wicked Witch of the West summons with her silver whistle might not have been arbitrary choices. All have connections with the history of witchcraft. Human beings have never been comfortable with wolves, those hunters and singers of the night. By contrast, stories presented wolves as agents of witches, unfortunates transformed by witches, or even witches themselves, prowling as ravenous werewolves. Crows and bees were occasionally mentioned in the annals of witch trials as familiars, lesser demons in animal form kept as pets by witches and who ran odious errands for their owners. In return for services rendered, a familiar might be permitted to snack on a witch's blood, a less than satisfactory exchange in the case of the Wicked Witch of the West, for she is so old her blood has dried up. Since superstition points to crows or a swarm of bees as harbingers of death, she is correct to choose these creatures for the mission of destroying Dorothy and her companions. The inquisitors did not mention monkeys as familiars, probably because these animals were not to be encountered in the villages of Europe during the heyday of the witch hunts. Thus it is quite proper that the Winged Monkeys, unlike the wolves, crows, and bees, are involuntary slaves of the Wicked Witch of the West, not her willing servants.

This witch remains the most popular of Baum's villains, even if she is dissolved by Dorothy. She has been reinterpreted a number of times, most notably by Margaret Hamilton in the 1939 MGM motion picture. There she no longer has the all-seeing eye with which Baum endowed her, but employs a crystal ball instead. Gone also are the braids and umbrella of W.W. Denslow's original illustrations. She has become a mean, cackling, green-skinned, dog-hating horror, sailing across the skies on that obligatory broomstick. Hamilton's witch remains an icon, despite the fact she was on screen no more than twelve minutes.

Even more distant from Baum's concept is Elphaba Thropp, Gregory Maguire's Wicked Witch of the West in his 1995 novel, *Wicked*. Maguire's Oz is magical, but also violent, corrupt, and rent by hostilities among classes, religions, ethnic groups, and species. It suffers under the growing tyranny of the Wizard. Born into Munchkin aristocracy, Elphaba is unaware her actual father is not her mother's husband, an itinerant preacher, but the Wizard of Oz himself, who drugged and raped her mother. Elphaba is thin, hatchet-faced, mysteriously emerald in color, and, of course, allergic to water. She is also cynical, sarcastic, and occasionally mean. She worships no god and claims to have no soul. Even so, she is not really guilty of any intentional wickedness, and she can show great kindness and compassion. At one point she confesses: "That's all I want—to do no harm" (Maguire 239). She favors Animal rights, the capital letter denoting beasts who reason and speak, and opposes the Wizard's brutal despotism. In this account of the story, it is the witch, not Dorothy, who sings of the faraway, fairytale land where life is better. She is not much of a witch either, generally favoring science over sorcery. Even her flying broomstick has been enchanted by another. Still, she does possess unconscious and uncontrolled occult powers, at times unleashed with deadly effect. In the end, hearing the very girl who killed her sister is now stalking her, Elphaba does become unhinged; even so, those shoes are her family legacy and do not belong to some child from Kansas, wherever that is.

Baum's original Wicked Witch of the West, a less complicated and tormented individual, primarily seeks through her magic to dominate or destroy others. Blinkie, another significant wicked witch in the Oz saga, applies her talents in a different traditional area of interest to the witches of western folklore: the inhibition of love. One of the most well-known functions of magic in the Middle Ages was to enflame passion, and the *grimoires*, the handbooks of Low Magic, were filled with bizarre recipes to this end. Popular opinion supposed that since witches knew how to kindle love or lust, they could also quell such emotions. Witches were commonly accused of producing sterility in women and impotence in men. There were concoctions for such purposes, including a heady beverage of ants boiled in daffodil juice. A favorite method for thwarting any affections between a man and woman involved ligature, the tying of knots in a cord or strip of leather. In *The Scarecrow of Oz*, Blinkie's technique of killing Gloria's love for Pon by dashing a potion on the girl's breast is rather unorthodox, but Blinkie is thereby fulfilling an expected role.

The three witches who assist Blinkie in mixing her elixir are the only ones in Baum's Oz stories who actually fly on broomsticks. The notion that witches can fly goes back to the Roman *strigae* and German mythology's rampaging nightriders in the sky. Witches astride airborne brooms were first depicted in Martin Le Franc's long poem *Le Champion des Dames* (*The Champion of Women*) from around 1440, but the idea did not appear in witch trials until a century and a half later. Before then witches were accused of transvection via other forms of transportation ranging from beanstalks and pitchforks to goats, dogs, and beehives. Probably in people's imaginations the broom became the preferred aerial steed for witches because it most patently symbolized women. Witches flew, said the experts, to attend distant sabbats. The wicked witches of Oz frequent no sabbats, so they need no broomsticks.

The third member of the trio of prominent wicked witches is Mombi, former autocrat of the Gillikins, who specializes in transformation or metamorphosis. She turns Ozma into the boy Tip and threatens to turn Tip into a marble statue. She changes Jellia Jam into her own likeness and herself into a rose, a shadow, an ant, and a griffin. Of course, she is not the only Oz witch to deal in shapeshifting. Blinkie makes Cap'n Bill into a grasshopper. Coo-ee-oh transforms Rora Flathead, a fellow witch, into a Golden Pig and the three Adepts into fish. In *The Road to Oz*, the Good Witch of the North turns ten stones into birds, lambs, and finally dancing girls as party entertainment. Glinda, in *Rinkitink in Oz*, returns Bilbil the Goat to his original form, the handsome Prince Bobo of Boboland. Still, Glinda does not approve of transformations when they are done maliciously. "[T]hey are not honest," she remarks, "and no respectable sorceress likes to make things appear to be what they are not. Only unscrupulous witches use the art" (Baum, *Land* 273).[6]

Glinda's reference to appearance touches on one of the major controversies about witch-induced transformations, namely: are such things real, with people actually becoming animals, or merely "glamour," hallucinations caused by befuddled and bewitched senses? The ancients argued for reality as did the testimony offered in the late medieval and Renaissance witch trials. The contrary point of view was advanced by St. Augustine, St. Thomas Aquinas, and other eminent Christian theologians. God, they said, can alter the nature of beings, but witches and demons cannot. At best demons can make men *think* they have been transformed or others have been. Since demons are not the source of Ozian magic, presumably the transformations in that land are usually more than glamour. The most obvious exception is Zixi, Queen of Ix, who appears young and beautiful but is always reminded by mirrors that she is really a bald, toothless, withered crone of 683 years.

There is one situation where Mombi does resort to glamour, staged special effects having no substance. She uses it in an effort to prevent Tip and his friends from reaching the Emerald City. The obstacles she puts in their way—a field of whirling sunflowers, the changing landscape, the rushing river, the wall of granite, the forty crossroads which rotate, and the grass fire—are all illusions, surmounted by being ignored. Fraud is to be expected from a witch who studied with the humbug Wizard of Oz.

Mombi does perform a bit of genuine magic when she glances into a mirror to discern the future. This is scrying, a form of divination in which a seer concentrates on a shiny surface, such as a crystal ball, a polished stone, or a bowl of water, to induce a trance. In that trance the seer gains access to hidden knowledge through visions of past, present, or future events. Glinda similarly looks into a mirror to discover the whereabouts of Button Bright in *Glinda of Oz*, while in *The Tin Woodman of Oz* Ozma gazes into a platter of broth to check on the activities of the treacherous giantess, Mrs. Yoop.

The Marvelous Land of Oz ends with Mombi being compelled by Glinda to down a drink which causes the witch to forget how to perform witchcraft; she becomes, as she puts it, "a helpless old woman" (Baum, *Land* 262). Ruth Plumly Thompson, in *The Lost King of Oz*, inflicts an even worse punishment. In that book Mombi flees her post as cook to the King of Kimbaloo in Gillikin country and plots to restore the evil old days before Ozma when she and other wicked witches controlled everything. This is treason, and on Dorothy's suggestion Mombi is put to death by having water splashed on her. Mombi thus becomes the only person in Oz eliminated on purpose by being dissolved.

In former times, Mombi and three collaborators had formed an alliance of evil to enslave Oz, but wicked witches generally do not cooperate. Consider, for instance, the relationship between Rora Flathead and Coo-ee-oh. They are both witches and neighbors in an isolated part of Gillikin country. Rora is the wife of the Supreme Dictator or Su-dic of the mountain-dwelling Flatheads; Coo-ee-oh is the queen of the Skeezers, who live on a submersible island in a lake to the south. The two women despise each other. When the Flatheads are denied fishing rights in Skeezer Lake, Rora plots to poison all the fish in that body of water. Co-ee-oh thwarts this bit of petty revenge by turning Rora into a pig first.

Poison in the Middle Ages was considered an essential part of the arsenal of any competent witch. Her cupboard was supposed to have an ample supply of lethal liquors and salves compounded from such horrific ingredients as hemlock, nightshade, human bones, toad glands, and bits of rat. These poisons could be administered orally, rubbed onto the victim's body, spread on the ground for the luckless to walk on, or poured into water supplies to wipe out whole populations. So close was the relationship between witchcraft and poison that the passage in Exodus (22:18) which reads "Thou shall not suffer a poisoner to live" often appears as "Thou shall not suffer a witch to live." With their profound skill in working with herbs, classic witches could also offer antidotes to poisons, if they so wished.

As for Coo-ee-oh, she proclaims:

> I have magic powers greater than any fairy possesses, and greater than any Flathead possesses. I am a Krumbic Witch—the only Krumbic Witch in the world—and I fear the magic of no other creature that exists! ... I rule one hundred and one Skeezers. But every one of them trembles at my word [Baum, *Glinda* 102–03].

These are audacious claims for a teen-aged girl who had only recently stolen the basics of magic from the three Adepts at Magic, at that time the benevolent rulers of the

Flatheads. (She used her ill-gotten skills to transform the Adepts into fish, leaving them to swim in Skeezer Lake.) For all of her grimoires, powders, and incantations, she is a witch of the Industrial Revolution. Her Krumbic witchcraft, a kind of supernatural technology, would have been unimaginable to those living in antiquity or the Middle Ages. Her magic is a means for launching submarines, operating the cumbersome mechanism that raises and lowers her glass-domed city in the lake, and sending a steel bridge, section by section, from the city to the mainland. With Coo-ee-oh there is a strange blend of science and conjuration. Appropriately for a narcissistic witch who casts spells by intoning one of the three syllables of her own name, Coo-ee-oh ends her Krumbic career as a self-absorbed swan.

The final wicked witch to be considered in this study is the Wicked Witch of the East, another example of Baum's willingness to reshape the traditions of witchcraft to suit his own purposes. She is associated with the Silver Shoes and enchanting an axe to dismember Nick Chopper, gradually turning him into the Tin Woodman as prostheses replaced each lost body part. Yet, silver and the iron in the axe head are metals which, according to folklore, ward off witches. The silver sixpence in a bride's shoe, a silver bullet, and a drink containing a silver coin all deflect a variety of evils, including witches. Witches were sometimes charged with hexing tools, but iron amulets, iron nails in one's pockets, an iron knife buried under the doorstep, or an iron horseshoe hung on the wall were all supposed to keep iniquitous magic at bay. Obviously such is not the case in Oz. The Wicked Witch of the West even trips Dorothy with an invisible iron bar and grabs one of the Silver Shoes.

The Yookoohoos, Mrs. Yoop the giantess in *The Tin Woodman of Oz*, and Reera the Red in *Glinda of Oz* are not systemically hostile to human beings as are the wicked witches but tend to be indifferent to the suffering and needs of others. They use their magic for their own entertainment and pleasure. Neither one enjoys having guests, preferring pets for company; with Mrs. Yoop, guests can become the pets, requiring only a bit of reshaping into animal form. She refers to herself as "an Artist in Transformations" (Baum, *Tin Woodman* 73). With some hand gestures Mrs. Yoop transforms a pitcher of water, a bunch of weeds, and a few pebbles into a breakfast of coffee, oatmeal, and fish. Through her magic Polychrome becomes a canary, the Tin Woodman an owl, the Scarecrow a bear, and Woot the Wanderer a green monkey. The giantess' flaw in enchanting people is her inability to restore them to what they were originally. Reera is more skilled and enjoys repeatedly altering her own appearance along with that of her many animal companions (or familiars) according to fancy.

Both Yookoohoos are attractive, courteous young women, but Mrs. Yoop, for all of her pleasant demeanor, is definitely more dangerous and prone to seething anger besides. Her attitude might be the result of having had an abusive husband.[7] Reera, on the contrary, displays a sense of humor. She flirts with Ervic and coyly allows herself to be manipulated by him into transmuting the three Adepts from fish back into tall, slender, pretty, and intelligent young women. Reera wishes them well and asks only that they keep her admirable deed secret; she does not want to be bothered by multitudes of supplicants coming to her door. She actually has some of the positive attributes of a good witch.

The good witches of Oz are very much akin to the wise women described by Matilda Gage in her *Women, Church & State*. The wise women, she said, were not agents of Satan at all but medieval disciples of the priestess-scientists who founded the earliest civilization and who had governed it with peace, justice, and morality; when men took over, the character of society deteriorated rapidly as did the status of women. According to Gage, medieval "witches" were actually talented women with the ability to exercise certain psychic powers unknown to most people. As masters of animal magnetism, a sort of spiritual electricity, the wise women could heal at a touch, defy gravity, and manage the weather. Borrowing from the historian Jules Michelet and the folklorist Jakob Grimm, Gage viewed the so-called witches' sabbats as nocturnal protest rallies by the peasantry against an oppressive Church. The sabbats were conducted by the wise women who kept alive, despite fierce persecution, ancient wisdom and pagan religious rites dedicated to the creative abilities of women, abilities which the Church sought to suppress. Gage's wise women essentially practiced High Magic. Baum made Oz the ancient matriarchy reborn; there remarkable women with extraordinary skills wield the ultimate authority.

The three mysterious Adepts, Audah, Aurah, and Aujah, fit the descriptions of both Gage's wise women and Baum's good witches.[8] In Theosophy an adept is an advanced student or master in the science of esoteric philosophy serving the welfare of humanity and employing the energies of the occult for unselfish purposes. The Adepts become rulers of the Flatheads, teaching them how to think and improve life in general. They also work with the Skeezers, building the glass-domed city in the lake. Out of jealousy, Coo-ee-oh turns the Adepts into fish, and the region descends into authoritarian government, militarism, rancor, and misery, precisely as Gage theorized happened to humanity with the fall of the prehistoric matriarchate.

The Good Witch of the North, called Locasta in Baum's 1902 stage production of *The Wizard of Oz* but unnamed in his Oz books, is also one of the wise women. She claims to be weaker than the wicked witches, yet defeats Mombi in the struggle for regional supremacy. She proves quite accomplished in teleportation, transformations, and divination. To protect Dorothy she insists the girl wear the silver shoes, silver offering defense against evil, and kisses her on the forehead, leaving a shining circle which will repel harm. Silver, according to lore, is a metal sacred to the moon and the glowing circle is symbolic of the full moon, the ultimate guardian of female magic. The fate of this witch, as presented in Thompson's *The Giant Horse of Oz*, is a bizarre one. After more than two decades living as Tattypoo, the kind, elderly Good Witch of the North, she discovers she is actually young, beautiful Orin, missing Queen of the Ozure Isles, victim of a spell gone awry cast by Mombi. Her real identity, memory, and royal husband all restored, she goes on to rule the Munchkins, but without the magic. The Good Witch of the North, then, is a peculiar accident. In a sense, she never genuinely existed.

The ultimate good witch and wise woman is, of course, Glinda, who goes far beyond the limits normally assigned to witches. Witches were alleged to have the facility of making themselves invisible, but no legendary witch ever had the ability to hide an entire country from the eyes of outsiders as Glinda does with Oz at the end of *The Emerald City of Oz*. When Glinda flies, she does not perch on a puny broomstick; she soars through the heavens like a Nordic goddess in a chariot drawn by storks. She is a High Magician who uses her talents to protect Oz and its Inhabitants from adversity, to promote the happiness of all, and to turn discord into harmony. She is far too selfless and perceptive to be classified as a mere witch. Baum even tried to distinguish her from the other witches by referring to her as a Sorceress, although actually the distinction between witchcraft and sorcery is unclear.

The most complex of the good witches is Queen Zixi of Ix, whom we know is a good witch because she is a guest at Ozma's birthday party in *The Road to Oz*. Zixi is fundamentally a kind-hearted sovereign—just, sagacious, generous, brave in war, and mild in her financial demands on her subjects. However, she can also be deceitful, selfish, and bitter when crossed. She is a sympathetic character because she is capable of intellectual and emotional growth. When the magic cloak refuses to grant her petty wish of seeing herself young in reflections, she comes to realize that one must accept one's lot in life and not yearn for the impossible. To everyone else she appears about sixteen years of age instead of more than six centuries old; she alone sees the truth. Zixi is fine as long as her common sense and reason keep tight rein on her emotions. As Baum put it: "When her mind was in normal condition the witch-queen was very sweet and agreeable in disposition" (Baum, *Zixi* 183). In her role as witch Zixi brews exotic potions, her incantations wonderfully obscure and filled with inscrutable phrases and paradoxes. She speaks the languages of animals, can render herself invisible, and knows how to achieve transformations. In short, she is an accomplished member of her profession. Above all, alone among the witches of Oz and its borderlands, Zixi actually does what medieval and Renaissance witches were executed for: she consults entities from the Other World to assist in working her magic, beings Baum calls "'i' imps." She summons them to weave a duplicate of the Magic Cloak she intends to steal, although they are unable to include the golden thread which enables the garment to grant wishes (a skill only possessed by fairies). She also consults them on how best to rid Noland of the obnoxious Roly-Rogues, with their advice involving a clandestine sleeping draught in the morning soup.

Medieval theologians affirmed the reality of imps, pointing out these creatures were minor demons, off-shoots of the Devil. Despite their diminutive size they could do considerable damage to mortals. Renaissance inquisitors often equated imps with familiars, suggesting that imps hid their grotesqueness by masquerading as animals or insects. Baum's imps, however, had no religious connections and returned to their pre–Christian, Germanic origins as mischievous domestic or nature spirits who delighted in playing not always harmless pranks. In "Ozma and the Little Wizard," one of the short tales included in Baum's *Little Wizard Stories of Oz*, three imps harass travelers on a mountain road in a fairly sadistic fashion until the Wizard turns them into metal buttons, promising to release the pests only when they repent and become respectable citizens of Oz. Imps bound to objects such as bottles, crystal balls, swords, or staffs are a common literary theme. These imps—bearing the punny names of Imp Olite, Imp Udent, and Imp Ertinent—resemble brownies from Palmer Cox's *The Brownies: Their Book* (1887) in appearance, with large mouths, flat noses, and form-fitting clothing. Whether Zixi's imps are similar cannot be said.

While discussing the persecution of accused witches in the past, Matilda Gage noted:

> Few women dared to be wise, after thousands of their sex had gone to death by drowning or burning because of their knowledge. The superior learning of witches was recognized in the widely extended belief of their ability to work miracles. The witch was in reality the profoundest thinker, the most advanced scientist of those ages [243].

This judgement certainly fits Baum's description of witches in Oz. Female practitioners of magic dominate the intellectual life of Oz and work their own variations on traditional witch activities, from intoning spells and inducing transformations to brewing potions and, in the case of Zixi, trafficking with otherworldly entities. Each of these women reflect a heritage which stretches back at least to the ancient Greeks and their dark goddess, Hecate. As previously mentioned, Hecate is a protector of the moon and of witches. Her personality combines the separate outlooks of the three categories of Oz witches: menace, benevolence, and indifference. She also oversees boundaries and cross-roads and so might appreciate Oz as a region where magic and science intersect, commingling to produce extraordinary results.

Notes

1. This essay is a revision of my 1994 publication "L. Frank Baum, the Witches of Oz, and the Witches of Folklore."

2. Baum's relationship to Theosophy has been explored in Algeo 270–73, Koupal 63–68, and Hearn xcii–xciv.

3. On March 1, 1890, he wrote Gage was the "most remarkable woman of her age, possessed of the highest literary ability, the brightest thoughts, the clearest and most scholarly oratory, the most varied research and intelligence and diversified pen of any public woman of the past twenty years" (*Pioneer* 4).

4. Hermetic magic was named after Hermes Trismegistus (Hermes "Thrice-Great"), legendary king of early Egypt, incarnation of the god Thoth, and alleged author of the mystical treatises which enjoyed considerable repute in the Middle Ages and Renaissance.

5. See, for example, his December 6, 1890, column in *The Aberdeen Saturday Pioneer* (4).

6. The Wizard of Oz agrees: "It is wicked to transform any living creatures without their consent..." (Baum, *Glinda* 249).

7. Mr. Yoop had a tendency to steal people's livestock and dine on the people themselves; for that he has been imprisoned in Quadling country. His wife has no desire to free him.

8. When intoned one after another, their names sound like a magic spell.

Works Cited

The Aberdeen Saturday Pioneer, 25 January 1890–21 March 1891.
Algeo, John. "A Notable Theosophist: L. Frank Baum." *The American Theosophist* 74, no. 8 (September–October 1986): 270–73.
Baum, L. Frank. *Glinda of Oz*. Reilly & Lee, 1920.
_____. *Little Wizard Stories of Oz*. Reilly & Britton, 1914.
Baum, L. Frank (Lyman Frank), and W.W. Denslow. *The Wonderful Wizard of Oz*. George M. Hill, 1900.
_____. *The Wonderful Wizard of Oz*. Dover, 1960.
Baum, L. Frank (Lyman Frank), and John R. Neill. *The Marvelous Land of Oz*. Reilly & Britton, 1904.
_____. *The Patchwork Girl of Oz*. Reilly & Britton, 1913.
_____. *Queen Zixi of Ix; or the Story of the Magic Cloak*. Century, 1905.
_____. *Rinkitink in Oz*. Reilly & Britton, 1916.
_____. *The Road to Oz*. Reilly & Britton. Reilly & Britton, 1909.
_____. *The Scarecrow of Oz*. Reilly & Britton, 1915.
_____. *Tik-Tok of Oz*. Reilly & Britton, 1914.
_____. *The Tin Woodman of Oz*. Reilly & Lee, 1918.
Gage, Matilda Joslyn. *Woman, Church & State*. Truth Seeker, 1893.
Hearn, Michael Patrick, ed. *The Annotated Wizard of Oz, Centennial Edition*. W.W. Norton, 2000.
Koupal, Nancy Tystad. "On the Road to Oz: L. Frank Baum as Western Editor." *Baum's Road to Oz: The Dakota Years*, Nancy Tystad Koupal, editor. South Dakota State Historical Society Press, 2000. 49–106.
Kramer, Heinrich, and James Sprenger. *The Malleus Maleficarum*. Trans. Montague Summers. Dover, 1972.
Luehrs, Robert B. "L. Frank Baum, the Witches of Oz, and the Witches of Folklore." *The Baum Bugle* 38, no. 2 (Autumn 1994): 4–10.
Maguire, Gregory. *Wicked: The Life and Times of the Wicked Witch of the West*. HarperCollins, 1995.
Thompson, Ruth Plumly. *The Giant Horse of Oz*. Reilly & Lee, 1928.
_____. *The Lost King of Oz*. Reilly & Lee, 1925.

Witch's Familiars or Winged Warriors?

Liberating the Winged Monkeys

DINA SCHIFF MASSACHI

For the past several years, I've had the privileged to teach *The Wonderful Wizard of Oz* at the University of North Carolina at Charlotte. Each semester, I begin by asking my students what they already know about Oz, and someone always mentions being scared of the MGM Flying Monkeys. Many Baum scholars reading this will likely note this as one of the many changes between the MGM film and Baum's *Wonderful Wizard*. In the introduction to his book, L. Frank Baum states his desire to leave out the "heart-aches and nightmares," and his love of humor, puns, and comical illustrations is well documented. However, others might suggest that my students are tapping into some of the darker reads that scholars have offered, including Henry Littlefield's well-known essay "The Wizard of Oz: Parable on Populism," which sees Baum's Winged Monkeys as a symbol for America's indigenous people (55). Even though Littlefield admitted in the Spring 1992 *Baum Bugle* that his essay was meant as a teaching aid and is not based on fact, this piece seems to reemerge in scholarship again and again, especially when placed alongside two editorials Baum wrote ten years before he penned *The Wonderful Wizard of Oz*—editorials which are often read as a call for the annihilation of America's indigenous people. Of course, this is not the only way these monkeys have been interpreted, but these readings view Baum's Winged Monkeys as a single symbol of the culture and time of his life, limiting their interpretation. When one looks at not only Baum's Winged Monkeys but also MGM's Flying Monkeys, *The Wiz*'s Winged Warriors, *Tin Man*'s Moats, *Wicked*'s Chistery, *Oz the Great and Powerful*'s Finley, and *Dorothy Must Die*'s Lulu, Ollie, and Maude, the Winged Monkeys move beyond a reading that may symbolize a specific moment in history and, instead, become a discussion about America's complex relationship with disenfranchised groups, the power structures that accompany this disenfranchisement, and who has the agency to liberate.

Before Baum's readers meet the Winged Monkeys, they see the object these monkeys are bound to—"a Golden Cap, with a circle of diamonds and rubies running round it. This Golden Cap had a charm. Whoever owned it could call three times upon the Winged Monkeys, who would obey any order they were given" (Baum 145). The Wicked Witch of the West gets this cap after she has exhausted her own magic. Her bees, crows, and wolves—realistic plights for farmers—are outmaneuvered by Dorothy and her friends, so the witch turns to something more magical. In his introduction, Baum notes a desire to eliminate "the stereotyped genie," yet, as Michael Patrick Hearn points out in

Winged Monkeys carrying Dorothy (W.W. Denslow illustration from *The Wonderful Wizard of Oz* [1960 edition]).

his *Annotated Wizard of Oz*, this cap seems to function like a modernized version of a genie's magic lamp (210). Under the right conditions the user is granted three wishes by the creature(s) bound to the magical object.

The idea of a modernized genie is interesting to consider when one thinks about how genies function within fairy tales. There is a "user beware" subtext when it comes to fairy tale wishes. Baum's Winged Monkeys are also trickster characters, recalling stories Baum may have read, like Palmer Cox's *The Brownies, Their Book*, where the brownies cause a bit of mischief, but no real harm. While using a trickster character might not seem modern on Baum's part, it is notable that the way Baum plays with the trickster relies on some elements of spiritualism. Matilda Gage, L. Frank Baum's suffragist mother-in-law, is credited with giving Baum the sort of foundation needed for creating the types of characters that broke gender stereotypes of both Baum's time and our own. She also introduced Baum to Theosophy. According to Michael Patrick Hearn's introduction to his *Annotated Wizard of Oz*:

> H.P. Blavatsky, founder of the Theosophical Society, described [...] "Elemental Spirits" in Isis Unveiled (Vol. 1, 1878, p.xxix) as "the creatures evolved in the four kingdoms of earth, air, fire and water and [....], may be termed the forces of Nature. [...] these spirits of the elements appear in myth, fable, tradition or poetry of all nations, ancient and modern. Their names are legion—peers, devs, dijinns [...]" [Hearn xcii].

While Hearn notes that "like many nineteenth-century critics, Baum lumps the Near Eastern tales of the Arabian Nights with European fairy tales" (6), it is interesting to consider how Baum's Winged Monkeys parallel the Islamic Jinn. In *Islam, Arabs, and the Intelligent World of the Jinn*, Amira El-Zein notes that Jinn "have mental faculties that allow them to access knowledge" (13), "hav[e] free will" (15), and "[i]t is generally believed those [jinn] who are enslaved by humans are the heretic jinn" (27). Though it should be noted that "Arabs in pre–Islam acknowledged animals could be the dwelling places for spiritual entities. They depicted jinn as taking animal shapes to hide from humans, or trick them, or deliver a message to them" (92). Despite the idea of shapeshifting for the pros of trickery, "people believed evil jinn could forsake their wickedness at any time and become good" (100). This redemptive quality becomes important when we consider the jinn as inspiration for Baum's Winged Monkeys.

While likely a coincidence, there are several ways that Baum's Monkeys overlap with the Islamic Jinn, including, but not limited to, the idea of punishment and the notion that they could become good even if they were not always that way. The Winged Monkeys' moral neutrality could relate to the jinn, or it could be another connection with Baum's mother-in-law, Matilda Gage. In her novel *Woman, Church and State,* Gage notes that "'magic' [...] is of two kinds, 'white' and 'black,' according as its intent and consequences are evil or good, and in this respect does not differ from the use made of the [...] laws of nature, which are ever of good or evil character, in the hands of good or evil persons" (Gage 238). Baum borrows this neutrality for his Winged Monkeys. As Suzanne Rahn notes in *The Wizard of Oz Shaping an Imaginary World*, "the power itself is morally neutral [...] we see the same Winged Monkeys used to commit cruel and destructive acts by the Wicked Witch of the West and helpful acts by Dorothy and Glinda" (Rahn 71). While there are many different interpretations as to what Baum's monkeys might symbolize, it is clear that they are morally neutral. Baum borrows this view of magic in his various magical Oz objects—the Golden Cap that controls the Winged Monkeys, and the Monkeys themselves, are morally neutral; it is the wisher who is good or evil.

This moral ambiguity is part of what makes Littlefield associate Baum's Winged Monkeys with America's indigenous people. Littlefield makes this connection when discussing the backstory that the King of the Winged Monkeys tells Dorothy as he carries her to the Emerald City. Littlefield notes that

> Baum makes these Winged Monkeys into an Oz substitute for the plains Indians. Their leader says, "Once ... we were a free people, living happily in the great forest, flying from tree to tree, eating nuts and fruit, and doing just as we pleased without calling any-body master." "This," he explains, "was many years ago, long before Oz came out of the clouds to rule over this land" (p. 172). But like many Indian tribes, Baum's monkeys are not inherently bad; their actions depend wholly upon the bidding of others. Under the control of an evil influence, they do evil. Under the control of goodness and innocence, as personified by Dorothy, the monkeys are helpful and kind, although unable to take her to Kansas. Says the Monkey King, "We belong to this country alone, and cannot leave it" (p. 213). The same could be said with equal truth of the first Americans [Littlefield 55].

There are quite a few issues with this read of the Winged Monkeys. The first is that Littlefield, likely in an effort to recreate the popular narrative during the times of populism, describes America's indigenous people as having their actions, and the goodness of those actions, depend wholly upon the bidding of others. Of course it is worth noting that Littlefield himself stated, "My intention in this article was to suggest another means to teach a difficult period in American history. The Populists appear less than real to modern urban students. But kids all know Oz, thanks to Judy Garland and television" (25). Littlefield used the Winged Monkeys (and many other Oz characters and objects) as a convenient symbol to fit his thesis.

If Baum's magical neutrality traces back to Gage, then it is unlikely that the neutrality of the Winged Monkeys relates to America's indigenous people because of Baum's connection with Gage. As Sally Roesch Wagner notes in the opening of the unabridged edition of *Woman, Church and State*, "During the 1870s Gage spoke out against the brutal and unfair treatment of Native Americans. She was adopted into the Wolf Clan of the Mohawk nation and given the name Ka-ron-ien-ha-wi (Sky Carrier)" (6). It is evident that Gage influenced Baum's thoughts on women's suffrage, Theosophy, witches, and writing, but it is less clear whether Gage influenced Baum's thoughts on America's indigenous people because of the two editorials he wrote during his time in the Dakota Territory. Regardless, the neutrality seems to be far more influenced by Gage's thoughts on magical neutrality, and the modernization of a genie character, than anything having to do with America's natives.

It seems impossible to discuss the Winged Monkeys without discussing Baum's editorials, though, primarily because they are cited in so many of the scholarly works that mention the characters. There seem to be three schools of thought on the editorials—those who find them atypical of Baum's thinking, as Michael Patrick Hearn suggests in his *Annotated Wizard of Oz* and Ranjit Dighe in his *The Historian's Wizard of Oz*, those who take the editorials as satire, as Jason and Jessica Bell suggest in their "Freeing the Slaves in Oz," and those, like Gretchen Ritter and Richard Tuerk, who believe that Baum meant the words to be taken as they are written. Ken Derry summarizes the various critical reads of these editorials in his article "'Like You Could Read What Was Inside of Me': Genocide, Hermeneutics, and Religion in *The Wizard of Oz*," and anyone seeking a bit more explanation would do well to look there. It's far too easy to leave Baum's Oz and fall into the rabbit hole of the editorials. The goal of this essay is not to explore Baum's thoughts on America's indigenous people, but on his Winged Monkeys, and what they have to teach us. It is also worth noting that, in his *Western Humanities Review* article "Lyman Frank Baum: Looking Back to the Promised Land," Tom St. John read the same monkeys as satire on the old Northwest Mounted Police.

Even leaving the Winged Monkeys as a symbol of the culture and time of Baum's life, scholars cannot agree on what, exactly, these monkeys function as a symbol *for*. In spite of the variety of symbols the Winged Monkeys have been interpreted to represent, it is interesting to note that scholarship hasn't made a significant effort to link them with other subjugated or enslaved people of Baum's time, namely Africans and African Americans—especially when one considers that works like John Kennedy's *Swallow Barn* and Caroline Gilman's "The Country Visit" both describe African slaves as monkeys. I state this not to open up a new claim on what Baum meant, but to illustrate how the characters of the Winged Monkeys easily overlap with longstanding depictions, especially in American literature, of disenfranchised groups. Therefore, in order to both focus on the characters of the Winged Monkeys and explore what they teach readers and viewers of Oz, we need to expand beyond Baum's *Wonderful Wizard* and see what other authors have done with these characters.

Before we move beyond Baum, though, let's return to *The Wonderful Wizard of Oz* and explore the relationship between Baum's Winged Monkeys and their Golden Cap. When asked how the Monkeys came to be at the mercy of the cap, the King of the Winged Monkeys tells Dorothy the following story:

> "Once," began the leader, "we were a free people, living happily in the great forest, flying from tree to tree, eating nuts and fruit, and doing just as we pleased without calling anybody master. [...] There lived here then [...] a beautiful princess, who was also a powerful sorceress. [...] Her name was Gayelette [...]. Everyone loved her, but her greatest sorrow was that she could find no one to love in return [...]. At last, however, she found a boy who was handsome and manly and wise beyond his years. [...] When he grew to manhood, Quelala, as he was called, was said to be the best and wisest man in all the land [...]. Gayelette loved him dearly, and hastened to make everything ready for the wedding. My grandfather was at that time the King of the Winged Monkeys which lived in the forest near Gayelette's palace, and the old fellow loved a joke better than a good dinner. One day, just before the wedding, my grandfather was flying out with his band when he saw Quelala walking beside the river. He was dressed in a rich costume of pink silk and purple velvet [...]. At his word the band flew down and seized Quelala, carried him in their arms until they were over the middle of the river, and then dropped him into the water." "Swim out, my fine fellow," cried my grandfather, "and see if the water has spotted your clothes." Quelala [...] laughed, when he came to the top of the water, and swam in to shore. But when Gayelette came running out to him she found his silks and velvet all ruined by the river. The princess was angry, and she knew, of course, who did it. She had all the Winged Monkeys brought before her, and she said at first that their wings should be tied and they should be treated as they had treated Quelala, and dropped in the river. But my grandfather pleaded hard, for he knew the Monkeys would drown in the river with their wings tied, and Quelala said a kind word for them also; so that Gayelette finally spared them, on condition that the Winged Monkeys should ever after do three times the bidding of the owner of the Golden Cap. This Cap had been made for a wedding present to Quelala [...]. Of course my grandfather and all the other Monkeys at once agreed to the condition, and that is how it happens that we are three times the slaves of the owner of the Golden Cap, whosoever he may be [172–174].

Many Oz scholars have pointed out the inconsistencies within Baum's fourteen Oz books, but one of the more consistent elements is the abolition of slavery whenever

Dorothy, Ozma, or any of the other hero-protagonists encounter it. However there is neither a move to "free" the monkeys nor do the monkeys seem to seek freedom. The Winged Monkeys "at once agree to the condition" of being "three times the slaves of the owner of the Golden Cap" (Baum 174). Perhaps slavery is preferable to drowning, but the monkey's description of Gayelette as beautiful, powerful good, beloved, and wise suggest that they harbor no ill feelings towards her. Rather, it is almost like how "[Louise Clarke] Pyrnelle notes in the preface [of *Diddie, Dumps, and Tot*] her hope 'to tell of the pleasant and happy relations that existed between master and slave'" (Hakala 24)—I stress *almost*, as the lack of fear and the fact that the Winged Monkeys speak as eloquently as Dorothy are enough to suggest a departure from works like Pyrnelle.

Regardless, there is something casual about how this particular example of slavery is treated within Oz, and we see this echoed within Dorothy, too. Dorothy reacts to this story as if it were a bedtime tale with a happy ending—which for her it is, as without the cap, she would not have the monkeys carrying her back to the Wizard. Further, though Glinda does give the monkeys, the cap at the end of *The Wonderful Wizard of Oz,* presumably freeing them, *The Marvelous Land of Oz* seems to negate this move when the Scarecrow tells Jack that "the Winged Monkeys are now the slaves of Glinda the Good, who owns the Golden Cap that commands their services" (117). We can try to logic this away—the monkeys are slaves in a limited sense, as they only have to listen to the owner of the cap three times; Scarecrow wasn't paying attention and missed Glinda giving the cap to the King of the Winged Monkeys, thus ending their slavery—but it stands out among the many examples of Oz heroes abolishing slavery. Even within *Wonderful Wizard*, Dorothy manages to free both the Munchkins and the Winkies from their enslavement.

One of the critiques of Oz is that while it is utopian for certain Oz citizens (farm girl Dorothy and the humbug Wizard rise in rank to princess and actual Wizard, respectively) it is not utopian for others (the suicidal Gump and the unloved Phonograph serve as two such examples). In "Utopian Tension in L. Frank Baum's Oz," Andrew Karp notes, "Baum's characters express [...] a desire for self-reliance and autonomy, a need to assert one's distinctness in the face of social pressures for conformity and uniformity, an urge to be free from society's efforts to inculcate specific mores, a 'yearning for leisure and freedom'" (106). However, Karp also notes the tensions that Baum's unique characters present, as they "suggest a devaluation of the group" (106) and some "express [...] elitism" (107) ultimately creating "a dramatic difference between the distinct individuals and the faceless, working masses" (109). When one begins dissecting the hidden hierarchies within Oz, several dichotomies pop up: unique individuals versus groups that function as a single character, objects or created characters versus those that are born, and human (or even human-like) versus animals. None of these labels are perfect—the Scarecrow isn't born, but he is afforded all of the utopian dues that Dorothy receives; the Lion is an animal, but, other than eating away from the group so as not to upset them, he, too, is afforded the utopian dues that Dorothy receives. It is notable, when considering this utopian versus less-than-utopian Oz, that the monkeys are a group that function as a single character. Only the King speaks, and none are offered a name.

The monkeys as a collective becomes something of a reoccurring theme as Oz adapts into new mediums. This is likely because the MGM film *The Wizard of Oz* uses them in this fashion, and, as the Library of Congress claims, the film "has been seen by more viewers than any other movie." The Winged Monkeys, or the Flying Monkeys as MGM calls them, almost weren't in the film, though. "Freed could not see how The Winged Monkeys could be filmed and suggested instead that Dorothy encounter some physical upheaval [...] similar to the earthquake in *San Francisco* (1936)" (Hearn, *Wizard of Oz Screenplay*, 14). Once MGM decided to use the monkeys, they went through several ideas, including a version where they become "a weapon for Dorothy. Summoned by Dorothy, who grabs the Golden Cap, they fight with her and Florizel against the Witch" (Harmetz 40). While this echoed some of the moral neutrality—the Flying Monkeys fight for the Witch when she has the Golden Cap and then for Dorothy when she takes ownership—ultimately the MGM Flying Monkeys become something darker. As Suzanne Rahn notes, there are echoes of an authoritarian dictatorship within the MGM witch's power. "There is more than a hint of military dictatorship in the regimentation of [the Wicked Witch's] joyless goose-stepping Winkies and bomber-like fleet of Flying Monkeys, reminding us that the militarization of Germany was very much in the news when the final version of the screenplay was written" (Rahn 120). Further, these Monkeys, treated as a collective, become solely associated with the Witch. Since the MGM film removed all traces of the bees, crows, and wolves that Baum's witch tried before using the cap (there's the deleted jitterbug scene, but it never made it to the final cut), and since the cap is never explained within the film, the Winged Monkeys become linked with the Wicked Witch's magic. "As for the Winged Monkeys, [in the MGM film] they are wholly evil; Nikko, their leader, is described in the screenplay as the Witch's familiar" (Rahn 121); when the cap is not explained as something like a genie lamp, the monkeys become part of the witch's magic. It is this collective witch's familiar version that seems echoed most often in adaptations.

The Monkeys as a collective are not only slaves to the Wicked Witch, but slaves towards whom even the reader (or viewer) is conditioned to be apathetic. In MoTown's *The Wiz*, these monkeys are a motorcycle gang—faceless because of their helmets and frightening because of their speed. While this version of *The Wiz* is often noted for having a cast comprised of African Americans, according to a conversation I had with Michael Patrick Hearn, the Winged Monkeys were actually portrayed by the New York City Chapter of the Hell's Angels, which had no Black members at the time. (His source was the late Sandy Alexander, President of the New York Chapter of the Hell's Angels.) This might account for the facelessness, but it does not explain the other connections readers, viewers and scholars make: when the monkeys become collective—they become part of the witch.

The clearest example of this monkey/witch connection is in the Sci-Fi miniseries *Tin Man* where the Wicked Witch character is this version's Dorothy's sister, possessed by an ancient witch. This possession includes a physical marking, tattoos of monkeys across her chest. As Alyssa Burger notes,

> The moats (short for monkey-bats) come to life from her very flesh when she calls upon them, playing on previous discourses of the flying monkeys as enslaved and literally commanded by another in Baum's book, and the maternal cross-species relationship between the Wicked Witch and her flying monkeys briefly depicted in MGM's *Wizard of Oz*, eliding themes of destructive control and unsettling maternalism in the figure of Azkadellia [Burger 51].

Even when the Monkeys are not a physical part of the Witch, or used as her familiar, their scene(s) are often used as a means to comment on the othering of the Witch, highlighting her evil. As Jesse Scott points out, "The Black Interior, Reparations, and African American Masculinity in *The Wiz*," "The Flying Monkeys and The Crows [are] under

[Evillene's] control along with everyone else" and this "excessive and unchecked power […] produces misery and despair in the lives in which she has influence and control" (78). Both Burger and Scott discuss elements around the monkeys to emphasize the unnatural, evil nature of the Wicked Witch of the West. They are not round characters in their own right, but rather they serve to underscore the witch's villainy.

While Gregory Maguire's 1995 novel *Wicked* keeps his Winged Monkey as something of a familiar or a child for his Wicked Witch, he does offer the character a name, and a bit of a backstory. In doing so, Maguire offers his readers a chance to explore this disenfranchised group with a touch more depth. Of course, given the novel's exploration of animals (as we know them) and Animals of the anthropomorphic variety, Maguire's monkey is hardly the only character with which Maguire explores the theme of disenfranchisement. In fact, Maguire makes those who are othered central by offering his reader Elphaba, his Wicked Witch of the West, as a protagonist. Elphaba's green skin aligns her with the MGM film villain, but her actions, especially early on, do not match the stereotypes one might attach to her appearance. Instead, Elphaba's otheredness makes her more sensitive to those who are disenfranchised. Her favorite teacher at Shiz University, Doctor Dillamond, is an Animal; Elphaba helps him research the biological differences between humans, animals, and Animals. This research is meant to help provide an argument against the restrictions the Wizard is placing on Animals, and leads to Doctor Dillamond being murdered. Elphaba continues this research after his death.

It is this research that ultimately leads to *Wicked*'s Winged Monkeys. Elphaba goes to the Emerald City to plead for Animal rights and, when that fails, drops out of school to work towards freeing Animals and overthrowing the Wizard. Her lover, Fiyero, is killed by the Wizard's secret police and she eventually makes her way to Fiyero's home with their lovechild in order to offer up a confession/apology to his wife. It is on the journey to Fiyero's home in the Vinkus that Elphaba finds a baby monkey. "It was a small monkey—of the variety called the snow monkey. A baby abandoned by its mother and its tribe, or maybe separated by accident? […] The monkey, who was called Chistery because of the sound he made, chittered and chattered now that he was warm and safe" (Maguire 242). Elphaba sees Chistery as an opportunity to continue her research. As Alyssa Burger notes:

> Elphaba's investment in the rights and intelligence of Animals culminates most powerfully in a creative impulse—when she works with her snow monkey Chistery to induce him to speech, and later when she gives him wings. […] building on the biological sciences of Dillamond, Elphaba "had found spells to convince the axial nerves to think skyward instead of treeward. And once she got it right, the winged monkeys seemed happy enough with their lot." Combining her own powers with the intellectual promise of Dillamond's truncated research, Elphaba is able to create a new race of creatures, though even the flying monkeys are not without their failures. They represent the intersection of two kinds of Animal—both animal and Animal—still proving largely unequal to the task of speech, as Elphaba reflects upon them in the dotage and revulsion of her unnatural motherhood [Burger 114–115].

If one switches the focus from Elphaba to Chistery, however, one can see how Maguire uses Chistery as a foil character for Elphaba's son Liir.

While this emphasizes Elphaba's feelings toward motherhood and her preference for scientific work over the work of nurturing her son, pairing well with Burger's observations, it also illuminates how both child and monkey are affected by Elphaba's lack of maternal feelings. Elphaba cares for the monkey, but she largely ignores her son, whom she does not claim as her child. When Liir is bullied by Fiyero's son Manek, and Liir tries to threaten that Elphaba won't be happy with Manek's teasing, Lirr is told, "She won't care. She likes the monkey more than she likes you. She won't even notice if you're dead" (Maguire 252). The other children in the Vinkus use Chistery to tease Liir and emphasize Elphaba's lack of maternal feelings toward her son. When the children discover Elphaba's adeptness with magic they claim that "Liir is Chistery's brother. Liir is what Chistery was like before she taught him how to talk. You're a monkey, Liir" (Maguire 273). With this teasing, Chistery becomes the means to other Liir—Liir is no longer seen as human if Chistery is his brother. This seems to recall the unnatural qualities presented in the MGM and *Wiz* versions of the Wicked Witch of the West. Though Elphaba is all about Animal rights, she is too wrapped up in her causes to notice how she is trapping both her son and Chistery in roles they do not want. Neither youth is able to claim the childhood (or animalhood) they might desire.

Chistery seems defined by what he is not. He is not Lirr, the Witch's son. He is also not Animal, though Elphaba does teach him to talk. Chistery even says in the sequel to *Wicked*, *Son of a Witch*, that he's "hardly a Monkey—more a monkey really" (194). While he is ordered to get Dorothy, much like every other Winged Monkey version, Chistery seems far more sympathetic than Baum's genie-like monkeys because it is his pseudo-mother making the request, not someone he is object-bound to. He also seems far less magical. Chistery is almost a science experiment gone wrong, yet he does not demonstrate any ill feelings toward Elphaba. Likewise, he seems overly forgiving of any ill feelings Liir directs his way, even "kiss[ing Liir's hand] with gummy affection" (Maguire, *SOAW*, 187) when the two reunite in *Son of a Witch*. If *Wicked*'s Elphaba dedicates her life to fighting for the disenfranchised Animal, Chistery almost disproves her goal. He is as loyal as Dorothy's Toto, and just as much an animal (especially when we consider that Baum ultimately granted Toto speech).

Wicked is not just one creation but two and, like Baum's book and the MGM film, Stephen Schwartz's stage musical *Wicked* might be the better known version. Like in Maguire's *Wicked*, Schwartz's Elphaba is an othered character who seeks to help those in a similar position. "*Wicked*'s producers, not surprisingly, emphatically stress its universality, asserting that Elphaba's 'difference' stands in for all difference. As producer Mark Platt is frequently quoted as saying, 'We all have a green girl inside of us'" (Wolf 11). However, while Stephen Schwartz borrows characters, plot elements, and settings for his musical version of *Wicked*, he changed quite a few things. One of those changes is Chistery. In the musical version of *Wicked*, the Wizard tricks Elphaba into casting a spell that causes Chistery and the other monkeys to sprout wings. The Wizard uses these Winged Monkeys to further the limits he continues to place on Animals until Elphaba endeavors to set the Monkeys free. Just as Elphaba in Maguire's *Wicked* comes to live in a non-traditional family with her monkey, her son, and her dead lover's widow and children, Alyssa Burger describes Schwartz's *Wicked*:

> Elphaba surrounds herself with a postmodern, non-nuclear family that consists of herself, her best friend Glinda, her lover Fiyero, and the flying monkey she created, Chistery. This family is far from harmonious [...] Elphaba regarding the flying monkeys she created with a volatile combination of love and anger at being tricked by the Wizard, seeing the monkeys as the personification and physical manifestation of her magical powers, both their strength and their lack [Burger 141].

What is interesting about each version of *Wicked*'s Winged Monkeys is how each serve to demonstrate the conflicted feelings of the liberating character. Elphaba is clearly on the side of those that help the disenfranchised, with Animals reading as a metaphor for any group whose civil liberties have been restricted by a patriarchal government leader, yet in both versions the Monkey is a minor character—the musical version of *Wicked* credits the role as an ensemble role. Through Chistery we see the ambivalence of the liberator—Elphaba's flaws as a mother in Maguire's novel and her mixed feelings toward Chistery because of her lack of consent in her creation within the musical offer a humanizing side to her work with Animals, yet this humanizing is not a flattering portrayal. Further, neither version makes Chistery particularly rounded, suggesting that though Elphaba can be read as a liberator, these disenfranchised animals are helpless if left on their own.

For all the ways that Disney's 2013 film *Oz the Great and Powerful* is "very much indebted" to *Wicked* as Henry Jenkins notes in his article ("All Over the Map: Building and Rebuilding Oz" 19), the screenwriters offer a far more rounded Winged Monkey than any other Oz version thus far explored within this essay. For the first time in a major Oz tale, viewers get to understand what motivates one Winged Monkey. In a homage to the MGM film, *Oz the Great and Powerful* offers a Kansas version and an Oz version for many of their main characters; Zach Braff plays both Frank, the assistant to James Franco's Oscar, and Frank's Ozzy counterpart, a Winged Monkey named Finley. Within their first interaction, Oscar yells at Frank and clearly withholds fair payment for his services as carnival barker and special effects man. Oscar views Frank as beneath him, stating that he's "just a trained monkey" (11:08–11:10). Meanwhile, Frank believes himself to be Oscar's friend. Oscar disagrees, telling Frank, "Friend? You're not my friend, Frank. I don't need a friend" (11:20–11:25). While not yet a Winged Monkey, these interactions set the tone for Frank/Finley's character arc. Frank, and Finley later in the film, plays a lesser, beta male to Oscar's toxically masculine alpha. His desire isn't to become the alpha, or have a love interest, or any of the other items that arc a traditional hero's role; Frank wants to be seen and valued by Oscar. In Baum's world of non-traditional male characters, this desire seems perfectly normal, but in the world of grand Hollywood films, especially the fairy tale love stories so common to Disney, this stands out as something different.

It would be easy to add Frank, and his desire to be appreciated by Oscar, to the long list of Disney's possible closeted characters. Baum's second novel, *The Marvelous Land of Oz*, is often used to highlight the homosocial intimacy between the Tin Woodman and the Scarecrow. In "The Utopia of Oz," S.J. Sackett examines the Scarecrow and Tin Woodman and hypothesizes that Baum used them to unite "the intellect and the emotion[al] in a harmonious relationship" (287)—together this "queerly made" (Baum, *Stories*, 135) pair represent emotional intelligence. While Baum likely meant queer as a synonym for strange or odd, Tison Pugh points out in his essay "John R. Neill: Illustrator (and Author) of L. Frank Baum's Queer Oz" that "if any couple stages the beauty of a long-term romantic relationship in Oz, it is the Scarecrow and the Tin Woodman—for no male-female friendships receive as much detailed attention and unqualified praise throughout the series" (64). This quote highlights how some people struggle with how to equate the traditionally male realm of rational thought and the traditionally female realm of emotional thought depicted in a harmonious relationship that isn't sexualized; it also serves to demonstrate the long, Ozzy history of non-traditional male characters in Oz and their possible homosexual readings. While I do not read this particular relationship as a homosexual pairing (certainly Oscar's womanizing ways limit any potential love between the men to "unrequited," if any), I do find it interesting that we code respectful friendships with subtextual romance. In my read of the relationship, Frank wants the respect that his loyalty and friendship deserve.

As Frank becomes Finley, his wishes and his submissive relationship with Oscar are echoed within Oz. While viewers are never privy as to why Frank works for Oscar, Oscar saves Finley during their first interaction, which ends with Finley pledging himself to Oscar for life. "My name is Finley. My master's home was ransacked by the Wicked Witch's baboons. And I've been hiding in these woods ever since. But now you've saved my life, oh, Wizard. So I hereby swear a life debt to you. […] From this moment on I shall be your loyal and faithful servant until death" (34:45–35:06). This debt is not like the Golden Cap, as Finley offers himself willingly, and he offers himself without limit (for life). Oscar appreciates this as much as he appreciated his relationship with Frank. He instructs Finley, "As my new assistant all you need to know are the three 'ups.' Show up, keep up, shut up" (37:04–37:08). Oscar is just as borderline abusive toward Finley as he was to Frank. This is as much a comment on Oscar as a character as it is for the trope of the Winged Monkey. It is not an accident that the writers chose to make Frank's counterpart the genie/slave of Oz, and this point is highlighted further when Finley is not allowed to ride to the Emerald City in the carriage with Oscar and the China Girl. He has to walk with the bags because he is taking on the role of the disenfranchised Winged Monkey—the lowest on the power totem, despite his ability to fly.

Like Baum's Winged Monkeys, Finley does not seek freedom from his enslavement. Finley's loyalty to Oscar borders on what readers see with Baum's monkey's description of Gayelette as beautiful, powerful, good, beloved, and wise. Finley knows Oscar is a fraud, yet he respects and admires him. In fact, rather than lament his servitude, Finley becomes a classic Disney sidekick, providing humor during the darker moments of the film. When Oscar, Finley, and the China Girl go to confront the supposed evil witch in the south, Finley provides his fair share of comic relief, sneezing away Oscar's dirt-drawn plans and mooing like a cow when he's supposed to provide a distracting animal noise. These moments make him seem simple, silly, and very much a beta, or lesser, male.

A character like Frank/Finley surely needs a leader instructing him, perhaps making his status seem justifiable to the viewer. Of course, there's a history behind this justification. In her book, *Slavery in American Children's Literature*, Paula Connolly notes how antebellum author Caroline Gilman presents slaves in *The Rose Bud* "as loyal, foolish, at times mischievous, but more often needing a master's protection" (57). Like Baum's monkeys, there is something casual about how this example of slavery is treated within Oz, but the "what" seems different. Baum's trickster monkeys were enslaved for a wrongdoing, and their punishment had limits—three wishes, bound to a cap. Finley is a "good" character to the point of being harmless; throughout the film he only does good or silly acts. Additionally, he is smaller than Oscar and several other characters, highlighting the power structure within the film. There are other flying simians in this film, as the Wicked Witch of the East has flying baboons that function more like the collective familiars from the MGM film or the *Tin Man* miniseries. Finley is physically smaller than the flying baboons, and clearly afraid of them. Oddly, the potential link between Finley and the baboons is never explored, even though each are flying simians. Finley is all good and the baboons are all villains.

In true fairy tale fashion, Finley's story seems to have a happy ending. At the conclusion of the film, Oscar offers several characters tokens, much like the Wizard offers a diploma, a clockwork heart, and a medal of bravery toward the end of the MGM film. Oscar offers Finley "'something that I've never given anyone. My friendship. Now you're my partner. You're my friend' [and Finley replies] 'That's all I've ever really wanted'" (2:01:26–2:01:47). The viewer is denied any friendship actions that could follow this statement. Connolly notes a propensity for forgiveness in abolitionist responses to slavery, quoting J. Elizabeth Jones's *The Young Abolitionists* as describing "a family of escaping slaves promises that 'our freedom is all we ask. [...] [W]e wish no harm to come upon [the white masters]'" (26–27). Finley is quick to forgive Oscar, and quick to believe his word. Viewers never see Finley treated as an equal, or what his friendship with Oscar might look like. Given the abundant differences in power structures and personality types, it is difficult to imagine how this partnership might work. Even when the named monkey character is rounded with his own wants and desires, the story concludes when he is freed. With his agency to liberate, befriend, or otherwise grant wishes, Oscar becomes the savior and Finley is never given the chance to actually experience, on screen, his freedom.

One year after the release of Disney's *Oz the Great and Powerful*, Danielle Paige's *Dorothy Must Die* offered readers the first text with several named Winged Monkey characters and offered agency to those characters. Paige's Oz focuses on Amy Gumm, a high schooler who hates her Kansas, trailer park life up until she is transported to a dystopian Oz in environmental peril from a dictatorial Dorothy. This flipped version, where Baum's hero characters are turned into villains, gives Paige the room to dig into how a character gains agency in a world set up against them. When readers meet the novel's first Winged Monkey, Amy finds him tied to a pole (very much like Baum's Scarecrow character) and the Munchkin she is traveling with tells Amy, "'Come on. Let's keep moving. Forget we even saw it.' I shook my head at her. *It* was wearing pants. *It* had dried blood all over it. *It* was in eardrum-bursting pain" (Paige, *Dorothy Must Die*, 61).

Amy immediately takes issue with the way the Winged Monkey is made lesser with the use of "it." She helps him and is rewarded with more knowledge—the knowledge that this Winged Monkey self-mutilated and cut off his wings. "Although I was still freaked out, I bent down to help him sit up. My fingers brushed against the jagged, stumpy nubbins poking out of his shoulder blades. 'Don't mind those,' he explained [...]. 'That's just where my wings used to be. Before I cut them off'" (Paige, *Dorothy Must Die*, 62). While this seems horrific and dystopian, the monkey's reasons add a new level of horror to the story. He cut off his wings to preserve his autonomy. As he tells Amy, "'My people have always been used by those who are more powerful,' he began to explain. 'Even before Dorothy rose to power, we were slaves to others. It's part of our enchantment. The wings are vulnerable to magic; they make us easy to control. [...] I would rather be free than fly'" (Paige, *Dorothy Must Die*, 64). If *Wicked* uses Animals as a metaphor for any group whose civil liberties have been restricted by a government leader, *Dorothy Must Die* uses its Wingless Monkeys to explore the length to which one with restricted liberties might go in order to gain back some sense of choice and control.

Paige does not make light of the sacrifices, both physical and social-emotional, that these Wingless Monkeys go through. Not every monkey chooses to cut off their wings, creating a divide within the species and even within families. Ollie, the monkey readers get to know best within Paige's first novel, is separated from his sister, who did not cut off her wings. Further, when he flees with Amy and is chased by Winged Monkeys, Paige pens Amy musing, "I wonder how it had felt for him to be so close to his people and to not even be able to look at them. The monkeys weren't evil: they were slaves, and some of them had probably been his friends once" (Paige, *Dorothy Must Die*, 74–75). Where *Oz the Great and Powerful* did not explore the possible connection between its named Winged Monkey and the nameless Winged Baboons, Paige connects her protagonist and antagonist monkeys. This allows readers another way to sympathize with her enslaved creatures while recalling Baum's morally neutral monkeys. Through Amy, Paige identifies that the Monkeys are enslaved rather than evil, and shows the emotional struggle Ollie goes through as a Wingless One.

Ollie is a more rounded character than any monkey previously examined—he is named, he has a family, and he has his own wants and desires. Paige offers him autonomy to the point that she allows him to leave Amy when they are confronted by the evil Tin Woodman. A sidekick would never leave the hero, and a slave would be powerless to whomever had control, but Ollie has his own agency. When he reunites with Amy, he apologizes the way a friend would: "'I'm sorry I ran off on you' [...] 'It's okay, Ollie.' I patted him on the head and he slowly released me [...] 'Where have you been?' I asked. 'How did you get away?' 'I made it to the Dark Jungle,' he said. 'There's a group of Wingless Ones there, and they've started a small resistance among the animals'" (Paige, *Dorothy Must Die*, 334). Not only is Ollie granted agency over his own actions, but Paige pens the entire species of Winged Monkeys as capable creatures with agency. They create their own safe space, and decide how much to help or intervene with the other characters. Ollie (with the help of his sister, Maude) eventually saves Amy, carrying her away from danger via fake wings. He chooses to help her, just as she chose to help him.

Choosing how much to help others, regardless of what is in one's own interest, becomes a major theme for the Wingless Ones in the next entry in Paige's *Dorothy Must Die* series, *The Wicked Will Rise*. In her second Oz novel, Paige develops her Winged Monkeys beyond Ollie and his family, showing her readers their Queendom and their queen when Amy and Ozma take refuge there. "The Queendom of the Wingless Ones was built high in the trees, just below the thick canopy of leaves that covered the Dark Jungle. The monkeys had known the path through the jungle by heart and commanded enough respect in these woods that we'd been able to share it with them" (Paige, *Wicked Will Rise*, 40).

While Paige leaves her Monkeys in a natural habitat, these characters are anything but. Like Zach Braff's Finley, Paige uses these Wingless Ones for a bit of comic relief—especially their seemingly eccentric queen. "Queen Lulu was sitting on a large throne constructed out of sticks and branches in the middle of a filthy room strewn with banana peels, clothes, and piles upon piles of newspapers, books, toys, and other junk. She wore bright red lipstick, a pouty pink tutu, and pink, rhinestone-encrusted cat-eye sunglasses" (Paige, *Wicked Will Rise*, 44). Like *Oz the Great and Powerful*'s Finley, there's something a little dark hiding behind the humor here. Connolly notes how in Louise Clarke Pyrnelle's *Diddie, Dumps, and Tot*, "slaves' attempts to dress and act as whites [...] is a site of humor" (110), and we seem to see this sort of humor echoed with Paige's Lulu. The audience is laughing at her as she attempts to dress like the dominant humans, but she can't quite manage to pull off a convincing version.

It might be easy to dismiss this questionable humor if it weren't for Lulu's backstory. Lulu wasn't always the Queen of the Wingless Ones. She began as Ozma's nursemaid and her "family had worked for the royal family for ages. She took care of Ozma, and after a time, Lulu came to think of Ozma as her own" (Paige, *Wicked Will Rise*, 72). Lulu recalls the Mammy character from white-authored postbellum literature, which certainly dampens whatever humor might be found in her non-traditional attire. In spite of this questionable humor, Paige keeps her monkeys fully rounded characters with their own unique moral code. Her Wingless Monkeys help those who help them, but otherwise stay to themselves. When Amy is among the Wingless Ones, the Queen suggests to her that they are even. "'Shall we call our debt all settled up here, then?' 'Debt?' I asked. 'Yeah, debt. You saved Ollie and Maude, they saved you. Even-steven. No more monkey business'" (Paige, *Wicked Will Rise*, 45). Paige's monkeys are good to those who are good to them, but, like Baum's sectionalized Oz characters, they wish to keep to themselves and not get involved in the larger happenings within Oz. This sectionalization might also recall antebellum America while playing with some of the less utopian concepts that some have read into Baum's Oz; certainly Paige is aiming for a dystopian novel.

Paige uses this idea of "keeping to one's own" as a means of exploring the political options that disenfranchised people have. Via Amy, the reader empathizes with the Wingless Ones removing themselves, as much as possible, from the dystopian conflicts within Oz. "Then I understood what Queen Lulu had been saying to me. This was why she wanted to stay out of it, why she wanted the monkeys to just keep to themselves and let the rest of Oz fight for power. The monkeys had made a place for themselves, and they wanted to enjoy it" (Paige, *Wicked Will Rise*, 55). Paige's Wingless Ones have sacrificed a great deal for their freedom. It is understandable that they might not want to sacrifice that freedom for some arbitrary greater good.

Of course, every action affects others, and Paige shows this when Mombi, one of the formerly wicked witches helping Amy start a revolution to save Oz, makes an impassioned speech to get Queen Lulu and the other monkeys to join them as allies against Dorothy.

> "But what of those who can fight, and choose not to? Wingless Ones, while you cavort mindlessly in the trees, far from the troubles below, your brothers and sisters are in chains, forced to serve their mistress's cruel whims. You turn your backs on them simply because you think that they are not as brave as you. Need I remind you what those backs look like now? Did you deform yourselves—pay the ultimate price—just so you could cover your eyes and ears to the truth?" [Paige, *Wicked Will Rise*, 90–91].

As Mombi points out, no one can really be free when others are enslaved. It isn't enough for Queen Lulu and the Wingless Ones to mind their own business for safety's sake. When members of your own community are disenfranchised, you disenfranchise yourself if you do not do something to help. In the end, her speech works. Lulu and her Wingless Ones show up in the final battle of *The Wicked Will Rise* to help Amy and to protect the Emerald City. As Lulu says when she finds Amy, "'You were right' Lulu told me as she approached [...]. 'You told me we couldn't just sit up there in the trees, waiting for bad things to come to us. We'd been ignoring the rest of Oz for too long'" (Paige, *Wicked Will Rise*, 269).

It is only by joining the combined efforts to retake and remake Oz that the Wingless Ones truly gain their freedom. However, like *Oz the Great and Powerful*, once they serve their part in the battle, their story basically ends. In Paige's third Oz novel, *The Yellow Brick War*, the Monkeys show up for a handful of pages to battle Glinda and then basically stop being part of the story. Once they resolve to be part of Oz, they lose their page time. Paige's Wingless Ones aren't given a happy ending within the novel. Though the reader may imagine them back in their Queendom, the fact that this isn't shown means that their highest purpose was to help, serve, or otherwise drive Amy's story, not their own.

When Baum created his Winged Monkeys, he created a morally neutral character who borrowed from genies and trickster characters of fairy tales and religious lore. Over time, however, they have been read as far more than magical hybrid animals. Scholars have posited these monkeys to be symbols for America's indigenous people, or even as satire on the old Northwest Mounted Police, but those readings attempt to read Baum's Winged Monkeys as a symbol of the culture and time of the author's life, limiting their interpretation. When one expands beyond Baum's Oz to include MGM's Flying Monkeys and *The Wiz*'s Winged Warriors, one can begin to see how elements of war, with a backdrop of totalitarianism, cause the Monkeys to become villainous witch's familiars. Expanding beyond that to include *Wicked*'s Chistery, *Oz the Great and Powerful*'s Finley, and *Dorothy Must Die*'s Lulu, Ollie, and Maude, one can see how the Winged Monkeys become a means for discussing America's complex relationship with any disenfranchised groups, the power structures that accompany this disenfranchisement, and who has the agency to liberate.

Even in the adaptations that seem the most modern, the Winged Monkeys either become part of the Wicked Witch of the West, or they can be read in a way that recalls slavery and antebellum literature. While they are often depicted as loyal, mischievous, and even foolish, their stories revolve around the needs, desires, and hero's arcs of other characters. In a land of anthropomorphic beings, they do not stand out as unique for being human-like, but they do stand out by the limits placed upon their humanity. In the introduction to *The Wonderful Wizard of Oz*, L. Frank Baum stated his desire to leave out the "heart-aches and nightmares," yet the Flying Monkeys from MGM still cause nightmares—likely because the heartaches and nightmares of the disenfranchised echo through the Winged Monkeys, especially as they have been adapted over time.

WORKS CITED

Baum, L. Frank. *The Marvelous Land of Oz*. Dover, 1969.
_____. *The Wonderful Wizard of Oz*. HarperCollins, 1987.
Burger, Alyssa. *The Wizard of Oz as American Myth: A Critical Study of Six Versions of the Story, 1900–2007*. McFarland, 2012.
Connolly, Paula T. *Slavery in American Children's Literature, 1790–2010*. University of Iowa Press, 2013.
Derry, Ken. "'Like You Could Read What Was Inside of Me': Genocide, Hermeneutics, and Religion in The Wizard of Oz." *Journal of Religion and Popular Culture* 26, no. 3 (2014): 293–309.
El-Zein, Amira. *Islam, Arabs, and the Intelligent World of the Jinn*. Syracuse University Press, 2017.
Fleming, Victor, dir. *The Wizard of Oz*. MGM, 1939.
Gage, Matilda Joslyn. *Woman, Church and State*. Humanity Books, 2002.
Hakala, Laura. "Beyond the Big House: Southern Girlhoods in Louise Clarke Pyrnelle's *Diddie, Dumps, and Tot*." *The Southern Quarterly* 54, no. 3 (2017): 23–40.
Harmetz, Aljean, and Margaret Hamilton. *Making of Wizard of Oz*. Chicago Review Press, 2013.
Hearn, Michael Patrick. Personal correspondence, 27 January 2021.
_____, ed. *The Annotated Wizard of Oz, Centennial Edition*. W.W. Norton, 2000.
Jenkins, Henry. "'All Over the Map': Building (and Rebuilding) Oz." *Acta Universitatis Sapientiae. Film and Media Studies* 9 (2014): 7–29.
Karp, Andrew. "Utopian Tension in L. Frank Baum's Oz." *Utopian Studies* 9, no. 2 (1998): 103–21.
Langley, Noel, Florence Ryerson, and Edgar Allan Woolf. *The Wizard of Oz: The Screenplay*. Michael Patrick Hearn, editor. Delta/Dell, 1989.
Littlefield, Henry M. "The Wizard of Allegory." *The Baum Bugle* 36 (1992): 24–25.
_____. "The Wizard of Oz: Parable on Populism." *American Quarterly* 16, no. 1 (1964): 47–58.
Lumet, Sidney, dir. *The Wiz*. Universal Pictures and Motown Productions, 1978

Maguire, G. *Son of a Witch: A Novel*. ReganBooks, 2005.

_____. *Wicked: The Life and Times of the Wicked Witch of the West*. ReganBooks, 2000.

Paige, Danielle. *Dorothy Must Die*. HarperCollins, 2014.

_____. *The Wicked Will Rise*. HarperCollins, 2015.

Pugh, Tison. "John R. Neill: Illustrator (and Author) of L. Frank Baum's Queer Oz." *Marvels & Tales* 29, no. 1 (2015): 64–86.

Rahn, Suzanne. *The Wizard of Oz: Shaping an Imaginary World*. Twayne, 1998.

Raimi, Sam, dir. *Oz the Great and Powerful*. Disney, 2013.

Sackett, S.J. "The Utopia of Oz." *The Georgia Review* 14, no. 3 (1960): 275–91.

St. John, Tom. "Lyman Frank Baum: Looking Back to the Promised Land." *Western Humanities Review* 36, no. 4 (1982): 345–60.

Scott, J. "The Black Interior, Reparations and African American Masculinity in *The Wiz*." *Pimps, Wimps, Studs, Thugs and Gentlemen: Essays on Media Images of Masculinity*, E. Watson, editor. McFarland, 2009. 68–84.

Willing, Nick, dir. *Tin Man*. RHI Entertainment and the Sci Fi Channel, 2007.

"The Wizard of Oz: An American Fairy Tale." To See the Wizard—Oz on Stage and Film. Library of Congress, 31 October 2016. http://www.loc.gov/exhibits/oz/ozsect2.html.

Wolf, Stacy. "'Defying Gravity': Queer Conventions in the Musical 'Wicked.'" *Theatre Journal* (Washington, D.C.) 60, no. 1 (2008): 1–21.

Glinda and Gender Performativity

Walter Squire

As noted by Michael Patrick Hearn in *The Annotated Wizard of Oz*, L. Frank Baum's mother-in-law Matilda Joslyn Gage was one of the leading feminists of the late nineteenth century (14) and, in the words of Mark I. West, "encouraged Baum to question societal assumptions about gender roles" (130).[1] Perhaps Gage can in part be credited for Baum having created a fantasy world where all the powerful figures are female, at least in his first Oz novel, *The Wonderful Wizard of Oz*. This, however, does not mean he equated their power with good. After all, two of the witches in that novel are wicked. Following Baum, adaptations of the novel have maintained a dichotomy of powerful feminine figures, some good, some wicked, with the occasional revisionist text, such as Gregory Maguire's *Wicked* or Danielle Paige's *Dorothy Must Die* complicating that dichotomy.

Film adaptations have largely maintained the cardinal points of *The Wonderful Wizard of Oz* by locating the good witches in the north and south, and the wicked witches in the east and west. Notably, only one witch in Baum's first Oz novel receives a name—Glinda, the Good Witch of the South and the most powerful figure in that novel. (A wicked witch, Mombi, has to wait until the second Oz novel, *The Marvelous Land of Oz*, to receive a name.) Furthermore, Glinda appears to be Dorothy's ideal mother figure,[2] blowing her kisses across the page (253) in W.W. Denslow's illustrations for the first edition of *The Wonderful Wizard of Oz*, to be matched by Aunt Em's embrace when Dorothy returns to Kansas (253), such affection from Em not being detectable prior to Dorothy's journey to Oz.

This essay will examine the gender performativity of Glinda across numerous versions of *The Wonderful Wizard of Oz*. Glinda is often presented as idealized femininity, yet each Oz text's presentation of that femininity varies. Drawing upon Judith Butler's concept of gender performativity, I will illustrate how various Glindas' representations of femininity arise from repetitive actions frequently associated with femininity and, in one notable case, contest association of specific actions with femininity. Texts examined will include *The Wonderful Wizard of Oz*; the 1939 MGM film adaptation *The Wizard of Oz*, directed by Victor Fleming[3]; the 1976 partially gender-flipped Australian glam rock film *Oz* (released in the United States as *20th Century Oz*), directed by Chris Löfvén; and the 2005 televised film *The Muppets' Wizard of Oz*, directed by Kirk R. Thatcher, the last of which features Miss Piggy as all the witches.

In *Gender Trouble*, Judith Butler notes that "the original identity after which gender fashions itself is an imitation without an origin" (138). That is, gender isn't innate,

Glinda and Dorothy blow each other a kiss (W.W. Denslow illustration from *The Wonderful Wizard of Oz* [1960 edition]).

essential, and unchanging but, rather, historically constructed and, through performative repetition, produces the illusion of being "natural." These performative repetitions include not only actions and behaviors on the part of the gendered individual but also vocalizations and visual appearances, for "[t]he effect of gender is produced through the stylization of the body" (140). Further elaborating the contrivance of gender, Butler stresses that societies police boundaries, "regularly punish[ing] those who fail to do their gender right" (140), as a means of preventing the "politically tenuous construction" of gender as "be[ing] revealed as a regulatory fiction" (141).

Baum dividing witches morally through cardinal points in *The Wonderful Wizard of Oz* suggests that their relative goodness or wickedness may also be linked to their performance of gender, for femininity and masculinity are often presented as "existing in a binary relation to one another" (Butler 140). Since readers of *The Wonderful Wizard of Oz* only encounter the Wicked Witch of the East after her death, there are none of her performative actions or appearances to observe, although readers do learn the Witch of the East held Munchkins in "bondage" (Baum 21), as the Wicked Witch of the West holds the Winkies in bondage and plans to do the same with Dorothy. These crimes may seem meritorious of the punishment of death, but the causes of the Wicked Witch of the West's execution are more complex. The Witch's death is precipitated by her stealing a silver shoe from Dorothy, which angers Dorothy enough that the girl fatally dowses the Witch with a bucket of water.[4] While theft and enslavement are not gendered crimes in the sense that one gender is punished for engaging in the crimes while others are not, other aspects of the Wicked Witch of the West do suggest she "fail[s] to do their gender right" (Butler 140). While the Dorothy of *The Wonderful Wizard of Oz* merely states, "But I thought all witches were wicked" (23), Dorothy's (Judy Garland) elaboration in the 1939 MGM film *The Wizard of Oz* that "witches are old and ugly" can be applied to Baum's witches as well. Age is not a determinant of a witch's relative goodness or wickedness, for Baum describes both the Good Witch of the North as a "little old woman" (21) and the Wicked Witch of the West as "old" (152), the latter's age reinforced through the image of "the blood in her ha[ving] dried up many years before" (152). Yet Glinda, the Good Witch of the South, appears "both beautiful and young" (254) to Dorothy and her companions. It is not so much age as imbalance and uncleanliness that visually link the Witch of the West to wickedness. Symmetry is often associated with beauty, and one of Baum's few descriptions of the Witch of the West is that she "had but one eye" (141). W.W. Denslow, illustrator of the first edition of the novel, compounds this lack of symmetry by depicting the witch as an obviously elderly woman, possessing few teeth and with a creased and wrinkled face as well as pigtails, a hairstyle usually associated with young girls (140, 149, 153, and 155). Further detracting from her appearance is her apparent lack of cleanliness. Since water is fatal to the Witch, she cannot bathe, and upon passing away the Witch becomes "a brown, melted, shapeless mass" that befouls "the clean boards of the kitchen floor" (154). The Wicked Witch of the West violates expected gender performances twofold—through neglecting her appearance and through soiling the domestic sphere. She maintains order in neither her body nor home, and thus may be considered an unruly woman, who, if she cannot be tamed, must be eliminated.

If Dorothy's relationship to the Witch of the West is examined, yet another aspect of the Witch's gender performance comes to light. The Witch's intention is to enslave Dorothy, and she "bade [Dorothy] clean the pots and kettles and sweep the floor and keep the fire fed with wood" (150), to which Michael Patrick Hearn remarks, "The worst she can think of is to make Dorothy do housework!" (219). The Witch acts as what Dorothy might consider a "bad mother," for "she refuses the self-abnegating role" (Kaplan 468), desiring Dorothy's shoes for herself and expecting Dorothy to do chores. The Wicked Witch is markedly contrasted by Glinda, both in appearance and in respect to Dorothy. Glinda serves as destination and reward for Dorothy in *The Wonderful Wizard of Oz*, as the Good Witch of the South does not appear until the penultimate chapter, long after Dorothy has vanquished the Witch of the West and has been abandoned by the Wizard of Oz. Glinda is Dorothy's last hope of returning to Kansas, and Dorothy and her companions reach Glinda after a series of perilous adventures. Baum restricts his description of Glinda to a single paragraph: "She was both beautiful and young to their eyes. Her hair was a rich red in color and fell in flowing ringlets over her shoulders. Her dress was pure white; but her eyes were blue, and they looked kindly upon the little girl" (254). Denslow extends Baum's description by adding hearts to the border of Glinda's dress and heart-shaped rubies to Glinda's crown (253). The Quadling guards who attend Glinda likewise have hearts on their hats and uniforms in Denslow's illustrations (249).

Denslow's addition of hearts to costuming foregrounds Glinda's performance of gender. Instead of taking and exploiting as the Wicked Witch does, Glinda bestows—transit, knowledge, and, most of all, affection. After arranging for the Scarecrow, Tin Woodman, and Lion to be carried to each of their domains, Glinda informs Dorothy of the power of the silver slippers to take Dorothy home to Kansas. Dorothy's adventures in Oz conclude with affectionate parting, foreshadowed by Denslow's illustration of Glinda blowing kisses to Dorothy at the beginning of the penultimate chapter of the novel (253), followed by Dorothy hugging and kissing the friends she has made in Oz, and returning at the end to Glinda, who "step[s] down from her ruby throne to give the little girl a good-bye kiss" (258). In the final chapter, Aunt Em then mimics the actions of Glinda, "folding [Dorothy] in her arms and covering her face with kisses" (261). Previously, no affection or even happiness is shown emanating from Em, from whom "sun and wind … had taken the sparkle from her eyes and left them a sober grey" (12), who "never smiled, now" (12), and who "would scream and press her hand upon her heart whenever Dorothy's merry voice reached her ears" (13). In "Dorothy and the Heroine's Quest," which appears as the Dorothy essay in this McFarland collection, Mark I. West notes that the one "significant difference" between Dorothy and the heroes of Joseph Campbell's monomyth "is that Dorothy does not 'bestow boons' when she returns to Kansas at the end of the book" (125), but I would suggest that affectionate gestures are the boons that Dorothy receives from Glinda and brings back to Kansas. If affection is missing from Dorothy's existence in Kansas, then despite the tornado being an accident of nature, the purpose of Dorothy's quest could easily be seen as the attempt to acquire a different relationship with her mother figure than she currently has. This can first be seen when the Witch of the North kisses Dorothy, albeit for Dorothy's protection, shortly after Dorothy arrives in Oz (27). Notably, Glinda's first action toward Dorothy is that she "looked kindly upon the little girl" (254). One could argue Dorothy wins that kindness through her own kindness to numerous residents of Oz, and then she acquires the mother figure she wants, one who gives both materially and emotionally. The title of the chapter devoted to Glinda, "The Good Witch Grants Dorothy's Wish" (251), couldn't be any clearer. A good witch, from Dorothy's perspective, is one who does or provides what Dorothy wants, and Glinda's performance of motherly provision and affection is replicated by Em, rendering her the affectionate good mother Dorothy always desired. Em's elderly appearance in contrast to Glinda's youthful one is unimportant, for in *The Wonderful Wizard of Oz* good witches/mothers are so designated through their providing Dorothy with kisses.

Dorothy's frustration with Em is more explicit in the 1939 MGM film *The Wizard of Oz*. Dorothy (Judy Garland) runs away from home due to Em's (Clara Blandick) refusal to defy the sheriff's order allowing Almira Gulch (Margaret Hamilton) to take Dorothy's dog Toto (Terry). Whereas Baum's Dorothy appears to desire affection from Em, Dorothy in *The Wizard of Oz* desires protection from those who would take something of value from her, whether the valued item be Toto in Kansas or the ruby slippers in Oz. Thus, the most significant repetition through which Glinda (Billie Burke) performs gender in *The Wizard of Oz* is protection of Dorothy. When the Wicked Witch of the West (Margaret Hamilton) makes a threat in Munchkinland, Glinda responds, "Be gone before someone drops a house on you, too," and wraps her arms tight around a trembling Dorothy. Later, when Dorothy, Toto, and the Cowardly Lion (Bert Lahr) fall asleep in the poppy field, Glinda returns to waken them with a snowstorm. Finally,

Glinda appears after the Wizard's (Frank Morgan) balloon has launched to Kansas, leaving Dorothy stranded in Oz. While the means of Dorothy getting back to Kansas are the same in the MGM film and Baum's novel, Glinda's role changes somewhat. In Baum's novel, Dorothy and her companions must undertake a perilous journey to find Glinda, making themselves worthy of her assistance, but in the film adaptation, Dorothy need only express her helplessness[5] through crying for Glinda to arrive and set everything right. Dorothy also performs her gender by hailing through helplessness, viewers having previously seen her gain a meeting with the Wizard through crying, which the Guard (Frank Morgan) cannot bear. *The Wizard of Oz* clearly depicts an idealized and gendered parent-child relationship between Glinda and Dorothy, whereby the mother (Glinda) will bestow absolute protection, provided the daughter (Dorothy) appear helpless and contrite. This dynamic is not only based upon age but also relative power, so that Dorothy adopts a motherly role to protect those she deems weaker than herself. Thus, Dorothy protects Toto from the Lion when the latter scares her dog, and when the giant projected head of the Wizard causes the Lion to faint, Dorothy chastises the Wizard, exclaiming, "You ought to be ashamed of yourself, frightening him like that when he came to you for help!" (1:11:44–1:11:52).

In contrast to Glinda, the Wicked Witch of the West is completely immune to Dorothy's tears, even mocking Dorothy's cries for her Aunt Em. The visage of Em being replaced by the Wicked Witch of the West in the Witch's crystal ball in this scene suggests that Dorothy still may hold Em's action of supporting the law against her and continues to consider her a wicked guardian who does not perform the maternal femininity Dorothy desires. Another parallel between Em and the Wicked Witch may be seen in attire. The Wicked Witch wears a long black dress that leaves only her hands and face exposed, and her costume is completed with a conical black hat. While Em's costuming is not as monochrome as the Witch's, it is similarly simple, composed of a solid dark skirt and a light printed, pleated, and collared blouse. In contrast, Glinda's attire is extraordinarily flamboyant, frilly, and delicate. Glinda's enormous hoop skirt gown, designed by Adrian Adolph Greenburg, "was made of layers of delicate pink tulle sprinkled with 'northern stars' and frosty snow crystals" (Scarfone and Stillman 139). Glinda's gown is accompanied by a silver butterfly necklace, and a much larger silver butterfly is incorporated into the front left shoulder of the dress. The transparent tulle of the shoulders of the dress are bunched in a fashion to suggest butterfly wings, as if Glinda is a fairy rather than a witch, although Glinda does not fly in a conventional sense but, rather, transports herself via an iridescent bubble.[6] Glinda's costume is completed by a tall, silvery, transparent crown and by a wand tipped with a glittering gemmed star.

While the pink hue of Glinda's gown, its composition of tulle, a fabric often used for veils and ballet tutus, and the star, bubble, and butterfly motifs may seem to replicate conventional adolescent and pre-adolescent femininity, Glinda's costuming also represents that which Dorothy does not possess in Kansas—excess, daintiness, and anything non-utilitarian. Most of the Kansas characters wear sturdy and plain clothing, as most live and work at Aunt Em's and Uncle Henry's farm. Likewise, Dorothy wears a simple blue and white gingham pinafore dress. The only character in Kansas who wears a flamboyant costume is Professor Marvel (Frank Morgan), who is clad in a ruffled shirt, jacket, vest, and tie, yet the patterns of the jacket, vest, and tie clash, and though his Prince Albert jacket "had a velvet collar, … the nap was all worn off the velvet" (Mary

Mayer qtd. in Harmetz 241–42). Still, we can tell Dorothy yearns for more than utility in dress, for she wears makeup as well blue ribbons in her hair.

Shortly after Dorothy arrives in Oz, Glinda transfers the ruby slippers from the Wicked Witch of the East's feet to those of Dorothy, and a long shot of Dorothy wearing the slippers is immediately followed by a medium close-up of the slippers, Dorothy modeling them by turning one foot and lifting up her heel so that the rubies glitter by catching the light. Long before Dorothy discovers the power of the slippers, they are presented as a desired object of beauty and one Dorothy could not possibly afford in Kansas, nor would they be sensible to wear there, considering the gems would soon be covered in dirt and mud. They are excessive, dainty, and non-utilitarian, at least until Dorothy learns their power. That Glinda is Dorothy's model of desired femininity is highlighted in the next shot, a medium close-up showing Dorothy and Glinda looking downward at the slippers, Glinda's hand resting upon Dorothy's shoulder. Both Dorothy and Glinda have red hair of the same length, although Dorothy's hair is of a darker hue and Glinda's is curlier. The similarity of appearance between Dorothy and Glinda in this shot suggests a familial relationship. Given the greater height of Glinda, one could even imagine them as mother and daughter.

If one combines Glinda's qualities of protectiveness and delicate beauty, one can see her performance of femininity as strength through fragility. Glinda's fragility is most notable through her mode of transportation, a bubble, which on the surface would seem to be easily eliminated by the Wicked Witch of the West, who first appears and disappears through smoke and fire. Yet Glinda appears to be the most powerful being in Oz, so certain of her powers that she never even raises her voice. During the interchange between the Wicked Witch of the West and Glinda in Munchkinland, Dorothy trembles within Glinda's arms, but Glinda smiles and laughs at all the Wicked Witch's threats. Glinda maintains a docility of demeanor that may represent Dorothy's attempts at negotiating gendered expectations of behavior whereby women are discouraged from expressing anger simultaneous with her desire to control situations that impact her and those who are important to her, such as Toto. That is, Glinda is a performance of powerful femininity, if said femininity is assumed to be pretty, pleasant, and delicate. Power exerted by the Wicked Witch of the West might be labeled toxic power, even toxic masculinity, although that toxic power/masculinity in the film is wielded by characters of multiple genders.

The first character in the film who clearly uses their power hegemonically and in a self-serving and destructive fashion is Almira Gulch. The wealth of Gulch, who "own[s] half the county," according to Em, enables her to weaponize the law against poorer residents. Not only does she acquire a sheriff's order to take Toto from Dorothy, but she also threatens to sue Em and Henry for their farm. Gulch's counterpoint in Oz, the Wicked Witch of the West, threatens Dorothy and Glinda within seconds of her first appearance engages in violence seemingly for the sheer pleasure of doing so (such as when she throws a fireball at the Scarecrow), enslaves the Winkies,[7] and is willing to engage in kidnapping and murder to acquire the ruby slippers.

Contrasts in the exertion of power are most obvious among the witches, given they are the strongest beings in Oz, but the contrast between toxic and gentle power can also be seen in male characters in Oz. The Cowardly Lion uses his size to terrify Toto and the Wizard uses technology to terrify, dismiss, and thus jeopardize the lives of Dorothy and her friends when he sends them to acquire the Wicked Witch of the West's broomstick.

Toto, the Scarecrow, the Tin Woodman, and the Cowardly Lion all act kindly toward Dorothy and one another once they become friends, but, while they use their abilities to assist Dorothy, none can be said to be powerful (once the Lion is revealed to be cowardly) in the sense that they do not realize until the end of the film they have strengths greater than others and which can be used benevolently or maliciously. However, the Guard does enact gentle power when he grants Dorothy and her companions a meeting with the Wizard, despite being charged with telling them, "The Wizard says go away!" (1:07:23–1:07:27).

To return to Glinda's visual performance of femininity in *The Wizard of Oz*, though, its excessiveness calls attention to itself much in the same way that drag performances call attention to the *performance* of gender as opposed to a mere identification of gender. Butler says of drag, "*In imitating gender,* [it] *implicitly reveals the imitative structure of gender itself—as well as its contingency*" (137, emphasis in original). Reflecting on the relationship between drag and *The Wizard of Oz*, Alexander Doty notes, "Camp's appreciation of the excessive also led me to reevaluate Glinda. She wasn't just *like* a drag queen, she was one! Artifice surrounded her like that pink (but of course) gossamer gown she wore" (50, emphasis in original).[8] Although Doty continues, "Who better to guide Dorothy along the road to straight womanhood" (50), his reading of *The Wizard of Oz* in *Flaming Classics: Queering the Film Canon* depicts Dorothy struggling with her lesbian desires and identification, oscillating between the femme Glinda and butch Wicked Witch of the West.

The Wizard of Oz has long been integral to American LGBTQ+ culture,[9] but less attention has been paid to queer gender and sexuality within Baum's original Oz series. Tison Pugh has performed queer reading of Baum's novels and notes Baum's frequent use of the adjective "queer" to describe characters and Oz itself (218–19), and then explores "[t]he impermanence of gendered identities and sexual morphism in Oz" (222), using as examples Tip/Ozma from *The Marvelous Land of Oz* and Billina the talking chicken, the latter who first appears in *Ozma of Oz*.[10] In *The Marvelous Land of Oz*, the sequel to *The Wonderful Wizard of Oz*, the male protagonist Tip is revealed to be and transformed back into Princess Ozma, an unpleasant shock to Tip, who had no memory of previously being the female Ozma. The third book in the Oz series, *Ozma of Oz*, features Billina the talking chicken who asks to be addressed as Bill and who does not distinguish their chicks by gender but rather bestows the name Dorothy upon all of them.

Considering the queer appeal of *The Wizard of Oz* and the fluctuations of gender in Baum's novels, it is surprising that explicitly queer or gender-flipped characters rarely appear in adaptations of either *The Wonderful Wizard of Oz* or *The Wizard of Oz*. One exception is *Oz* (1976, dir. Chris Löfvén), an Australian partially gender-flipped glam rock adaptation of *The Wizard of Oz*.[11] In this film, Dorothy (Joy Dunstan) is a groupie who is knocked unconscious in a motor accident while traveling with the band Wally and the Falcons. She is transported to Oz, which visually is almost a carbon copy of the Australia she left behind (although more desolate), where she meets Glynn the Good Fairy (Robin Ramsay), who supplies her with ruby heels. Dorothy then travels with a surfer (Bruce Spence), a mechanic (Michael Carman), and a biker (Gary Waddell), and attempts to avoid a thuggish trucker (Ned Kelly). Her quest is to meet the Wizard (Graham Matters), a glam rock star whose final performance is the same day she arrives in Oz.

Oz mimics the frame narrative of *The Wizard of Oz* in that the actors who portray Dorothy's traveling companions, the Wizard, and the Wicked Witch of the West (not labeled as such in *Oz*, but the thuggish trucker fulfills this role) all appear as characters in Australia previous to Dorothy's journey to Oz, and all those actors reappear as their frame characters at the end of the film except for Ned Kelly.[12] In the frame narrative, the surfer, mechanic, biker, and Wizard are all members of Wally and the Falcons, with Bruce Spence performing the dual roles of bass player and surfer, Michael Carman portraying drummer and mechanic, Gary Waddell as guitarist and biker, and Graham Matters playing Wally and the Wizard. Like Frank Morgan in the 1939 *Wizard of Oz*, Matters has several roles beyond Wally and the Wizard, including the doorman who initially prohibits Dorothy and her friends from seeing the Wizard's final performance. Ned Kelly, in addition to being the thuggish trucker, is a bouncer in the frame narrative. As with Glinda in *The Wizard of Oz*, Glynn has no counterpart in Australia. Another similarity between the films is Dorothy's transport to Oz kills the sibling of the Wicked Witch of the West figure. In the case of *Oz*, Wally and the Falcons' van kills the thuggish trucker's brother.

The depiction of Dorothy's traveling companions does vary from that in *The Wizard of Oz* in that *Oz* seems to take those characters' perceived lacks literally. The surfer, who corresponds to the Scarecrow, seems unintelligent, the mechanic, corresponding to the Tin Man, is frequently labeled as heartless by other characters, and the biker, who is the Cowardly Lion figure, remains aggressive long after he first meets Dorothy. Nor do any of these characters desire for the Wizard to change them in any way. However, the most noticeable difference between the set-up of the two films is that in *Oz* Dorothy's aunt and uncle are only mentioned offhandedly once and do not appear. With the exception of Dorothy, *Oz* is largely bereft of female characters, for Dorothy's friend Jane (Paula Maxwell) does not travel with her to Oz, resulting in Dorothy having to navigate toxic masculinity with only the assistance of a few effeminate men.

Several men at the Wally and the Falcons concert Dorothy and Jane attend at the beginning of the film initiate the toxic masculinity by making unwanted passes at the two women. Wally also makes an unwanted pass at Dorothy in the band's van by stroking her thigh with his hand, which Dorothy pushes away. While the drummer makes out with Jane, his bandmates laugh and gawk at them, their distraction leading to an accident. Once Dorothy is transported to Oz upon being knocked unconscious, the toxic masculinity intensifies. The mechanic sexually objectifies Dorothy and the trucker attempts to rape her, the biker threatens all males with whom he interacts, and music business figures at a party at the Wizard's hotel suite plot to prevent the Wizard's retirement so that they can continue to make money off of him. One of those businessmen says, "I don't let nobody cut me out of my percentage."

Glynn offers Dorothy protection from said toxic masculinity, and mirrors Glinda of *The Wizard of Oz* in that his performance of femininity centers on his being a protective maternal figure. He provides Dorothy with a pair of ruby heels, of which he says, "They'll protect you." When the trucker enters Glynn's shop seeking revenge upon Dorothy for the death of his brother, Glynn snaps, "You'll leave her alone if you know what's good for you." Later in the film, when Dorothy goes to a beach, takes off her ruby heels (thus voiding their protection), and then falls asleep after getting high with the biker, there is a suggestion that the mechanic, who has been interested in Dorothy since she and the surfer showed up at his garage earlier, may plan to sexually assault her while she is unconscious. The mechanic says to the biker, "It's just you and me and the sheila."[13] Glynn promptly arrives to wake and rescue Dorothy, taking her to the city in his red Mustang.

Similar to Glinda in *The Wizard of Oz*, Glynn offers not just protection for Dorothy but also glamour. In an otherwise desolate and dusty town, Glynn's boutique "Good Fairy" sticks out, first through the neon sign that draws Dorothy's attention and next through the ruby heels in the window that Dorothy stops to admire. Glynn's glossy white high-waisted bell-bottomed slacks and unsnapped shirt, revealing the multiple necklaces he wears, could be considered an upgrade of Dorothy's similar attire of high-waisted blue jeans, bland white buttoned shirt tied at the bottom to reveal her midriff, and unadorned neck. Likewise, Glynn's well-maintained light brunette curls resemble and improve upon Dorothy's frizzy blond hair. Glynn's Mustang is far newer and more expensive than the vehicles in which Dorothy has previously traveled, whether the band's van prior to the accident or those driven by the surfer, the mechanic, and the biker. Finally, Glynn is the means by which Dorothy may achieve glamour, first-hand through the red heels Glynn gifts her and second-hand through urging her to see the Wizard, whom Glynn labels "the most sensational thing ever to hit Oz."

Whereas Glynn resembles Glinda of *The Wizard of Oz* through performing femininity by protecting Dorothy nonviolently and without anger and through presenting a glamorous image to which Dorothy aspires, Glynn diverges from Glinda, both of *The Wizard of Oz* and *The Wonderful Wizard of Oz*, in two key ways. Most notably, Glynn is male. Glynn's performance of femininity is unconnected to his gender/sex, fitting for the androgynous glam context of the film. Femininity in *Oz* is linked to protectiveness, gentleness, desirability, and vulnerability, whereas masculinity in the film is linked to self-centeredness or "heartlessness," violence, desire, and invulnerability. These qualities can be performed by characters of any gender, although with the witches in *Oz* being male and no other characters gender-flipped, performances of femininity and masculinity are performed almost exclusively by male characters.

Glynn is the first character to protect Dorothy, but over time her traveling companions the surfer, the mechanic, and the biker become protective of her, eventually rescuing her from the trucker, the stand-in for the Wicked Witch of the West. As does Glynn, the surfer depicts the gentleness aspect of femininity, for he assists Dorothy without recourse to violence or anger. Desirability is represented through the items in Glynn's shop, Glynn's glamorous appearance, and his apparent wealth, all of which are desired by Dorothy. However, the Wizard is the character most desired in the film, both by numerous screaming female fans during his performance in the film, where his costume and makeup accentuate his nearly nude body, and by the male business figures who desire the capital he produces. Despite his power and wealth, Glynn is also feminine in that he is vulnerable to the insults lobbed at him due to his gender performance and assumed sexuality. Upon meeting Glynn, Dorothy asks his name, to which Glynn responds, "People call me all sorts of names," and when the trucker enters the boutique, he addresses Glynn by saying, "Shut up, fairy." Despite the physical similarity between Glynn and Dorothy, Dorothy's greater vulnerability to sexual exploitation is more closely mirrored by the vulnerability of the Wizard, who is financially exploited.

Several male characters in the film are self-centered, whether motivated by desire for sex, desire for wealth, or desire to project a masculine image. Two characters in the film, the drummer for Wally and the Falcons in the frame narrative and his corresponding character in Oz, the mechanic, are labeled heartless by other characters due to the drummer's and the mechanic's placing their sexual desires above concern for anyone else, including those they desire.

While no female character in *Oz* is self-centered or heartless to the degree that they exploit other characters, Dorothy at key moments in the film uses violence, first by kicking the mechanic to gain his attention so that he will pump petrol into the surfer's car and later by kicking the trucker in the groin in order to flee the house in which he has kept her captive. Interestingly, both kicks are delivered while Dorothy wears the heels Glynn provided her. Glynn himself does not act with violence, but since he transgresses in his gender performativity, his gift of the ruby heels to Dorothy enables her also to transgress in her gender performativity, although her desire for rock stars indicates that she had already been transgressive. She and her friend Laura are sexually aggressive in that they seek out male partners instead of waiting to be approached. At the end of the film, Dorothy even enters the Wizard's bathroom while he is showering without previously being invited. One could claim the ruby heels Dorothy wears makes her invulnerable, but the constant threat of sexual assault suggests otherwise. Rather, certain male characters provide the illusion of invulnerability, whether the biker until he is actually challenged, or the trucker until Dorothy and the biker team up on him after he abducts Dorothy.

Strangely, the one character in the film who seems invulnerable is Glynn, despite the homophobic slurs directed at him. The end of the film reveals Glynn to not be the fairy godmother Glinda historically has been presented as. After Dorothy joins the Wizard in his shower, Glynn walks into the bathroom to chastise the Wizard for hiding away and not attending to important publicity. The Wizard reveals to Dorothy that Glynn is his agent and Glynn dismissively says to Dorothy, "Sorry, dear, but there are thousands of you and only one Wizard." Glynn is hardly selfless in his guidance, for the Wizard appears to be his meal ticket. As is fitting for a more adult version of *The Wonderful Wizard of Oz*, Glynn is not an ideal or perfect representation of femininity but, rather, a human with his own desires, who may help those in need sometimes, but is not averse to exploiting others to get what he wants. In other words, Glynn combines feminine and masculine qualities rather than existing solely within one gender.

Glinda barely makes an appearance at all in *The Muppets' Wizard of Oz*, a made-for-television film directed by Kirk R. Thatcher, which first aired in May 2005 on ABC. Glinda is briefly onscreen to inform Dorothy (Ashanti) that the magical silver slippers will return her to Kansas. Unlike in *The Wonderful Wizard of Oz*, Glinda isn't really a destination, for Dorothy and her companions don't engage in a perilous quest to reach Glinda but, rather, just return to Munchkinland, where Glinda is visiting her sister Tattypoo, the Good Witch of the North. Despite the brevity of her presence in *The Muppets' Wizard of Oz*, Glinda's performance of femininity is highly complex. All four witches, including both Wicked Witches, are portrayed by Miss Piggy (Eric Jacobson), and the witches repeat actions and qualities of Miss Piggy with which viewers of Muppet media are already familiar. Miss Piggy is a diva character, glamorous and vain, demanding and at times violent, yet also protective and affectionate, although the aggressiveness of her affection sometimes distresses other Muppets.

Miss Piggy's portrayal of Glinda begins with glamour and self-centeredness, as she sports long blond hair, wears a lavender gown, lavender boa, and a pearl necklace, and knocks Munchkins out of her way as she approaches Dorothy, commanding, "Shoo! Shoo! Shoo!" She wows the Scarecrow, played by Kermit the Frog (Steve Whitmire), who is immediately smitten and is further intrigued yet somewhat embarrassed when she mentions "a roll in the hay" to him. Glinda further reveals her forwardness by apparently goosing the Scarecrow, as he jumps forward after standing in front of her and turns back to look at her in some dismay. Key to Miss Piggy's portrayal of Glinda is her characteristic vocal delivery, which includes snippets of French and elevated diction spoken in a high-pitched voice when trying to impress others, but when she becomes angry or irritated, the pitch of her voice drops significantly and she delivers threats and warnings in a staccato of one- and two-syllable words. Thus, her first words upon seeing the Scarecrow are "Enchanté," followed by "And who is this sophisticated and distinguished gentleman?" spoken in a high, lilting, sugary manner. When Pepe the King Prawn (Bill Barretta), as Toto, mistakenly believes Glinda is addressing him, her voice drops and she snarks, "Not you," accompanied by a karate chop.

Miss Piggy's performance of Tattypoo is similarly complex, for she alternates between lavishing affection upon the Munchkins and knocking them over when they get in the way of her being center stage. The Wicked Witch of the East appears so briefly that she only has time to spew anger and demonstrate superhuman strength, but the Wicked Witch of the West has ample time to demonstrate a range of femininity. While her violence and vanity are more pronounced than among the good witches, for she relishes her planned murder by circular saw of Dorothy and Toto, which is being filmed for her reality television show, she also dotes upon her dog. The overlapping appearances and behaviors of the witches are partially explained through all four being sisters, yet the complex portrayal of all except the Wicked Witch of the East also suggests that any idealized femininity (or masculinity, for that matter) is necessarily restrictive, for it prohibits certain behaviors among those performing the femininity. Likewise, any demonization of a character who "fail[s] to do their gender right" (Butler 140) relies upon a simplification of performance that stresses only those behaviors and appearances deemed pejorative for one's gender. Miss Piggy hardly presents ideals in her portrayals of the witches, yet those portrayals are oddly human in their complexity, considering Miss Piggy is a puppet representation of an anthropomorphized sow voiced by a male.[14]

In *Gender Trouble*, Judith Butler argues that drag "suggests a dissonance not only between sex and performance, but sex and gender, and gender and performance" (137), with the end result being the exposure of gender performance being unrelated to biology. The androgynous glam rock context of *Oz* previously depicted an Oz whereby traits coded feminine or masculine easily appear within both women and men, yet, while Glynn is not punished for gender transgression in the film, the revelation of his (toxic) masculine exploitation of the Wizard propels Dorothy away from her previous pursuit of rock stars, and when she returns to consciousness among the members of Wally and the Falcons she tries to warn them not to pursue fame and fortune. Before Glynn arrives, the Wizard confesses to Dorothy that "it's good not to act like a freak for a change," which indicates he is uncomfortable with the androgynous image he presents publicly. The dissonance between sex, gender, and performance is even greater in *The Muppets' Wizard of Oz*, for not only is Miss Piggy a drag character in that a male performs her, but she is also a cross-species character that bridges the animate/inanimate divide. However, there is no punishment for any of the witches on the basis of gender performance, as the witches have the same mixture of behaviors. Rather, the fate of the witches is determined by the consequences of their actions.

While fuller depictions of Glinda's femininity developing over time across adaptations might be expected, some of the most complex depictions of Glinda's gender performativity may be due to more than the dissonance Butler perceives in drag. Women's cultural, economic, and political power have increased immensely in the century since

Baum published *The Wonderful Wizard of Oz*, and yet the behavioral expectations for women may not have changed to the same degree. Thus, women may be in more jeopardy of being punished for "fail[ing] to do their gender right" (Butler 140) than men who perform femininity, especially if those men are performing as comic puppet characters.

NOTES

1. After Elizabeth Cady Stanton and Susan B. Anthony, Matilda Joslyn Gage is perhaps the most significant American feminist of the nineteenth century, though now largely forgotten. Of note is her examination of and resistance to the historical role theology has played in the subjugation of women. See her *Woman, Church, and State*, originally published in 1893 and reprinted, with an introduction by Sally Roesch Wagner, by Humanities Press in 2002.

2. Although their focus is on the 1939 MGM film adaptation *The Wizard of Oz*, Agnes Curry and Josef Velazquez have similarly explored Glinda as a good mother figure (and the Wicked Witch of the West as an evil mother figure), even alleging that "Glinda, in fact, might actually be Dorothy's deceased mother" (28).

3. Victor Fleming is credited as director of *The Wizard of Oz*, but three additional directors also worked on the film—Richard Thorpe, George Cukor, and King Vidor. For an extensive chronicle of the production of the film, see Harmetz.

4. Unlike in the 1939 film *The Wizard of Oz*, there is no suggestion in Baum's novel that the wicked witches are sisters, and thus the Wicked Witch of the West has no claim to the silver shoes.

5. The Scarecrow (Ray Bolger) and Tin Man (Jack Haley) likewise hail Glinda through helplessness, their cries of "Help! Help!" precipitating Glinda's snowstorm.

6. Both a 1938 script for the film and "Burke herself referred to Glinda as a 'fairy' instead of a 'witch'" (Scarfone and Stillman 140).

7. Whether the Winged Monkeys are enslaved, too, is not clear in *The Wizard of Oz*, although the monkey that verifies the Witch is dead seems to clap. An early script for the film had Dorothy grabbing the Golden Cap that controls the monkeys and ordering them to fight with her against the Witch (Harmetz 40). No mention is made of the Golden Cap in the final cut of the film, but, after Glinda creates the snowstorm to counteract the effect of the poppies, a monkey hands the Witch a golden cap, which the Witch promptly throws across the room.

8. Contrary to this depiction of Glinda, Margaret Hamilton suggests Billie Burke performed herself as Glinda: "She had a pink and blue dressing room, with pink and blue powder puffs and pink and blue bottles filled with powder and baby oil. And pink and blue peppermints. And an infinite number of perfectly beautiful clothes, all lace; and everything was pink and blue" (qtd. in Harmetz 127).

9. For an overview, in addition to Doty see Brantley, Bunch, and Michel, both *Friends* and "Not in Kansas."

10. Pugh also discusses the Phanfasms of *The Emerald City of Oz*, who possess the ability to change sex.

11. There is a brief drag performance by Frederick Ko Vert (as the Phantom in the Basket) toward the beginning of the 1925 silent film *The Wizard of Oz*, directed by Larry Semon. Tina Landau's play *1969*, first staged in 1994, is another work that queers *The Wizard of Oz*. See Zank for more on 1969. Pamela Robertson argues that the Australian road film *The Adventures of Priscilla, Queen of the Desert* (1994, directed by Stephan Elliott), "which tells the story of two drag queens and one transexual travelling from Sydney into the Australian outback" (273), while not an adaptation, parallels *The Wizard of Oz*.

12. This frame narrative structure with actors aside from those portraying Dorothy appearing in both Kansas and Oz was not new with the 1939 *Wizard of Oz*. The 1925 *Wizard of Oz* featured Larry Semon, Oliver Hardy, and Spencer Bell as farmhands who traveled to Oz with Dorothy (Dorothy Dwan) and then for their own protection pose as the Scarecrow, Tin Man, and Cowardly Lion, respectively. In the 1910 silent short *The Wonderful Wizard of Oz*, directed by Otis Turner, Dorothy (Bebe Daniels) first meets and rescues the Scarecrow (Hobart Bosworth) in Kansas, and they journey to Oz together.

13. "Sheila" is an Australian slang term for "woman."

14. Fran Brill was the original voice for Miss Piggy, but since 1974 Miss Piggy has been performed by men (Fisher and Cox 186–87).

WORKS CITED

Baum, Frank L. *The Emerald City of Oz*. 1910. SeaWolf Press, 2019.

———. *The Marvelous Land of Oz: Being an Account of the Further Adventures of the*

———. *Scarecrow and the Tin Woodman* 1904. HarperCollins, 1985.

_____. *Ozma of Oz*. 1907. HarperCollins, 1989.

_____. *The Wonderful Wizard of Oz*. 1900. HarperCollins, 2000.

Brantley, Ben. "Why Oz Is a State of Mind in Gay Life and Drag Shows." *New York Times*, 28 June 1994, p. C15.

Bunch, Ryan. "'The Wizard of Oz' in the LGBT Community." *Philadelphia Gay News*, 20 October 2016, https://epgn.com/2016/10/20/the-wizard-of-oz-in-the-lgbt-community, accessed 17 December 2021.

Butler, Judith. *Gender Trouble: Feminism and the Subversion of Identity*. Routledge, 1990.

Curry, Agnes, and Josef Velazquez. "Dorothy and Cinderella: The Case of the Missing Prince and the Despair of the Fairy Tale." *The Universe of Oz: Essays on Baum's Series and Its Progeny*, Kevin K. Durand and Mary K. Leigh, editors. McFarland, 2010. 24–53.

Doty, Alexander. *Flaming Classics: Queering the Film Canon*. Routledge, 2000.

Durand, Kevin K., and Mary K. Leigh, editors. *The Universe of Oz: Essays on Baum's Series and Its Progeny*. McFarland, 2010.

Fisher, Maryanne, and Anthony Cox. "The Uniquely Strong but Feminine Miss Piggy." *Kermit Culture: Critical Perspectives on Jim Henson's Muppets*, Jennifer C. Garlen and Anissa M. Graham, editors. McFarland, 2009. 181–201.

Fleming, Victor, dir. *The Wizard of Oz*. MGM, 1939.

Gage, Matilda Joslyn. *Woman, Church, and State*. 1893. Humanities Press, 2002.

Harmetz, Aljean. *The Making of The Wizard of Oz*. 1977. 75th anniv. ed. Chicago Review Press, 2013.

Hearn, Michael Patrick, ed. *The Annotated Wizard of Oz, Centennial Edition*. W.W. Norton, 2000.

Kaplan, E. Ann. "The Case of the Missing Mother: Maternal Issues in Vidor's *Stella Dallas*." *Heresies* 4, no. 4 (1983). Rpt. in *Feminism & Film*, E. Ann Kaplan, editor. Oxford University Press, 2000. 466–78.

Löfvén, Chris, dir. *Twentieth Century Oz* (originally called *Oz* and also called *Oz—A Rock 'n' Roll Road Movie*). Greater Union, 1976.

Maguire, Gregory. *Wicked: The Life and Times of the Wicked Witch of the West*. HarperCollins,1995.

Michel, Dee. *Friends of Dorothy: Why Gay Boys and Gay Men Love The Wizard of Oz*. Dark Ink Press, 2018.

_____. "Not in Kansas Anymore: The Appeal of Oz to Gay Males." *Baum Bugle* 46, no. 1 (Spring 2002): 31–38.

Paige, Danielle. *Dorothy Must Die*. HarperCollins, 2014.

Pugh, Tison. "'There lived in the Land of Oz two queerly made me': Queer Utopianism and Antisocial Eroticism in L. Frank Baum's *Oz* Series." *Marvels & Tales* 22, no. 2 (2008): 217–39.

Robertson, Pamela. "Home and Away: Friends of Dorothy on the Road in Oz." *The Road Movie Book*, Steven Cohan and Ina Rae Hark, editors. Routledge, 1997. 271–86.

Scarfone, Jay, and William Stillman. *The Wizard of Oz: The Official 75th Anniversary Companion*. Harper Design, 2013.

Semon, Larry, dir. *The Wizard of Oz*. Chadwick, 1925.

Thatcher, Kirk R., dir. *Muppets' Wizard of Oz*. Fox Television Studios, 2005.

Turner, Otis, dir. *The Wonderful Wizard of Oz*. Selig Polyscope Co., 1910.

West, Mark I. "The Dorothys of Oz: A Heroine's Unmaking." *Story and Society: Children's Literature in Its Social Context*, Dennis Butts, editor. Macmillan, 1992. 125–31.

Zank, Ronald. "'Come out, come out, wherever you are': How Tina Landau's *1969* Stages a Queer Reading of *The Wizard of Oz*." *The Universe of Oz: Essays on Baum's Series and Its Progeny*, Kevin K. Durand and Mary K. Leigh, editors. McFarland, 2010. 61–76.

Ozma, Sorceresses, and Suffrage

Women, Power, and Politics in L. Frank Baum's Land of Oz

M ARY L ENARD

In L. Frank Baum's Oz books, unlike traditional folk and fairy tales, women rarely, if ever, are relegated to a passive role. Instead of waiting in castles for men to rescue them, they take center stage as major players. The main character of each book tends to be an American girl, first Baum's most famous heroine Dorothy Gale, and then her later analogs Tiny Trot and Betsy Bobbin. Most of the Oz books follow a girl heroine through her adventures in Oz and/or another magical land. We see these young heroines exercise courage, common sense, and a certain kind of generous open-mindedness, as they accept and value the contributions made by a vast collection of odd companion characters like the Scarecrow, the Tin Woodman, Tik-Tok the machine man, and so on, and it is usually with the cooperation of these diverse characters that the girls' adventures end happily. Taken in itself, Baum's repeated use of these plucky girl heroines seems to suggest a kind of latent feminism.[1]

In my opinion, however, this focus on the girl heroines has obscured something even more significant: the fact that Baum's Oz books have a great many female characters who possess and exercise power—most importantly, the fairy princess named Ozma who rules the Emerald City and presides over the four territories of Oz. The most powerful magic-worker in Oz, or indeed any of its neighboring countries, is the Sorceress Glinda the Good, ruler of the Quadling country of Oz. And these are only two examples of the numerous queens, princesses, fairies, witches, and Yookoohoos who populate the world of Oz.

The presence of Ozma and these other powerful female characters is particularly striking from an American perspective because when the Oz books were originally written and published, women were almost entirely without direct political power or influence. It was not until 1920, the year after Baum's death, that all American women even gained the right to vote with the ratification of the Nineteenth Amendment to the U.S. Constitution. Jeanette Rankin, the first woman to serve in Congress, was not elected until 1916—more than fifteen years after Baum's first Oz book, *The Wonderful Wizard of Oz*, was published. The domestic ideology of the day confined the sphere of women's influence largely to the home. The notion of a woman holding political office or wielding political power was therefore one that would have been at least highly controversial and arguably even beyond the imaginative powers of most of Baum's contemporaries. Even the opponents of women's suffrage in the nineteenth century did not devote much

Princess Ozma (John R. Neill illustration from *Ozma of Oz* [1907]).

serious attention to the issue of women holding political office, possibly because the notion of a woman president or senator would have been considered so ludicrous at the time that it was not worthy of notice.

When Belva Lockwood, the first American female lawyer admitted to practice before the U.S. Supreme Court, ran for President in 1884 and 1888 as the nominee from the National Equal Rights Party, her campaign received some serious coverage from a few newspapers, but the barrage of ridicule from most American newspapers reveals a great deal about nineteenth-century American conventional attitudes regarding women and politics. Some articles treated the whole campaign as an absurdity: for example, the *Jackson Citizen-Patriot* stated that Lockwood had been nominated as "presidentess" and "now that she has the nomination it would be interesting to ascertain what she means to do with it" ("Mrs. Belva Lockwood," *Jackson* 2). An exasperated New Jersey journalist complained that "Belva really takes the persimmon. She talks as if she were elected already and is busy picking out her Cabinet. She proposes to make women Judges of the Supreme Court and send the present Judges into the kitchen and woodshed" ("Mrs. Belva Lockwood," *Trenton* 2). A large number of newspapers only reported on one thing about Lockwood: the fact that she used a tricycle instead of a carriage to get around Washington, D.C., for her legal practice. *The Kansas City Times* jokingly reported that "Belva Lockwood is the latest nomination for the presidency, but ... she is mixed up with an open, palpable, and atrocious scandal. She rides a tricycle" ("Belva Lockwood" 4), and the *Macon Telegraph and Messenger* confirmed that "if elected, Belva will make the trip from the capitol to the White House upon her distinguished tricycle at the rate of twenty miles an hour" ("Mrs. Belva Lockwood," *Macon* 2). Other newspapers chose to belittle Lockwood by implying she should only be expressing ideas about fashion, as in the *Wheeling Register*: "It is announced that Mrs. Belva Lockwood intends to have her cabinet made a la pompadour, cut bias, with seven rows of knife plaiting down the front and a jabot of Spanish lace" ("It is Announced" 2). *The Cincinnati Commercial Tribune* opined that "no woman can ever be elected to the Presidency of the United States who wears a false bang. That settles it for Belva" ("Only Belva Lockwood" 4). On the other hand, Lockwood's campaign attracted a great deal of public interest, and she traveled throughout the United States speaking to interested audiences: "The lady candidate was a curiosity and people were willing to pay to hear her" (Norgren 135). The interest and notoriety that Lockwood's campaign attracted show that Americans were fascinated by the notion of a woman wielding political power, but also that they were at best deeply ambivalent about the prospect of females participating fully in the political process as voters and as candidates. Despite the interest raised by Lockwood's candidacy, American women would not win the right to vote in every state for another thirty-six years. For twenty of those years, L. Frank Baum was also writing and publishing his popular fantasies about the woman-ruled Land of Oz.

The Oz books have never gotten the critical attention they deserve, compared to the works of other fantasy writers like Lewis Carroll, C.S. Lewis, and J.R.R. Tolkien. But this is one issue on which he was far in advance of his fellow children's fantasy writers. Several critics have suggested that fantasy fiction should be seen not as a form of escapism, but as a genre that is capable of commenting on social reality—sometimes to an even greater degree than realistic fiction. Jack Zipes argues that "criteria for judging works of fantasy depend on the artful, innovative manner in which a work reformulates and reconstructs our personal and social experience, so that we can grasp those forces and values which govern our existence. [...] The more meaningful works of fantasy compel us to read them in a socio-historical light" (Zipes 189). One might even argue that the form of fantasy literature could be a more fruitful genre for social commentary than adult realistic fiction, because, as Ann Swinfen has explained:

> All serious fantasy is deeply rooted in human experience and is relevant to human living. Its major difference from the realist novel is that it takes account of areas of experience—imaginative, subconscious, visionary—which free the human spirit to range beyond the limits of empirical primary world reality. In a sense then, fantasy provides the writer with greater scope to construct his own scheme of morality, his own time structure, his own political and social order. But at no time does this apparent freedom permit the author to escape from contemporary reality. Indeed the fundamental purpose of serious fantasy is to comment upon the real world and to explore moral, philosophical and other dilemmas posed by it [231].

The fact that Baum explored the issue of women and power to such an extent in his fantasy fiction—at the very historical moment when women were poised to gain the right to vote—is therefore crucially important, and is worthy of more study than it has received up to this point.

I am certainly not the first critic to note that Baum's fantasy novels may have been influenced by the feminist political agenda of his wife Maud and her mother, Matilda Joslyn Gage, who, along with Susan B. Anthony and Elizabeth Cady Stanton, was one of the three major leaders in the women's suffrage movement and author of the radical *Woman, Church, and State*. In fact, historian Sally Roesch Wagner has read the Oz books primarily as a vehicle for Gage's ideas, even calling Matilda Joslyn Gage "the Wonderful Mother of Oz" (Wagner). The problem with this hypothesis is that it tends to turn into an academic version of a mother-in-law joke, because the whole controversy hinges on the relationship that L. Frank Baum may or may not have had with his actual mother-in-law. This has led to wildly varying interpretations. Journalist Daniel P. Mannix argued in his 1964 *American Heritage* article on Baum that Gage was a "militant suffragette" who was "violently opposed" to Baum's marriage to her daughter, with the result that "Baum and his mother-in-law had never gotten along well." Gage's only contribution to the Oz books, according to Mannix, was that she "ordered" Frank to try publishing his fairy tales, and that both she and Maud "nagged" Baum until he did so (Mannix 38, 43).

The preponderance of the actual evidence tends to support historian Sally Roesch Wagner's contradictory claim that L. Frank had a respectful and affectionate relationship with his mother-in-law, but since Matilda Gage died in 1898, almost two years before Baum began writing *The Wonderful Wizard of Oz*, a feminist analysis of the Oz books may be better served by looking at the evidence in the texts themselves rather than focusing solely on Gage's relationship with her son-in-law. In fact, I argue that the Oz books, despite their seeming contradictions, express a coherent feminist political philosophy about leadership, gender, and power, and that this feminist political philosophy is embodied primarily by Ozma of Oz.

The first tenet of the feminist political philosophy represented in the Oz books is that Baum's leaders and rulers—at least the good ones—always rule with the consent or approval of the ruled, making them more analogous to democratically elected politicians than traditional, fairy-tale kings or queens. Although the connection to feminism in particular may not at first be obvious to the modern reader, John Locke's Enlightenment idea of government as a contract between the ruler and the ruled was actually as foundational to early American feminism as it was to early American democracy. The Declaration of Sentiments (the manifesto adopted by the first Seneca Falls women's rights convention in 1848) echoes the Declaration of Independence when it accuses men of "compelling [woman] to submit to laws, in the formation of which she had no voice" (Anthony 70). In fact, Susan B. Anthony, Matilda Joslyn Gage, and Elizabeth Cady Stanton chose the Declaration's "governments derive their just powers from the consent of the governed" as the epigraph to the first volume of their monumental *History of Woman Suffrage.* So, the Lockean idea that rulers should rule with the consent of the ruled was one that Baum's original readers might have associated not only with American political history, but also specifically with women's suffrage.

In the Oz books, this democratic idea would seem to be contradicted by the fact that Ozma's claim to the throne is, at first, presented in *The Marvelous Land of Oz* as being based on the right of inheritance from her father, the king who was deposed by the Wizard. As Glinda tells the Scarecrow, "Pastoria had a daughter, who is the rightful heir to the throne of the Emerald City" (235). Glinda even argues that this right of royal inheritance takes precedence over the Scarecrow's having been confirmed by "the choice of the people" (234) after being appointed by the Wizard. However, this idea of royal blood was either rejected or forgotten by Baum because later in the Oz series he completely changed the rationale for Ozma's rulership of Oz. Readers are told in *The Scarecrow of Oz* (1915) that Ozma comes from "a long line of fairy queens" (256), and in *The Tin Woodman of Oz* that a fairy queen named Lurline made Oz a fairyland and left one of her fairies to rule over it (156–58). In *Glinda of Oz* (1920), this idea is elaborated on further when Ozma says,

> What and who I am is well established, and my authority comes from the Fairy Queen Lurline, of whose band I was a member when Lurline made all Oz a Fairyland. There are several countries and several different peoples in this broad land, each of which has its separate rulers, Kings, Emperors, and Queens. But all these render obedience to my laws and acknowledge me as the supreme Ruler [100].

This revised basis for Ozma's authority closely resembles Gage's theories about pre–Christian matriarchal societies in which descent (and authority) ran "in the female line" (Gage 42). These are entirely different and contradictory explanations for Ozma's rule, and Baum made no effort to reconcile them; in fact, according to Michael Patrick Hearn, the idea of a former king named Pastoria was actually invented not by Baum, but by Julian Mitchell, who directed the vastly altered theatrical, musical version of *The Wizard of Oz* put on in 1902 (Hearn, "Introduction," lviii). More importantly, the sudden and unexplained change in Ozma's backstory in the Oz books implies its lack of consequence as an explanation for her status.

In contrast, the idea that people should approve of and even choose their rulers is repeatedly and consistently shown in the Oz series. At the end of the first book, *The Wonderful Wizard of Oz* (1900), the Scarecrow remains in Oz to rule the Emerald City because "the people like me" (232), the Tin Woodman to rule the Winkies because ""the Winkies were very kind to me, and wanted me to rule over them when the Wicked Witch died" (232), and the Cowardly Lion asks to be returned to a forest in the Quadling country because "all the beasts that live there have made me their King" (233). Similarly, in *Ozma of Oz* (1907), the dowager Queen of Ev presents her son Evardo to be approved by the people's acclaim (240–41), while the reign of his cousin Princess Langwidere by right of inheritance is presented as a joke earlier in the book. When Dorothy asks the Wheeler who rules Ev, he replies:

There is no ruler ... because every member of the royal family is imprisoned by the Nome King. But the Princess Langwidere, who is the niece of our late King Evoldo, lives in part of the royal palace and takes as much money out of the royal treasury as she can spend. The Princess Langwidere, is not exactly a ruler, you see, because she doesn't rule; but she is the nearest approach to a ruler we have at present [70].

This example pokes fun at the idea of royal blood making one fit for leadership. And the scenario of a group of people choosing or approving of their leader is repeated over and over in the Oz books: in *The Scarecrow of Oz* (1915), the Scarecrow asks the people of Jinxland to choose their ruler by acclamation (242–43), and at the end of *Glinda of Oz* (1920) the Skeezers formally vote for Lady Aurex to be their new Queen (274).

The second, and more gendered, aspect of Baum's political philosophy is the idea of ruling by kindness, love, and a familial care for the people's welfare:

Ozma, the beautiful girl Ruler of the Fairyland of Oz, was a real fairy, and so sweet and gentle in caring for her people that she was greatly beloved by them all. She lived in the most magnificent palace in the most magnificent city in the world, but that did not prevent her from being the friend of the most humble person in her dominions. She would mount her wooden Sawhorse, and ride out to a farm house and sit in the kitchen to talk with the good wife of the farmer while she did her family baking; or she would play with the children and give them rides on her famous wooden steed; or she would stop in a forest to speak to a charcoal burner and ask if he was happy or desired anything to make him more content; or she would teach young girls how to sew and plan pretty dresses, or enter the shops where the jewelers and craftsmen were busy and watch them at their work, giving to each and all a cheering word or a sunny smile.

And then Ozma would sit in her jeweled throne, with her chosen courtiers all about her, and listen patiently to any complaint brought to her by her subjects, striving to accord equal justice to all. Knowing she was fair in her decisions, the Oz people never murmured at her judgments, but agreed, if Ozma decided against them, she was right and they were wrong [*The Magic of Oz* 241–42].

Baum's description of Ozma's rule could be seen as a kind of benevolent despotism, but it has a distinctly domestic and feminine tendency, with care for women and children mentioned before any other social group. *The Emerald City of Oz* (1910) describes Ozma's rule even more literally in maternal and familial terms: "There were no poor people in the Land of Oz, because there was no such thing as money, and all property of every sort belonged to the Ruler. The people were her children and she cared for them" (30). As both Dina Schiff Massachi and Sally Roesch Wagner have pointed out, the matriarchal utopia of Oz is clearly influenced by the feminism of Matilda Joslyn Gage.[2]

In *The Patchwork Girl of Oz* (1913), the reader gets a more detailed treatment of law and order in Oz when the protagonist, a Munchkin boy named Ojo, picks a forbidden six leaf clover, which is one of the ingredients he needs for the antidote to the Petrifaction spell that has turned his grandfather to stone. After Ojo is arrested by the Soldier with the Green Whiskers, he resents his arrest, "blaming Ozma for making foolish laws and then punishing folks who broke them" and thinks that she must be "a bad and oppressive Ruler" (195). His resentment is based on a sexist bias that Ozma is "only a girl" (165) and that her law therefore must be "silly," "unjust and unreasonable" (229). He is surprised to find, however, that his prison is "very pleasant and comfortable" (198), and that his jailer is a kindhearted, motherly woman who cooks him a good meal, reads him stories, plays games with him, and puts him to bed, just like any mother with an erring child. When he asks her why he is being treated so kindly, she explains Ozma's criminal justice policy:

> We consider the prisoner unfortunate. He is unfortunate in two ways—because he has done something wrong and because he is deprived of his liberty. Therefore we should treat him kindly, because of his misfortune, for otherwise he would become hard and bitter and would not be sorry he had done wrong. Ozma thinks that one who has committed a fault did so because he was not strong and brave; therefore she puts him in prison to make him strong and brave. When that is accomplished he is no longer a prisoner, but a good and loyal citizen and everyone is glad that he is now strong enough to resist doing wrong. You see, it is kindness that makes one strong and brave; and so we are kind to our prisoners [200].

When Ojo appears in front of Ozma for judgment, he at first hopes that because of her "lovely and sweet" appearance she will be "merciful" (225).

However, it is not emotion, but reason, that decides the case. Ojo first finds out that Ozma's seemingly capricious law against the six leaf clovers has a rational basis: it was outlawed to "protect all the people and guard their welfare" (229) because the land of Oz was formerly troubled by rogue witches and magicians who used the six leaf clovers "to make their magic charms and transformations" (230). Ozma had first limited magical practice to Glinda and her assistant, the Wizard of Oz, because she trusts them to "use their arts only to benefit my people and make them happier" (230), but later she also had to make the clover itself illegal because some witches and wizards were still practicing their mischievous magic on the sly. When this basis for the law is explained to him, Ojo immediately realizes that it is wise and just and is "mortified to realize he had acted and spoken so ridiculously" (230). When he admits his error and apologizes, he is immediately forgiven. This incident presents a view of law based on kindness and on reason, where the ultimate goal is the welfare of all concerned. This relationship between the ruler and the ruled has a distinctly parental cast which Ojo's age emphasizes: since Ojo is a child, a child reader can identify with him and see someone who breaks the law as the equivalent to a child who breaks a household or parental rule and then matures by learning to understand the rational basis behind the rule.

To further drive home the point that effective government must be based on love and kindness, Baum's Oz books provide a wonderful contrastive example in the form of a recurring villain: the ruler of the underground world, the Nome King. The Nome King first appears in the third novel in the series, *Ozma of Oz* (1907), when Ozma and her companions and army travel to Ev to free the Queen and royal children of Ev. They have been transformed into ornaments by the Nome King as the result of a Faustian bargain made by King Evoldo of Ev, who sold his family to the Nome King in exchange for a long life, which he then destroyed by jumping into the sea in a fit of remorse (117). When Ozma and Dorothy first meet the Nome King, they are surprised to find that he appears to be "kindly and good humored" (151). He claims that he has treated his "delicate and tender" prisoners with "great kindness" because instead of being obliged to labor, they have been transformed into "articles of ornament and bric-a-brac … to decorate [my] apartments" (156). This transformation reinforces the point that both Evoldo and the Nome King have treated the Queen and her children as commodities, rather than agents in their own right, like a traditional nineteenth-century marriage in which the wife (and her property) are conveyed from the care and control of her father to a husband. Baum here slyly parodies such a traditional "separate spheres" idea of marriage, in which the wife is supposed to be an ornamental "Angel in the House," except that in *Ozma of Oz* the Queen has literally been transformed into an ornament.

Moreover, suffrage activists and their supporters were well aware that this domestic ideology was used as an argument against women's suffrage by writers like Congregationalist minister Horace Bushnell in 1870:

> The unlikeness between men and women is radical and essential. It runs through all the spheres. Distinct as they are in bodily form and features, they are quite as distinct in mental and moral characteristics. They neither think, feel, wish, purpose, will, nor act alike. They take the same views of nothing. The old statements that one is passive, the other active; one emotional, the other moral; one affectionate, the other rational; one sentimental, the other intellectual, are likely to be more than verified by science. […] Accordingly, if the two sexes are so very unlike in *kind*, there can, so far, be no predication of equality between them [36–37].

As if he had just finished reading Horace Bushnell, the Nome King immediately condescends to Ozma and Dorothy as inferior females, calling them "dears" and telling Ozma that "you are as brave as you are pretty" (157). His manner of responding to their demands is again a parody of a traditional nineteenth-century husband dealing with a young wife: "I am so kind-hearted that I cannot stand coaxing or wheedling. If you really wish to accomplish anything by your journey, my dear Ozma, you must coax me" (160).

Baum quickly reveals, however, that the Nome King's seeming benevolence masks a regime of oppression and cruelty. His power is based on wealth and military might, with "solid ranks of Nome soldiers" (157) all standing phallically with "their weapons held erect and true" (158). To make them even more perfect an allegory of patriarchy, the Nomes are all male, and are afraid of only one thing: eggs.[3] To provide the eggs and further emphasize the contrast, *Ozma of Oz* has, besides Dorothy and Ozma, a third female heroine in the form of Dorothy's feisty yellow hen, Billina. Baum's choice of a chicken for Dorothy's companion animal in this story is particularly significant, because the early advocates for women's rights were often compared to hens. For example, an 1852 story in the *New York Daily Herald* compared them to "hens that crow" (Hoffert 116).[4] And in spite of telling Dorothy that the difference between roosters and hens is that hens do not "crow or fight" (19), Billina is definitely a hen that crows, as her first appearance in the book is to wake up the sleeping Dorothy with her morning cackling. She also introduces herself to Dorothy as being named "Bill," and it is Dorothy who insists on changing her name to the more feminine "Billina" (19). When banished by the Princess Langwidere to the palace barnyard, Billina proceeds to beat up the flock's rooster "in a whirling ball of feathers" (110). When reproached by Dorothy for being unladylike, Billina says, "Do you think I'd let that speckled villain of a rooster lord it over ME, and claim to run this chicken house, as long as I'm able to peck and scratch?" (111). Rather than any of the male Ozites, or Dorothy or Ozma for that matter, it is Billina the courageous and assertive hen who defeats the Nome King by finding out the secret behind his transformations, providing the egg that the Scarecrow throws to disable him, and then prompting Dorothy to take away the Magic Belt that is the source of his magical power. In *Ozma of Oz*, then, the battle of the sexes is firmly decided in favor of the females—whether they have wings or not.[5]

In contrast to the king's violence and incompetence, Baum argued in one of his Dakota newspaper editorials that if women were to be allowed to vote and participate in government, that they would institute a "pure and just political policy that would be impossible to refute and difficult to improve upon" (Koupal 209). Oz novels show female characters who are more than capable of leadership, contradicting the argument made by Bushnell and other anti-suffragists that "women lack authority, and never bear it well when they assume it" (Bushnell 21).

When the boy Tip is revealed at the end of *The Marvelous Land of Oz* to be the lost princess Ozma, Tip objects to being returned to his proper form: "I want to stay a boy, and travel with the Scarecrow and the Tin Woodman, and the Woggle-Bug, and Jack—yes! And my friend the Saw-Horse—and the Gump! I don't want to be a girl!" (266). Reassured by the Scarecrow that girls are "just as nice" as boys, and by the Woggle-Bug that "they are equally good students" (266), Tip agrees to the transformation. After he is re-transformed into "a young girl, fresh and beautiful as a May morning," s/he says, "I hope none of you will care less for me than you did before. I'm just the same Tip, you know; only—only…" and when Jack Pumpkinhead interrupts with the artless statement, "Only you're different!" Baum's narrator reaffirms: "everyone thought it was the wisest speech he had ever made" (271). Tip/Ozma's gender seems immaterial to the ability to rule. In fact, Michael Patrick Hearn has contended that Tip's storyline may have been inspired by Baum's successful 1902 Broadway musical version of *The Wizard of Oz*, which featured a pretty actress in tights playing a male role. Since Baum wrote *The Land of Oz* with the intention of staging it as another musical, it probably made sense to have another such "trouser role" for an actress (Hearn 28), which suggests that Baum always intended for the ruler of Oz to be a girl.

The Oz books not only show women who are capable of effective government; the series even suggests that women who confine their powers and abilities to the home are acting selfishly by not using these gifts to better society. In the world of Oz, a Yookoohoo is a worker of magic who specializes in transformations (Baum, *The Tin Woodman of Oz* 73). There are two Yookoohoos in the series: the giantess Mrs. Yoop in *The Tin Woodman of Oz* (1918), and Reera the Red in *Glinda of Oz* (1920). Both are described as confining their magical activities to the home, which would seem to be virtuous womanly behavior, as it conforms to the Victorian domestic ideology in which, as Dinah Mulock Craik dictated, a woman should have "something to do" but should confine her sphere of influence to the home: "Generally—and this is the best and safest guide—she will find her work lying very near at hand: some desultory tastes to condense into regular studies, some faulty household to quietly remodel, some child to teach, or parent to watch over" (21). However, unlike those of most of the other female magic workers in the Oz series, the Yookoohoos' magical activities are described with explicit moral disapproval.

Mrs. Yoop is a giantess who is left alone in a lonely castle when her husband, Mr. Yoop, is captured and imprisoned by the Ozites. In *The Tin Woodman of Oz*, the Tin Woodman, the Scarecrow, and their companion Woot the Wanderer, are unfortunate enough to stumble into her hands. They have done nothing to her, but she decides to keep them for her own entertainment: "For I mean to keep you here as long as I live, to amuse me when I get lonely" (75). She decides to "transform [them] all into other shapes, so that [they] cannot be recognized" (78), but the transformations are also due to their entertainment value: "I will give you all new forms, such as will be more interesting to me than the ones you now wear" (84). Mrs. Yoop has confined herself to her castle for fear of the same enemies who captured Mr. Yoop. She shows no desire to leave ""[her] own private castle" to grasp for power elsewhere, and her mantra is to "stay at home and mind my own business" (83), yet being restricted to her own home has clearly resulted in boredom and loneliness. Even worse, her confinement to the domestic sphere has heightened her disregard for the needs and desires of others besides herself. She does not at first appear cruel, but she is deaf to pleas for mercy (88). When the travelers protest, she replies that "I am not expecting to satisfy you, but intend to please myself … and my pleasure is to give you new shapes" (88).[6]

The character of Reera the Red is more ethically ambiguous, as Reera does not act as a villain in *Glinda of Oz* in the way Mrs. Yoop does in *The Tin Woodman of Oz*. However, her magical activity is just as self-interested in that it is all for her own entertainment:

> The cottage is the home of a powerful Yookoohoo, named Reera the Red, who assumes all sorts of forms, sometimes changing her form several times in a day, according to her fancy. What her real form may be we do not know. This strange creature cannot be bribed with treasure, or coaxed through friendship, or moved by pity. She has never assisted anyone, nor done wrong to anyone, that we know of. All her wonderful powers are used for her own selfish amusement [206].

Like Mrs. Yoop, Reera keeps to herself and lives isolated from others: her cottage is "a lonely place—no other buildings were anywhere about and the ground was not tilled at all" (189). The untilled ground could suggest a lack of social utility—Reera produces nothing that can contribute to the welfare of any community. Again, Reera does not act malevolently or cruelly, but her lack of interest in helping others is still an obstacle to the book's happy outcome because the three Adepts of Magic who originally ruled the Flatheads and helped the Skeezers have been transformed into fish, and must be returned to their original forms and powers in order to avert further conflict between the Skeezers and Flatheads. Ervic, the young Skeezer who is helping the Adepts, skillfully uses reverse psychology to trick Reera into performing the transformations of the Adepts into their original forms (226–27). Reera does not regret having given her assistance in this particular case, but admits that she would have responded negatively to a straightforward plea for help. She still refuses to use her magical powers for social good: "I make it my rule never to perform magic to assist others, for if I did there would always be crowds at my cottage demanding help" (229). Because of her rejection of social responsibility, Reera is called "selfish" not just once, but twice in the book, once by the fishes and once by Ervic—"I am told that you only work magic for your own amusement. That seems to me very selfish. Few people understand magic" (210). Through the characters of Ozma, Glinda, and the Adepts, Baum shows how females can exercise magical and/or political power for communal good, and to better the lives of others. In the case of both Mrs. Yoop and Reera the Red, the women's concentration on their own households is shown in a negative light in contrast to Ozma's willingness to risk herself to improve the lives of the Skeezers and Flatheads, and this contrast is a direct contradiction to the domestic ideology of Baum's time.

In addition to showing that women are capable of effective government and should use these abilities for social good, the books also sometimes challenge the Victorian essentialist dogma that women are categorically more gentle, kind, and loving than men. The novels poke irreverent fun at the "Angel in the House" idea that women are the morally superior sex. In *The Road to Oz*, for example, Dorothy is relieved to find that the vicious Scoodlers are ruled by a queen because she thinks that she and her companions will be better treated by a woman. She is shocked when the Scoodler's queen turns out to be a cannibal. In her article "The Comedians of Oz," Celia Catlett Anderson identifies the number of "attractive but narrow-minded and vain female villains" in the Oz books (63) as a recognizable category of Oz villains. The rebellious General Jinjur of *The Marvelous Land of Oz* is probably the best example of this group, which also includes the Princess Langwidere of Ev in *Ozma of Oz*, Queen Ann of Oogaboo in *Tik-Tok of Oz*, and Queen Coo-ee-oh of the Skeezers in *Glinda of Oz*.

The Oz books' political ideology is not essentialist; it shows that women are more than capable of successful leadership, but it emphasizes the ideas and character qualities that make that leadership successful (compassion, fairness, equity, responsibility, etc.) even more than physical gender. And even though some of these qualities were culturally feminized at the time, Baum makes the distinction clear by including female characters who are totally lacking in those qualities. In *Rinkitink in Oz*, Queen Cor of Coregos, wife and co-ruler with her husband King Gos, is described as being "so stern and cruel … that the people could not decide which of their sovereigns they dreaded most" (111). A more in-depth characterization of Queen Coo-ee-oh in Baum's last Oz book, *Glinda of Oz*, emphasizes this point that feminist political ideology is more important than gender. Like the Nome King, Coo-ee-oh rules primarily by fear. Comparing herself to Ozma, she says, "You say you rule thousands. I rule one hundred and one Skeezers. But every one of them trembles at my word" (103). This statement that her subjects' fear of her is more meaningful than their actual number begs comparison to the Nome King's extreme punishments and intimidation of his underlings.[7]

Coo-ee-oh is also like the Nome King in her desire to keep her power entirely to herself. The Skeezers' island is in the middle of a lake and covered by a glass dome, only reachable by an extendable bridge. Coo-ee-oh submerges the island under water to protect herself from an[8] attack by the neighboring Flatheads. The Flathead leader transforms her into a Diamond Swan, however. Coo-ee-oh's egotism, now made physically manifest in her new form, places her people in grave danger, because the Skeezers (and now Dorothy and Ozma) are trapped under water, without anyone knowing how to raise the island (138). All the island's machinery is controlled by magic words known only to Coo-ee-oh herself. It is Dorothy who figures out that the former queen's self-absorption is the key to the mystery: the three syllables of her name, Coo, ee, and oh turn out to be the magic words.

That same egotism is presented in the character of another of Baum's "bad" female rulers, the Princess Langwidere of Ev in *Ozma of Oz*. The Princess, as explained earlier in this article, does nothing to "rule" except to spend the money in the royal treasury. She is described as "a very vain creature [who] lives mostly in a room surrounded by mirrors, so that she can admire herself whichever way she looks" (71). It turns out that Langwidere has an even more extreme outlet for her vanity than Coo-ee-oh, as she has thirty heads to choose from: "the thirty heads were in great variety, no two formed alike but all being of exceeding loveliness" (80). At first she appears to be merely conceited and silly, but her vanity takes a more sinister turn when she decides that she wants Dorothy's head for her collection (84). Fortunately for Dorothy, her friends from Oz cross the Deadly Desert just in time to rescue her, so that she can join their expedition to retrieve Ev's royal family from the Nome King. However, this incident shows the danger of providing someone who is unfit to rule with unlimited power: although Langwidere is wearing her No. 17 head, with its "fiery, harsh and haughty" temper, there is no one to stop her from beheading Dorothy, as "in the Land of Ev my will is law" (86).

All of these vain, cruel, and selfish female rulers have one thing in common: they see leadership as the right to fulfill their desires and/or impose their will on others. Unlike Ozma, they have no reasoned ideology or philosophy of government. Ozma constantly occupies herself with the welfare of her subjects, as in the beginning of *Glinda of Oz*, when Dorothy finds her in conversation with Glinda, "talking earnestly about the condition of the people, and how to make them more happy and contented—although they were already the happiest and most contented folks in all the world" (15–16). Baum's Oz can be seen as a political matriarchy showing what women could do if elected to political office. It implies that women could be better "caretakers" of the nation's welfare than male politicians, but it also shows the need for a thoughtful and carefully executed political agenda that applies feminist principles to the work of government.

Sadly, the character of Ozma as the benign ruler of Oz is often absent from pop culture iterations of Oz in the years since Baum's books were published. For example, although the film *Return to Oz* (1985) uses character and plot lines from Baum's novels *The Marvelous Land of Oz* and *Ozma of Oz*, both of which prominently feature Ozma, her character only appears in the film as a shadowy damsel in distress who is held prisoner by "Princess Mombi" (an amalgamation of the Princess Langwidere and the witch Mombi). After being rescued by Dorothy, Ozma is established as the ruler of Oz at the end of the film, but in a very ambiguous way because, as David and Karen Diket have suggested, it is not clear whether she is a separate character from Dorothy but only Dorothy's alter ego or even Dorothy's "imaginary friend" (Diket 15). In the film, Dorothy wishes to use the ruby slippers so that she could be ""in both places at once" (Oz and Kansas), and it is only then that Ozma appears as Dorothy's reflection in the mirror. It is also not at all clear that Oz is "real" in the film, as it could all be a figment of Dorothy's imagination like it is in the famous 1939 film musical. The importance of Ozma as the idealized ruler of a feminist utopia is therefore lost from the film.

Baum's own emphasis on female wisdom and strength, especially in the character of Ozma, makes it impossible to conclude that his Oz series was intended in any way as an attack on women's suffrage or women's leadership abilities. The books do not suggest that women are unfit to rule, in fact the reverse, but that women must articulate and enact a deliberate and effective feminist political philosophy that addresses injustice and takes care of the people's needs. Taken as a body of work, the Oz fantasy series may have provided a "safe space," one that is relevant both to Baum's time and our own, where both author and readers might speculate about what it would be like to have women fully participating in the political realm and what a wholly realized feminist government might look like. And for that, we owe him, and the Land of Oz, an immeasurable debt of gratitude.

Notes

1. Critic Paula Kent has suggested in her article reading Dorothy's quest in *The Wizard of Oz* as a female version of a Joseph Campbell-esque hero (Kent). Carl Vogel also pointed out in "The Amazonia of Oz" that Dorothy "is unlike the usual little girl in much children's fiction in that she is a doer not a beholder" (5).

2. Massachi compares Baum's Oz utopia to Charlotte Perkins Gilman's *Herland*, arguing that both are influenced by Gage: "[I]t is evident that the woman rulership in both Oz and Herland are fictional representations of the matriarchate that Gage described in detail in the first chapter of *Woman, Church, and State*" (Massachi 213).

3. And as Matilda Joslyn Gage herself pointed out in *Woman, Church, and State*, the egg is a symbol of femininity:

> Anciently motherhood was represented by a sphere or circle. The circle like the mundane egg which is but an elongated circle, contains everything within itself and is the true microcosm. It is eternity, it is feminine, the creative force representing spirit. [. . . .] The perfect circle of Giotto was an emblem of divine mother hood in its completeness [47].

4. Chicken metaphors seem to have been fairly common in the discourse over women's suffrage in the nineteenth century. Sylvia Hoffert opens her book on the antebellum women's suffrage movement, *When Hens Crow*, with a barnyard women's rights fable attributed to Lillie Devereux Blake, a friend of Matilda Roslyn Gage (1). Hoffert also provides an illustration of an 1858 anti-suffrage cartoon showing a crowing hen in front of an audience of other hens (5).

5. In *The Emerald City of Oz*, the Nome King's aggressive and violent temperament is further emphasized: he demands instant and unquestioning obedience and when dissatisfied with his underlings, he uses humorously exaggerated punishments at one point telling his servants to "please take General Crinkle to the torture chamber. Then you will kindly slice him into thin slices. Afterward you may feed him to the seven-headed dogs"(41). With the help of his new General Guph, the King builds alliances with other evil powers to form an army to march through a newly built tunnel and conquer Oz. Following the Scarecrow's advice, Ozma uses the power of the King's own former possession, the Magic Belt, to make the tunnel so dusty that the conquerors arrive crazed by thirst and immediately drink out of the Fountain of Oblivion, causing them to forget their evil intentions and dreams of conquest. Once back in his own kingdom, however, the King resumes his "old evil ways" (*The Magic of Oz* 265). In *Tik-Tok of Oz*, and now called Ruggedo instead of Roquat, he is again characterized by using violence and fear to control others: "the nomes trembled at the sound of the King's gong and whispered fearfully to one another that something unpleasant was sure to happen; but none dared to pause in his task" (93). Rejoicing in the fact that "I hate everybody, and everybody hates me" (96), Ruggedo's violent temper leads to his destruction, as Titti-Hoochoo sends a dragon back through the Hollow Tube to depose him and exile him from his underground kingdom. Claiming to be "sorry" and "harmless" at the end of the book, he says that he will lead "a blameless life" as a "common nome" (246). In his last appearance in *The Magic of Oz*, though, Ruggedo is back to his old self, this time tricking a mischievous boy named Kiki Aru, who possesses a secret magical spell of transformation, into helping him with a dastardly plot of revenge against Oz. Ruggedo lies to the beasts of Oz, telling them that Ozma plans to enslave them and force them to work for the people of Oz, and offers to have Kiki transform them into men and women so that they can switch places with the people of Oz, who will also be transformed into beasts (92–93). He is thwarted in this plan by the timely arrival of Dorothy and the Wizard, which causes the panicked Kiki to transform everyone in sight, including Ruggedo himself, and run off with the Wizard's bag of magical tools. Throughout *The Magic of Oz*, Ruggedo and Kiki are hampered by their inability to trust each other: "This is always the way with wicked people. They cannot be trusted even by one another. Ruggedo thought he was fooling Kiki, and Kiki thought he was fooling Ruggedo; so both were pleased" (49).

6. Ruggedo's next plan is to use the transformation spell to transform the forest monkeys into giant soldiers—"You will transform each monkey into a giant man, dressed in a fine uniform and armed with a sharp sword" (162)—but the "wicked old Nome" is once again thwarted by the Wizard. At the end of the novel, Ozma decides to again use the fountain of Oblivion to return her old enemy to a childlike state—this time keeping him in Oz where he will "learn no evil and be as innocent of guile as our own people" (266). Baum's characterization of the Nome King consistently reinforces the idea that the King's hyper-masculine form of leadership, in addition to being violent and oppressive, is ineffective and always serves to eventually undermine his own plans. He is unable to trust or cooperate with others, and his "rash and reckless" rage (*Tik-Tok of Oz* 92) leads to his being expelled from his own realm. In short, he's an extended object lesson in toxic masculinity in political leadership.

7. Fortunately, the travelers are able to escape, but with some difficulty. Although Yookoohoo magic is "peculiar and hard for others to understand," Ozma succeeds in reversing Mrs. Yoop's enchantments (162).

8. Coo-ee-oh's admission that her Skeezers are "already becoming difficult to manage" also illustrates Baum's argument that ruling by force is not effective (*Glinda of Oz* 102).

Works Cited

Anderson, Celia Catlett. "The Comedians of Oz." *L. Frank Baum's World of Oz: A Classic Series at 100*, Suzanne Rahn, editor. Scarecrow Press, 2003. 53–66.

Anthony, Susan B., Elizabeth Cady Stanton, and Matilda Joslyn Gage. *History of Woman Suffrage: 1848–1861*. Vol. I. Arno & *The New York Times*, 1969.

Baum, L. Frank. *The Emerald City of Oz*. Chicago: Reilly & Britton, 1910. Rpt. Rand McNally, n.d.

_____. *Glinda of Oz*. Chicago: Reilly & Lee, 1920. Rpt. Rand McNally, n.d.

_____. *The Magic of Oz*. Chicago: Reilly & Britton, 1919. Rpt. Rand McNally, n.d.

_____. *The Marvelous Land of Oz*. Chicago: Reilly & Britton, 1904. Rpt. Rand McNally, n.d.

_____. *Ozma of Oz*. Chicago: Reilly & Britton, 1907. Rpt. Rand McNally, n.d.

_____. *The Patchwork Girl of Oz*. Chicago: Reilly & Britton, 1913. Rpt. Rand McNally, n.d.

_____. *The Road to Oz*. Chicago: Reilly & Britton, 1909. Rpt. Rand McNally, n.d.

_____. *The Scarecrow of Oz*. Chicago: Reilly & Britton, 1915. Rpt. Rand McNally, n.d.

_____. *Tik-Tok of Oz*. Chicago: Reilly & Britton, 1914. Rpt. Rand McNally, n.d.

_____. *The Tin Woodman of Oz*. Chicago: Reilly & Lee, 1918. Rpt. Rand McNally, n.d.

_____. *The Wonderful Wizard of Oz*. Chicago: Reilly & Lee, 1956.

"Belva Lockwood." *The Kansas City Times*, 6 September 1884. American's Historical Newspapers. 27 March 2012.

Bushnell, Horace. *Woman's Suffrage: The Reform Against Nature*. Scribner's, 1870.

Craik, Dinah Maria Mulock. *A Woman's Thoughts About Women*. Follett, Foster, & Co., 1864. Google Books. 23 July 2012.

Diket, David, and Karen. "Did Dorothy Return to Oz?" *The Baum Bugle* (Autumn 2015): 12–16.

Egoff, Sheila A. *Worlds Within: Children's Fantasy from the Middle Ages to Today*. ALA, 1988.

Gage, Matilda Joslyn. *Woman, Church, and State*. Sally Roesch Wagner, editor. Humanity Books, 2002.

Hearn, Michael Patrick. "Return to *The Marvelous Land of Oz* One Hundred Years Later." *The Baum Bugle* 48:3 (Winter 2004): 26–36.

_____, ed. *The Annotated Wizard of Oz, Centennial Edition*. W.W. Norton, 2000.

Hoffert, Sylvia D. *When Hens Crow: The Woman's Rights Movement in Antebellum America*. Indiana University Press, 1995.

"It Is Announced. . ." *The Wheeling Register*, 18 September 1884. American's Historical Newspapers. 7 March 2012.

Kent, Paula. "A Feminist Stroll Down the Yellow Brick Road: Dorothy's Heroine's Adventure." *The Universe of Oz: Essays on Baum's Series and Its Progeny*, Kevin K. Durand and Mary K. Leigh, editors. McFarland, 2010. 179–90.

Koupal, Nancy Tystad. "The Wonderful Wizard of the West: L. Frank Baum in South Dakota." *Great Plains Quarterly* 9:4 (1989): 203–15.

Massachi, Dina Schiff. "Connecting Baum and Gilman: Matilda Gage and her Influence on Oz and Herland." *The Journal of American Culture* 41, no. 2 (2018): 203–214. *Project Muse*. Accessed 30 December 2021.

"Mrs. Belva Lockwood." *Jackson Citizen-Patriot*, 5 September 1884. America's Historical Newspapers. 7 March 2012.

"Mrs. Belva Lockwood." *Trenton Evening Times*, 8 September 1884. American's Historical Newspapers. 7 March 2012.

Norgren, Jill. *Belva Lockwood: The Woman Who Would Be President*. New York University Press, 2007.

"Only Belva Lockwood." *Cincinnati Commercial Tribune*, 11 September 1884. America's Historical Newspapers. 7 March 2012.

Swinfen, Ann. *In Defence of Fantasy: A Study of the Genre in English and American Literature Since 1945*. Routledge, 1984.

Vogel, Carl S. "The Amazonia of Oz." *The Baum Bugle* 26 (Autumn 1982): 4–8.

Wagenknecht, Edward. *Utopia Americana*. University of Washington Book Store, 1929.

Wagner, Sally Roesch. "The Wonderful Mother of Oz." The Matilda Joslyn Gage Foundation, 2003.

Zipes, Jack. "The Age of Commodified Fantasticism: Reflections of Children's Literature and the Fantastic." *Children's Literature Quarterly* 9 (Winter 1984–5): 187–190. Project Muse. 27 June 2012.

A Living Thing

The Very American Invention of Jack Pumpkinhead

Paige Gray

What a weird, wonderful *thing*.

That's what I think when I think about Jack Pumpkinhead.

Like so many, I first encountered Oz as a little girl through the 1939 film. It enchanted and dazzled me, but I have no memory of my initial encounter—Oz was just always *there*. But I *do* remember first seeing Jack Pumpkinhead, a hallowed occasion during which mini-me lay sprawled out on the carpet floor next to my older sister, mesmerized by our television screen that revealed the strange delights of *Return to Oz* (1985). And the strangest delight was the thing with the long, tree-limbed body dressed in loud-yet-dapper attire and topped with a giant jack-o-lantern. The idea of Mombi's Powder of Life left me transfixed and bemused—can object-things have a life? Is that life just *waiting* to come alive, thanks to magic powder and magic words? Do we create life when we make an object-thing—when we make art? I wasn't sure, but I never stopped wondering about the essence of Jack. Did his dead-vegetable dome make him more or less like a living thing?

At some point after many, many viewings of *Return to Oz*, I decided to journey to Oz through Baum's books, which gave me a new imaginative space to call home. Most significantly, I then discovered Jack's origin story, which only introduced more existential questions—questions that I continue to explore.

Not long after Tip and Jack Pumpkinhead escape from Old Mombi in *The Marvelous Land of Oz* (1904), Jack—a thingly construction assembled by Tip and brought into being thanks to Mombi's Powder of Life—proclaims to his human-boy companion, "[Y]ou must be my creator—my parent—my father!" (28). To this, Tip counters, "Or your inventor" (28). Jack, an ostensibly dim-witted creation given his empty jack-o'-lantern head, replies with a concise, cogent explanation of human power dynamics: "Then I owe you obedience ... and you owe me—support" (28). Jack seemingly outlines the more-or-less understood relationship between parent and child, but what about the relationship between artist (or "inventor") and artwork? What constitutes the "life" of art and who, if anyone, should oversee it? Indeed, Jack presents the fascinating case in the universe of Oz in which we see a character's site and manner of origin. We see a *thing* brought to life, a feat underscored by Mombi's cry of "He lives! He lives! He lives" (15) after she sprinkles the Powder of Life over Jack "in the same way one would pepper a baked potato" and recites the magic words (13). This extraordinary inception brings forth

122

the fantastical and fascinating Jack Pumpkinhead, a figure who, through his sheer being, animates concepts central to the Oz series—authorship, hybridity, performance, thingness. In essence, Jack Pumpkinhead forces us to ask *what defines human life*—and is this (whatever "*this*" is) less significant than lives "brought to life" through creative production? Indeed, *what is it to be alive*?

Those are complex questions that many may scoff at given what is inspiring them—a walking, talking thing with a giant pumpkin head. To most, the tall, gangly Jack exists as a character who is ridiculous and, perhaps, slightly stupid—and Baum's text refers to Jack as "stupid" several times. But undoubtedly, Jack also presents a sense of horror, or at least suggests the possibility of horror, which we can glean from the generations of children petrified by Jack's live-action manifestation in Disney's *Return to Oz* (1985), a film that has achieved something akin to "cult classic" status even though it was largely seen as a critical and box-office failure. And fans of both the Oz book series and Disney's stop-motion feature *The Nightmare Before Christmas* (1993) have speculated that Jack Pumpkinhead influ-

Jack Pumpkinhead (John R. Neill illustration from the *Oz Toy Book* [1915]).

enced the spooky-yet-harmless character of Jack Skellington, with some attributing this directly to *Nightmare* producer Tim Burton (albeit without verifiable support to such a claim from Burton) (@TheLegacyofOz).

Jack's weirdness and potential terror arise from his thingly corpus—he embodies the fraught relationship between creation and creator. As figurative parents of the art they birth, artists have to grapple with the "life" they produce and their roles in those lives. This is a story often told, dating back to the Prometheus tale in Ovid's *Metamorphoses*, notably reconceived in Mary Shelley's *Frankenstein* (1818). The notion of our creations' autonomy continues to fascinate storytellers, including the likes of Nobel Prize–winner Kazuo Ishiguro in his contemplative, melancholic-yet-hopeful novels *Never Let Me Go* (2005) and *Klara and the Sun* (2021), as well as Stanley Kubrick in his film *2001: A Space Odyssey* (1968), all works which wrestle with the anxiety of creativity, be it in spaces of art or technology.[1] In these spaces, broadly speaking, creative production is often viewed as the "unnatural" to the "natural" of biological reproduction, if we look to classical notions of art and nature. In the interesting case of Jack Pumpkinhead, his identifying jack-o'-lantern feature arguably celebrates, or at least epitomizes, American agriculture and harvest but does so in a way that complicates general perceptions of "nature," problematic as that word may be.

To wit, children's literature scholars have considered the ways in which Oz questions nature and presents us with a "queer" world. Notably, Tison Pugh writes, "*Queerness* bears a double meaning in studies of children's literature, in that these fictions often depict a world where oddness—which can be understood as asexual queerness—is embraced as a chief narrative value" (218, emphasis original). Given the reveal at the end of *The Marvelous Land of Oz* that Tip is really Ozma, the book allows for nuanced readings of gender, queerness, and identity, as, indeed, do many of the series' other books. For, as Pugh argues, the Oz books "display an antinormative sensibility in their celebration of the unique, the eccentric, and the downright peculiar, but antinormativity as oddness at times intriguingly merges with hints of sexual queerness, resulting in texts that subvert constructions of gender and sexuality from their supposedly normative foundations" (218). Within the structure of the fantastical Oz world, the books confront and trouble conceptions of the natural, be it with gender and sexuality, or the validity of *things*. The living thing that is Jack Pumpkinhead challenges the notions of natural and unnatural, and in so doing, forces consideration on the ontological framework of these terms rooted (no pun intended) in the very concept of life—or, more specifically, American life.

Celebrating Jack as a thing that disrupts ideas of what we consider natural places him in the posthumanism conversation, a particularly rich field within children's literature. Through investigating the delineations of thing life, we also expand the possibilities of human life. "Posthumanism acknowledges there is viable life in non-human entities, and that the human itself is not easily defined as living organic matter separate to the inorganic or discursive philosophical," Patricia MacCormack contends (112). She reads posthumanism and queerness as working along similar parallels, as both interrogate the arbitrary nature of systems of power masquerading as truth (112). Posthumanism, writes Zoe Jaques, "probes and critiques long-standing and debilitating humanist assumptions" (154). She argues that while the "humanist subject is invested in drawing lines between itself and 'others,'" the posthumanist subject confuses and confounds such distinctions (154). Such a subject, like Jack Pumpkinhead, "rejects an anthropocentric worldview that essentializes 'man' (in both its species-based and gendered terms) and instead sees the human as an 'assemblage'… entangled with technology, other species, and our environments as part of a shared coevolving planet" (154). Considering Jack through this lens pushes us to interrogate the centrality of humans and to ponder the possibilities of things.

But I also want to underscore that Jack is a very Ozian thing, and therefore a very American thing. Pop-culture writers and children's literature scholars have often detailed the ways in which *The Wonderful Wizard of Oz* and the Oz series created the American fairy tale. "[I]t is in *The Wizard of Oz* that we meet the first distinctive attempt to construct a fairyland out of American materials" (14), writes Edward Wagenknecht in *Utopia Americana* (1929), one of the earliest engagements with Oz through literary criticism. "Baum's long series of Oz books represents thus an important pioneering work: they may even be considered an American utopia," Wagenknecht asserts (14). For in addition to crafting a distinctly national brand of fantasy, the Oz books capture the changing landscape of America in the early twentieth century. For Michael O. Riley, Oz, in many ways, "is 'America'—an idealized and less overly civilized version maybe, but some form of America all the same" (56).

Much like the rapidly expanding United States, Oz evinces both the urban and pastoral, the futuristic and the rustic, as seen, respectively, in the technological wonder of the Emerald City and the fertile crops of Munchkin Country. Using the lens of utopia and utopian communities, Andrew Karp grapples with these dichotomies that define Oz. Karp finds that the magic and wide-ranging weirdness of the Oz books, qualities often more readily accepted by young people than adults, produces a society that thrives as a result of its multiplicity:

> Utilizing a child's perspective—a perspective that blurs the distinction between animate and inanimate, and reaches effortlessly for the commonality underlying diversity—Baum suggests a potential harmony based not just on fellow-feeling among disparate peoples but on a recognition of the consanguinity between human beings, nature, and the artificial and mechanical worlds [105].

The Oz books and, certainly, Baum's own biography mirror the notion of "consanguinity between human beings, nature, and the artificial and mechanical worlds."

Baum's "greatest passion" was the theater, a site that continually questions the boundaries between spaces of actuality and performance, spaces often deemed *natural* and *unnatural*, respectively. His love for display and spectacle evinced itself through Oz as well as pursuits like his brief editorship of *The Show Window: A Journal of Practical Window Trimming for the Merchant and the Professional*, which sought to help store owners improve a certain type of illusion-making (Culver 97). Indeed, as Stuart Culver argues, Baum shows us "a different relation between fantasy and reality" throughout his varied professional careers in that he "doesn't rigorously distinguish the space of fantasy from that of the real but leaves the worlds standing side by side" (99). Moreover, Baum also moved readily between the rural and urban—between places like Aberdeen, South Dakota, and Chicago—a discourse we see in the composition of Oz with its farmers and Emerald City denizens, its pastoral panoramas and futuristic wonders. And with the introduction of Jack Pumpkinhead and his wonderful noggin, we see the collapse of living thing and object thing, as well as these tensions between agricultural and industrial—rural and urban—that have defined so much of American life.

I want to explore how Jack functions as an existential American trickster figure in his ability to trouble our understanding of natural and unnatural, and therefore our understanding of life itself, through the cultural vehicle of his pumpkin head. To do this, I will consider the cultural history of the pumpkin against the backdrop of American literature's relationship with art and nature, most specifically with Nathaniel

Hawthorne's "Feathertop," which depicts a Jack Pumpkinhead predecessor, before close reading and contextualizing Jack himself.

The Jolly Great Pumpkin

To understand Jack Pumpkinhead as an American trickster figure, we need to understand the significance of the pumpkin in American life, a significance that intersects folklore, farming, and modern consumerism, among other key categorizations. "For centuries the pumpkin's huge size, animated growth, and malleable flesh have made it both a staple crop and a formidable cultural symbol," writes historian Cindy Ott (4). But the really fascinating aspect of the pumpkin that Ott points out is that despite "its almost complete lack of utilitarian function in contemporary life … its outsized physical presence inspires deep human attachments" (4). Such attachments indicate a complicated history. Indeed, centuries ago, while some Native Americans "held festivals in honor of the vegetable," Ott writes that many white settlers "stigmatized the pumpkin as food for the rural poor" (6). However, despite this elitist smear on the pumpkin, it still becomes romanticized by early America, and "[p]umpkin pie appeared in the first American cookbook, published just after independence, because it was a native food tradition but also, already, because of what it meant" (Ott 6). And even in the early days of the United States, the pumpkin had already come to represent the "American agrarian myth—the idea that farming inculcates good values of hard work and self-sufficiency" (Ott 6). The agrarian myth is part of Oz's identity as well, a myth that evolves in response to the physical environment of the American landscape, as well as the tension between that landscape's enchantment and its possibilities for exploitation.

Throughout the nineteenth century and into the twentieth, periodicals around the country chronicle the agrarian myth by way of the pumpkin and its cultural symbolism within which we find seemingly contradictory ideologies. "The pumpkin's natural proclivities made it a potent harvest symbol" while it also simultaneously absorbed the ideals of a growing capitalist society, Ott explains (6). For the pumpkin's "economic status as a subsistence crop endowed it with power as an agrarian icon for a nation of people who liked to think of themselves as farmers at heart, even as they moved into big cities and built more factories" (Ott 6).

The hybrid status of pumpkin as icon of harvest as well as a market commodity made for commercial, non-utilitarian purposes can be traced through American periodicals. Many poetic odes and sketches of pumpkins heralding their mythic American status can be found in nineteenth and early twentieth-century newspapers, particular in fall. *Our Boys and Girls* children's magazine published fireside poet James G. Whittier's "The Pumpkin" in its December 1, 1871, issue. Whittier's poet-narrator connects the pumpkin to youth, recalling "[w]hen wild, ugly faces we carved in its skin" ("The Pumpkin"). The poem becomes stranger as the poet-narrator venerates the "fruit loved of boyhood," essentially anthropomorphizing the pumpkin before enacting violence on it. Because of the way in which the poem humanizes the pumpkin, it seemingly cannibalizes the formerly adored "fruit"-friend in its pie form:

> Then thanks for thy presence! None sweeter or better
> E'er smoked from an oven or circled a platter!

> Fairer hands never wrought at a pastry more
> fine,
> Brighter eyes never watched o'er its baking
> than thine! ["The Pumpkin"].

In a piece that reflects similar ambivalence about the pumpkin as living thing or unliving object, the poem "Song of the Pumpkins," published in the October 5, 1872, issue of *The Portland Transcript*, opens by making the case for the pumpkin above other romanticized fruits and vegetables:

> Thousands of poets have sung the vine
> With its ruby juice and its thrills divine;
> But I tune my strain to a different thing—
> The pumpkin, the jolly great pumpkin, I sing ["Song of the Pumpkins"].

Here, the writer, interestingly, refers to the pumpkin specifically as a "thing," giving it something of an undefinable existential quality, especially since it is a "*different* thing"—what does that mean? The poem doesn't exactly answer this and instead adds to the mystique of this "thing." In one curious stanza, the writer puts forward that if "pumpkins had grown on the Tree of Life" instead of apples, "We shouldn't have fallen through Adam's wife" ("Song of the Pumpkins"). As with its being described as a "thing," here, in suggesting the pumpkin did not grow on the biblical "Tree of Life" communicates the pumpkin's removal from "Life" in general; the pumpkin hovers between natural and unnatural.

Closer to the publication of *The Marvelous Land of Oz* (1904) that acquaints American readers with Jack Pumpkinhead, illustrations of pumpkins occasionally predominate periodicals in autumn months, with these illustrations ascribing both objectivity and subjectivity to the pumpkin. On the cover of *The Minneapolis Journal* from September 3, 1904, a four-panel comic depicts a giant pumpkin that excites a farmer, given the crop's likely success at a county fair ("Farmer Brown's Prize Pumpkin Goes to the Fair"). However, also because of its size, it proves a desirable home for clever animals and vagabonds. The cartoon presents the pumpkin as agricultural prize and commodity crop, but also as an almost *living* feature of the rural landscape in its ability to nurture and house those looking for shelter. The cover of the *Sunday Magazine of the Sunday Star* (Washington, D.C.) on October 29, 1905, shows the pumpkin in, perhaps, its most recognizable form—the jack-o-lantern (*Sunday Magazine*). This particular image also works to erase distinction between subject and object, living thing and dead thing, with the jack-o-lantern projecting an eerie candescent light. This glow animates the pumpkin, imbuing it with life while rendering the drawing of the human girl who holds the pumpkin into something closer to a zombie or ghost figure.

Almost Too Good for a Scarecrow

The contradictions of the "agrarian myth" that Ott contends are baked into the American understanding and cultural resonance of the pumpkin can also be seen in the wider trajectory of American literature. In his well-known and oft-cited scholarship, Leo Marx argues that nineteenth-century romances hover around the concept of the "machine in the garden," or the ways in which the country's emerging industrialism breaks through the idyll of nature. Marx further outlines the inherent contradictory problem with the American "attracti[on]" to "pastoralism … [and] the felicity represented by an image of a natural landscape" and the need for social and scientific progress (9). In American literature throughout the long century, this theme manifests through characters and ideas that entangle concepts of America with the desire to both accommodate and destroy the natural world. (Thinking specifically of the pumpkin as a marker of this, readers could consider Washington Irving's "The Legend of Sleepy Hollow" as a kind of jeremiad, with the Headless Horseman warning young America of its growing schism between country and city with its smashing of the pumpkin.)

Emerson notably approaches nature as tool by which to explore his philosophy of the individual. In "Nature" (1836), Emerson finds compromise between civilization's progress and the natural world in that he sees the individual, progress, and society's works as a *product of* nature. All living things and phenomena belong to a process; "[t]he stars awaken a certain reverence" and "natural objects make a kindred impression" from which the gifted among us—"the poet"—"can integrate" into something of meaning and significance (28). Emerson goes on to proclaim that the "greatest delight which the fields and woods minister is the suggestion of an *occult relation between man and the vegetable*" (29, emphasis mine). That "relation" may develop through technology or artistry; for Emerson, the product of this relation always functions as part of nature because humankind is a representation of nature as well. He sees the natural world as a source of creativity and inspiration for the individual to obtain his or her utmost potential. But, as positioned by Emerson, there is something distinctively and exceptionally American in this relationship.

Emerson's friend and neighbor Nathaniel Hawthorne further builds on and muddies American notions of nature work through extolling the powers of the imagination in his works, which help usher in the American romance. Through his reliance on the contrast between religious dogma and that of the magical or superstitious in early rural American communities, his stories uproot and destabilize perceptions of "the natural." In particular, "Feathertop: A Moralized Legend," published in *Mosses from an Old Manse* (1846) concerns itself with invention and matters of bringing forth life from non-human things such as that of a pumpkin. Certainly, it's hard not to read the story as an inspiration for Jack Pumpkinhead, regardless of whether Baum himself knew the Hawthorne tale. It presumably permeated the cultural and literary atmosphere, and thus worked to help familiarize (or, at the least, introduce) readers and the public-at-large with questions about invention, artistic genesis, and being. "Hawthorne is writing a tale about illusion and reality, but he is also writing about the creation of a work of art," argues Mark W. Estrin (172). He sees Hawthorne's careful "oscillation between levels of reality" as the defining element that gives the story "its force" (172). It is this exposure of these varying "levels of reality" in Hawthorne, and later in Baum, that I want to consider for both "Feathertop" and Baum's Jack Pumpkinhead challenge the framework of "reality" by contesting what we deem natural.

In "Feathertop," an old woman named Mother Rigby constructs a "scarecrow" of sorts, pulling together, among other things, a "broomstick, on which Mother Rigby had taken many an airy gallop at midnight," a "hoe handle," a "miscellaneous stick from the woodpile," and "a meal bag stuffed with straw" (175). For the head, Mother Rigby makes use of a "somewhat withered and shrivelled pumpkin" into which she "cut two holes for the eyes, and a slit for the mouth, leaving a bluish-colored knob in the middle to pass for a nose" (175). Hawthorne's narrator verifies to readers that the pumpkin head displayed "really a quite respectable face" (175). Mother Rigby becomes quite enamored with her creation, believing her pumpkin-topped invention is "almost too good for a scarecrow" (176). She soon comes back to this thought, telling herself that the "scarecrow" remains "too good a piece of work to stand all summer in a corn patch, frightening away the crows and blackbirds" (177). She's come to believe that "[h]e's capable of better things" (177).[2]

Certainly, Mother Rigby is an artist proud of her creation. Hawthorne's Mother Rigby and Baum's Mombi *are* creative women—artists of alchemy—yet each text suggests ambivalence about these characters. Because of her creative powers, each woman is presented as unnatural, as a witch—a common theme throughout history and literature that Sandra Gilbert and Susan Gubar revealed to us in their landmark study *The Madwoman in the Attic* (1979). But is the text challenging or perpetuating these ideas of gender? Baum's Oz texts provide for rich, but complicated, feminist readings, especially given his portrayal of witches and his notable mother-in-law Matilda Gage, a leader in the women's suffrage movement. Elsewhere, I have argued that while "the persecution of witches and subsequent propaganda against women who strayed from traditional religious dogma concerning gender roles effectively marginalized women over the course of history, Baum revises the witch figure in his fantasy" (Gray, 94). Yet, again, it's complicated. For even with "its liberating gender possibilities, *Oz*, its women rulers, and even Dorothy's capability to send herself home cannot escape the hegemony of patriarchy" (Gray, 96). But I contend that Baum's text "heralds the opportunities for cultural change that lie within fantasy, invention, and artifice" and that it "invites patriarchy's dismantling" (96). Hawthorne perhaps presents more indeterminacy than Baum, never mind his infamous "damned mob of scribbling women" jab (Hawthorne, *Letters* 75). For while the text suggests a fluidity between art and nature, Mother Rigby still, ultimately, feels like a maligned character for her "unnatural" ways—that is, ways that do not conform to nineteenth-century notions of domesticity and femininity.

Hawthorne's story, while musing on creative invention and the artificial life created by the artist, quickly takes away such celebration of artificial life, making Feathertop bemoan it. Near the story's end, he cries to Mother Rigby, "I've seen myself, mother! I've seen myself for the wretched, ragged, empty thing I am! I'll exist no longer!" (191). Clayton Holaday suggests that, with this utterance, Feathertop "becomes a genuinely pathetic figure" (105). Holaday praises this moment, as he sees it elevating Feathertop from being "merely a device through which Hawthorne can satirize the gullibility of the multitude" (105). He humanizes Feathertop by making him face his "wretched" non-human self. This interpretation doesn't engage with Estrin's questions about the "levels of reality" that an artist or writer can create and, perhaps because of its 1954 publication, Holaday's article certainly does not consider ideas of the posthuman. But Baum's work *does* consider these ideas. While Feathertop laments his non-humanness, Jack Pumpkinhead normalizes it, allowing us to ruminate over the "nature" of his thingness.

A Man or a Pumpkin?

The Marvelous Land of Oz introduces Jack Pumpkinhead, but it also establishes Oz as a series—something which Michael Riley argues was *maybe* not in Baum's original plan. Riley suggests that with *The Marvelous Land of Oz*, "it was not the popularity of *The Wonderful Wizard of Oz* that Baum was most desirous of repeating, but the popularity of *The Wizard of Oz* musical extravaganza," which premiered in 1902 (98). Indeed, Riley writes, "the theater was the greatest passion of Baum's life" (98). If this is the case, Jack Pumpkinhead was created to eventually become a character for the stage. The idea of a Jack Pumpkinhead on stage would be in keeping with Baum's love of spectacle, but it also reifies Jack as an American trickster in that his thingness would not be abstract, but actualized, whether in puppet form or through a costumed actor. His queer-object self would not just be an oddity restricted to the imagination, but would be walking and talking *in reality*, even if only through the conceit of the theatrical production. Nevertheless, even if Baum's hope for another stage extravaganza never came to be, Jack Pumpkinhead still debuts in all his strangeness in the book.

The opening chapter of *The Marvelous Land of Oz*, "Tip Manufactures a Pumpkinhead," depicts a scene likely familiar to many children reading the story, with Tip looking for the perfect pumpkin in Mombi's cornfields "to make a 'Jack Lantern' and try to give the old woman a fright with it," since Tip "frankly hated her" (3). We then witness the invention of Jack, with Tip carefully selecting "a fine, big pumpkin—one with a lustrous, orange-red color" and then carving a face that "wore a smile so big and broad, and was so jolly in expression, that even Tip laughed as he looked admiringly at his work" (3). Tip's idea to make the pumpkin into a man-figure arises from his desire to terrify Mombi. It's this moment when Jack's thingness comes into fruition. Tip seeks to "manufacture the form of a man, who would wear this pumpkin head" (4). But what constitutes the "form of a man"? Tip takes to the woods in order to assemble various parts so he can craft something similar in appearance:

> So he took his axe to the forest, and selected some stout, straight saplings, which he cut down and trimmed of all their twigs and leaves. From these he would make the arms, and legs, and feet of his man. For the body he stripped a sheet of thick bark from around a big tree, and with much labor fashioned it into a cylinder of about the right size, pinning the edges together with wooden pegs. Then, whistling happily as he worked, he carefully jointed the limbs and fastened them to the body with pegs whittled into shape with his knife [4].

Jack, perhaps, has two origin stories: one in which he comes "alive" thanks to the Powder of Life, but also this one—a birth from a very "workmanlike manner" in terms of artistry (5). It's not idealized or dreamy or fantastical. In comparison to the conceit of the Powder of Life, here we have an unromantic, naturalized notion of creativity. It's not magic or inspiration from the muses, but diligence and patience. After Tip builds Jack's body, he works on his man further. He "rounded all the edges of the joints and smoothed the rough places" before going to the forest again to get a neck for Jack (5). As a prolific writer, Baum certainly knew the routine mundanity and required patience of the artistic life. But this extended description of Jack's construction suggests his invention as a piece of creative work is as important as his animation through the Powder of Life.

Throughout *The Marvelous Land of Oz*, the focus on Jack, and the frequent jokes about him, often surround his sheer being, his "assemblage," to use Zoe Jaques' term. As they embark on their escape from Mombi, Jack notices how very different Tip's composition is as compared to his. "I don't seem to be made the same way you are," he tells the boy (27). Later, when Jack greets the guard in the Emerald City, the guard asks, "What are you, a man or a pumpkin?" (58). To this, Jack smartly answers, "Both, if you please" (58). What does it mean for Jack to be both? Is he a human-thing? An object-thing? Or does it matter? The text indicates the latter, suggesting Jack is a thing with life—he *is*. To this point, when Jack meets the Scarecrow, "His Majesty" takes care to let Jack know he is a "dummy" (71). Jack responds, "I am!—I surely am!" (71). While ostensibly he is simply agreeing with the Scarecrow, his reply, printed on its own separate line of text, feels like an existential cry, a justification of his significance. He *is*, so he matters.

But the thing about Jack, in particular, is that pumpkin head. This is what separates him from something like the Sawhorse, another creature who becomes animate thanks to the Powder of Life. His pumpkin head makes him a walking, talking embodiment of our associations with the harvest symbol, be it Halloween, pie, or American agriculture. The collapse between natural world and unnatural world manifests through this sentient pumpkin, which works to further underscore the pumpkin's own commodification in American culture that undercuts its use as an icon of rural farm life. For by the late nineteenth century, "the pumpkin's meanings were alienated from its uses" (Ott 87). Ott unpacks this fascinating shift wherein the pumpkin becomes a sign for something it doesn't really signify. "No longer was its symbolism sustained by material and practical functions—that is, by actual farmers raising actual pumpkins for human and animal sustenance," Ott asserts (87). As pumpkin lore filled the pages of newspapers like *The Portland Transcript* and *The Washington Star* during autumn months, Ott writes that the U.S. Agricultural Census "did not even bother to include pumpkins in its reports through the end of the [nineteenth] century" (87). As such, in the pumpkin and in Jack Pumpkinhead exists an exquisite distillation of American contradiction in its nostalgia for small farms and rural countrysides and its dependence on urban mass production. But Jack, and Oz as a whole, seem to suggest, why not both? Do we not contain multitudes?

The trickster figure of Jack further defies ideas of natural and unnatural, object and subject, and life and death through his thingness and pumpkin head in *The Road to Oz* (1909). In this fifth book in the Oz series, Dorothy discovers "Jack Pumpkinhead's private graveyard" (162). Throughout the graveyard, etched in each little tombstones reads the same message—"Here lies the mortal part of Jack Pumpkinhead, which spoiled" followed by the date of that pumpkin's demise (163). Dorothy, who "had hoped to see" Jack again, laments what she perceives as his death. But the Tin Woodman tells her "Jack is now a farmer and lives in this very pumpkin field" (164).[3] Soon enough, Dorothy finds the "queer man" who retains his notable attire of "a spotted shirt, a red vest, and faded blue trousers" and "whose body was merely sticks of wood, jointed clumsily together" (164). The great invention of Jack, "queer" in his ability to undo (or at least slacken) ideological constraints, has now also become an inventor—he is a farmer who can grow his own head. In this very bizarre scene, the natural world and that of the manufactured or artificial are wholly conflated. The text presents us with the idea that maybe there is no distinction between natural and unnatural; maybe everything is a constructed piece of art, from the curated work of farming to the constructed assemblage of Jack. Indeed, Jack seemingly questions *us* for questioning him. It doesn't matter that he must bury his pumpkin head after it spoils and find a new one. "I am still Jack Pumpkinhead, no matter how often I change my upper end," he tells Dorothy (166). Jack's assembled, hybrid being suggests new, improved conceptions of life beyond the human.

Jack's cameo appearance in *The Emerald City of Oz* (1910) humorously comments on the edible potential of Jack's head, but in doing so, troubles any accepted belief system of ontological hierarchies in terms of comestible consumption. When Dorothy and company visit Jack near the end of the novel, the "pumpkin-headed man welcomed his visitors joyfully and offered them several delicious pumpkin pies to eat" (264). Calling to mind Whittier's aforementioned "The Pumpkin" that promotes young people eating an entity that the poem so lovingly imbues with human qualities, Jack explains, "I don't indulge in pumpkin pies myself," going on to say that "were I to eat pumpkins I would become a cannibal" (264). The verity of this concept depends on the reader accepting the living being of Jack—that a pumpkin thing is sentient and possesses a life that is as valid as that of a human. "The impossibility of a pumpkin eating a pumpkin makes this scene amusing, yet it also upends the dining rules of real life, in which one should never see a dining companion devour a food item cooked from the same material as the host," says Tison Pugh in unpacking the passage (326). Pugh admits that while "it is ridiculous to argue that pumpkin-eating represents cannibalism," part of the "sheer pleasure of much of children's literature arises in the contradictory and precarious balance between the rules of the real world and the rules of the fictional and fantastic 'reality' of the text" (326–327). What's more, here we're made to think about thingness, sentience, and, indeed, cannibalism—what or who gets to eat what or whom? If it's cannibalism for a sentient Jack to eat a pumpkin pie, what makes it acceptable for Dorothy or Aunt Em to consume a thing that once had the potential to feel and think (albeit, with the help of magic powder)?

Readers can find Jack Pumpkinhead throughout the Oz series, including "Jack Pumpkinhead and the Sawhorse," one of six tales comprising *Little Wizard Stories of Oz* (1914). In this adventure, the text emphasizes Jack's strange being while also stressing his affability, as to seemingly link the two. Jack is described as "one of the queerest of the queer inhabitants of Oz," but also as "good-natured and a general favorite" (111). In this Oz episode, Jack and the Sawhorse save two children, but Jack's head gets smashed in the process. However, the Wizard helps the two find their way back to Jack's house and its pumpkin field so that a new head can be selected and affixed to Jack's thingly form.

Jack eventually gets his own titular novel from Ruth Plumly Thompson in 1929. *Jack Pumpkinhead of Oz*, the twenty-third book in the series, follows Jack and Peter Brown, a Dorothy-esque character introduced by Plumly in *The Gnome King of Oz*, as they encounter a variety of new and familiar Oz marvels. One of Jack's oft-noted features, his idiocy, is again highlighted here, with him lamenting at one point, "I am only a poor stupid pumpkin head with only a few dried seeds for brains" (168). However, Jack's very awareness of his supposed stupidity somewhat weakens the case for him being a wholly mindless thing.

Thinking back to my awe upon first seeing Jack Pumpkinhead in *Return to Oz*, I now realize that in addition to being overwhelmed by the spectacle of this unfamiliar living thing, a feeling of recognition also tugged at me. Vivian Wagner has argued that "[h]ome forms the core of *Wizard of Oz* mythology" (27). I believe she's right, but I don't interpret home in the traditional sense—a stationary place of bricks and mortar. No, home, as many of us know, is a feeling. And what the Oz books show us again and again—and what I see Jack Pumpkinhead exemplifying—is that the creative space is home. Jack Pumpkinhead and Oz remind us that there's nothing so natural as the unnatural.

NOTES

1. Writing for *The Atlantic* on *Klara and the Sun*, Judith Shulevitz connects the novel to *Frankenstein*, but also underscores the bigger questions offered by artificial life: "Ishiguro leaves us suspended over a rift in the presumptive order of things. Whose consciousness is limited, ours or a machine's? Whose love is

more true? If we ever do give robots the power to feel the beauty and anguish of the world we bring them into, will they murder us for it or lead us toward the light?" (Shulevitz).

2. Interestingly, Mother Rigby twice refers to the pumpkin-headed scarecrow as a "puppet." The *Oxford English Dictionary* provides us with the now-common definition of puppet, that of "a model of a person or animal that can be manipulated to mimic natural movement; a figure with jointed limbs moved from above by strings or wires, a marionette" ("puppet, n."). But it also provides the older usage of a puppet as an "image of a human being or a person or thing resembling one" ("puppet, n."). In "Feathertop," we can read Mother Rigby's invention as a "figure" that she manipulates through her magic, as well as a "thing" resembling a human life. Either way, thinking about Feathertop and Jack Pumpkinhead as puppets proves productive, especially given the puppet Jack of *Return to Oz*, performed and voiced by Brian Henson. Feathertop, as a "puppet" ("I've made many a puppet since I've been a witch" [176]; "'That puppet yonder,' thought Mother Rigby" [177]) is a "thing" resembling a human, but he is also a "thing" with some sort of life, with his pumpkin head giving him more of a sense of the botanical.

3. In what may be the first critical commentary on Jack Pumpkinhead, Edward Wagenknecht writes in *Utopia Americana*:

> Jack Pumpkinhead is a Hallowe'en prank, a body of wood with a pumpkinhead on top of it, bought to life by means of the Magic Power [*sic*] of Life. At first, Mr. Baum apparently believed that when Jack's head spoiled that would be the end of him, but when fully embarked upon in the Oz series, he decided that the Pumpkinhead was much too good to lose: accordingly he made a farmer of him whose business is to raise pumpkins for heads. The upper part of Jack Pumpkinhead has died and been buried several times but he is nevertheless very much alive [26].

Works Cited

Baum, L. Frank. *The Emerald City of Oz*. 1910. Ballantine-Del Rey, 1979.
_____. *The Land of Oz*. 1904. Ballantine-Del Rey, 1979.
_____. *Little Wizard Stories of Oz*. 1914. Project Gutenberg eBook, 2008.
_____. *The Road to Oz*. 1909. Ballantine-Del Rey, 1979.
Culver, Stuart. "What Manikins Want: *The Wonderful Wizard of Oz* and *The Art of Decorating Dry Goods Windows*." *Representations* 21 (1988): 97–116.
Emerson, Ralph Waldo. *Emerson's Prose and Poetry*. Joel Porte and Saundra Morris, editors. W.W. Norton, 2001.
Estrin, Mark W. "Narrative Ambivalence in Hawthorne's 'Feathertop.'" *The Journal of Narrative Technique* 5, no. 3 (1975): 164–73.
"Farmer Brown's Prize Pumpkin Goes to the Fair." *The Minneapolis Journal*, 3 September 1904: 1. Accessed 4 September 2021.
Gray, Paige. *Cub Reporters: American Children's Literature and Journalism in the Golden Age*. SUNY Press, 2019.
Hawthorne, Nathaniel. "Feathertop; A Moralized Legend." *Mosses from an Old Manse*. 1846. The Modern Library, 2003. 175–94.
_____. *Letters of Hawthorne to William D. Ticknor, 1851-1864, Volume 1*. The Carteret Book Club, 1910. Google Books. Accessed 30 November 2012.
Holaday, Clayton A. "A Re-Examination of Feathertop and RLR." *The New England Quarterly* 27, no. 1 (1954): 103–05.
Jaques, Zoe. "Posthuman." *Keywords for Children's Literature*. New York University Press, 2021. 154–56.
Karp, Andrew. "Utopian Tension in L. Frank Baum's Oz." *Utopian Studies* 9, no. 2 (1998): 103–21.
@TheLegacyofOz. "Tim Burton was once asked about Jack Skellington, & how he came up with such an iconic character. Burton credited L. Frank Baum's creation, Jack Pumpkinhead. Not only do they both have the name, Jack, but while one is a "Pumpkinhead" the other is "The Pumpkin King." Twitter, 10 August 2021, 3:28 a.m., https://twitter.com/thelegacyofOz/status/1424995961428926466.
MacCormack, Patricia. "Queer Posthumanism: Cyborgs, Animals, Monsters, and Perverts." *The Ashgate Research Companion to Queer Theory*, Noreen Giffney and Michael O'Rourke, editors. Routledge, 2009. 111–128.
Marx, Leo. *The Machine in the Garden: Technology and the Pastoral Idea in America*. Oxford University Press, 1964.
Ott, Cindy. *Pumpkin: The Curious History of an America Icon*. University of Washington Press, 2012.
Pugh, Tison. "'Are We Cannibals, Let Me Ask? Or Are We Faithful Friends?' Food, Interspecies, Cannibalism, and the Limits of Utopia in L. Frank Baum's Oz Books." *The Lion and the Unicorn* 32, no. 3 (2008): 324–43.
_____. "'There lived in the Land of Oz two queerly made me': Queer Utopianism and Antisocial Eroticism in L. Frank Baum's *Oz* Series" *Marvels & Tales* 22, no. 2 (2008): 217–39.

"puppet, n." *OED Online*. Oxford University Press, September 2021, www.oed.com/view/Entry/154792, accessed 16 October 2021.

Riley, Michael O. *Oz and Beyond: The Fantasy World of L. Frank Baum*. University Press of Kansas, 1997.

Shulevitz, Judith. "The Radiant Inner Life of a Robot." *The Atlantic* (April 2021). Accessed 19 September 2021.

"Song of the Pumpkins." *The Portland Transcript*, 5 October 1972. *Chronicling America*, Library of Congress. Accessed 28 July 2022.

Sunday Magazine of the Sunday Star, 29 October 1904: 1. *Chronicling America*, Library of Congress. Accessed 4 September 2021.

Thompson, Ruth Plumly. *Jack Pumpkinhead of Oz*. 1929. Ballantine-Del Rey, 1980.

Wagenknecht, Edward. *Utopia Americana*. University of Washington Chapbooks, Vol. 28, 1929. Department of Special Collections, Stanford University. 20 July 2021.

Wagner, Vivian. "Unsettling Oz: Technological Anxieties in the Novels of L. Frank Baum." *The Lion and the Unicorn* 30, no. 1 (2006): 25–53. *Project Muse*. Accessed 4 January 2014.

Whittier, James G. "The Pumpkin." *Our Boys and Girls*, 1 December 1871. *GALILEO*. Accessed 28 July 2021.

Trading Knitting Needles for Pistols

The Feminist, Violent, and Sexual Evolution of General Jinjur

SHANNON MURPHY

Throughout Baum's Ozian series, there is an emphasis placed on female characters, their roles in society, and fashion and accoutrement: readers encounter magical shoes, female armies equipped with knitting needles, and gown-wearing good witches that help guide the heroine through her journey. Many of Baum's references to female clothing are satirical and multilayered. In his second novel *The Marvelous Land of Oz* (1904), readers are introduced to General Jinjur, the leader of an all-female army that uses knitting needles as weapons. This is a sly nod to his commitment to the suffrage movement of the time; Baum was heavily influenced by women's rights activists Maud and Matilda Gage—his wife and mother-in-law, respectively—and used the knitting needles to give his female characters a means of reclaiming traditionally-feminine accoutrement, thereby a means of social movement. Baum's depictions—though satirical, multilayered, and empowering—are transformed by many authors. Three faithful yet diversified depictions of General Jinjur include Gregory Maguire's violent yet overshadowed General Jinjuria in *Out of Oz* (2011) and Olga Grushin's anthropomorphized war general mouse named General Gertrude, a fierce fighter who saves the lives of fellow house mice. These representations of Jinjur perpetuate the feminist fighter that Baum strove to create and further showcase historical female warriors and the rejection of the Angel of the House stereotype.

However, Danielle Paige in her *Dorothy Must Die* series problematizes this feminist message by replacing or adding to Baum's use of female clothing and accoutrement in a manner that ultimately confines or constricts the female subject instead of liberating her. By doing so, Paige morphs the feminist female fighter into a graphically violent and sexual entity. This essay will focus on various articles of clothing and accoutrement, depictions of protest, and historical background used by Baum, Grushin, Maguire, and Paige to discuss both female empowerment and confinement. The discussion will center around the ultimate shift from knitting needles to pistols and over-sexualized dress in General Jinjur's army. This, coupled with the varying emphases on violence, gendered language, and historical undertones, will be used to show how the depictions of stereotypically female items and gender roles represent female confinement, oppression, and over-sexualization rather than female liberation.

Baum's feminist stances were heavily influenced by two women who were themselves great feminist revolutionaries: his wife Maud Gage and her mother Matilda Gage.

Maud, one of the first female enrollees at Cornell University, met Baum in 1882 and became the practical and confident female figure that supported Baum in his many artistic adventures (Hearn xix, xxv). Matilda Gage was a "prominent feminist" and had "helped draft the Woman's Bill of Rights and, with Elizabeth Cady Stanton and Susan B. Anthony, produced the first three volumes of the *History of Woman Suffrage* (1881–1886)" (Hearn xx). More than just a strong feminist influence, Matilda challenged Baum and they "grew to admire each other and shared many of the same liberal ideas" (Hearn xx). Though Baum shared many of the feminist ideals, Michael Patrick Hearn does point out that "this did not prevent him from frequently satirizing the 'new woman' in is writings, notably in the character of General Jinjur and her Army of Revolt" (xx) and, therefore, dissecting feminism and its representation.

General Jinjur (John R. Neill illustration from the *Oz Toy Book* [1915]).

As this essay uses the term repeatedly, it is of note that there is no one definition for the word "feminism" and, as feminist scholar Chris Beasley aptly states, "there can be no final answer to the question, 'What is feminism anyway?'" (117) nor do I hope to create one with this work. Feminism is multifaceted and only a small portion of the greater feminist term will be focused on here. However, there are two distinct views on feminism that are used as a point of departure in this essay, the first adapted from Joan Kelly's "Early Feminist Theory and the *Querelle des Femmes*." Kelly defines feminism as "an outlook that transcended the accepted value systems of the time by exposing and opposing the prejudice and narrowness; a desire for a truly general conception of humanity" (Treichler 7). The element "accepted value systems at the time" is paramount; with four books spanning over a century, it is important to note their historical influences. This paper will touch upon the "general conception of humanity" and what it means to be a woman within society. The term feminism here will include its historical context and how it influences the depictions of gender.

The second viewpoint used for the definition of "feminist" is from Catherine Belsey and Jane Moore. They argue that

> [a] feminist does not necessarily read in order to praise or to blame, to judge or to censor. More commonly she sets out to assess how the text invites its readers, as members of a specific culture, to understand what it means to be a woman or a man, and so encourages them to reaffirm or to challenge existing cultural norms [1].

Assessment and the encouragement to notice and enact change are the approaches taken in this essay. A feminist children's novel "is a novel in which the main character is empowered regardless of gender. A key concept here is 'regardless': in a feminist children's novel, the child's sex does not provide a permanent obstacle to her development" (Trites 4). By focusing on the attributes given to the character and not their assigned gender or performed gender roles, a feminist novel will teach young readers the effect of the empowered female character. As Roberta Seelinger Trites says, "[n]o organized social movement has affected children's literature as significantly as feminism has" (ix).

These notions of feminism and the "organized social movement" on behalf of women's choice were at the forefront of the suffrage movement, though the term "feminism" was not coined until the 1960s. In 1848—eight years before Baum's birth—suffragists Elizabeth Cady Stanton, Susan B. Anthony, and Matilda Gage published "The Declaration of Sentiments and Resolution," a document that elucidates the rights desired by women in the United States during this time. These authors change the wording of the Declaration of Independence to explicitly include women: they state that "[w]e hold these truths to be self-evident: that all men *and women* are created equal" (emphasis added). Stanton, Anthony, and Gage recognized the power dynamic between men and women during this time, noting that "[t]he history of mankind is a history of repeated injuries and usurpations on the part of man toward woman, having in direct object the establishment of an absolute tyranny over her." Women were objects controlled by the patriarchy, living under laws that were not voted upon by women. Despite the attention these suffragettes drew to inequality and the necessity for change between men and women, rigid stereotypes about the ideal woman persisted.

In her book *Waking Sleeping Beauty: Feminist Voices in Children's Novels*, Roberta Seelinger Trites notes that "[f]or the feminist reader, reading a feminist text is an exercise in immersing herself or himself with a community of women" (98). As a female reader of fairy tales—looking, in particular, at many well-known European fairy tales from the 1700–1800s—it can be difficult to find a feminist fairy tale where feminist readers can immerse themselves, as Trites suggests. However, Baum, according to Dina Schiff Massachi, helped to create a new character to whom audiences relate: "[f]eminist Baum did not believe that girls could not go on adventures. With Dorothy, he created one of the first American feminist child-heroes. […] With Dorothy, Baum forever changed the role of girls in children's fiction, which helped change how young readers imagined gender roles" (6). Though Baum has created a new type of female protagonist that has shaped the way writers create female protagonists today, scholars such as Paula Kent have noted that "[w]hile researching feminist perspectives of *The Wonderful Wizard of Oz*, it became painfully clear that not much has been written specifically about L. Frank Baum's Dorothy Gale from a feminist standpoint" (179); while scholars have begun exploring the connections between Dorothy and Matilda Gage, General Jinjur remains largely unexplored. This essay will not only discuss feminist elements present in Baum's novel—thereby adding to scholarship on Baum's work—but it will discuss how authors Maguire, Grushin, and Paige transform Baum's feminist elements to fit varying definitions of feminist social movement.

Alongside his use of the female protagonist, Baum desired to create a fairy tale that did not revolve around violence. In his book *Fairy Tales and the Art of Subversion*, Jack Zipes notes that Baum "absorbed himself in the tales of Grimm and Andersen but disliked their violence, cruelty, and sadness. Baum was bent on seeing the brighter side of life, for he never knew how much more time he would have to appreciate the world around him" (123). Though Baum did not indulge in violence to the extremes that European fairy tales do, he did incorporate situations where violence was portrayed in a more humorous fashion. In *The Marvelous Land of Oz*, Baum introduces an all-female army that desires to dethrone the Scarecrow, who has become Oz's ruler after the Wizard's departure. Tip—a village boy around whom *The Marvelous Land of Oz* revolves—analyzes General Jinjur's appearance upon meeting her:

> She wore a costume that struck the boy as being remarkably brilliant: her silken waist being of emerald green and her skirt of four distinct colors [....] The splendor of the gown was almost barbaric [....] Yes, the face was pretty enough, he decided; but it wore an expression of discontent coupled to a shade of defiance or audacity [*Marvelous Land* 166].

General Jinjur here is gendered, but not overtly sexualized. Her gown is described as "barbaric" in appearance, which can be interpreted as being bizarre or unsophisticated; this description does not include any recognition of the sexualized body beneath the gown. Though her face is deemed "pretty enough" to Tip—neither overly attractive nor unattractive—the description does not detail the specificities of why it is beautiful, nor does it illustrate a desire for the woman to be beautiful. In fact, Baum writes that she wore a look of "discontent [...] defiance or audacity" (166) which mars the pretty face. Prettiness and attention to dress are not mentioned again in the novel, which shows their insignificance in Baum's narrative. By avoiding an outright discussion of beauty, Baum avoids labeling his female characters primarily by their appearance. He creates female characters that are marked by their audaciousness and defiance, not by their physical features. The only other evidence of beauty and fashion pertaining to General Jinjur and her army that readers receive is through illustrations.

In her article "Fashion History Timeline: 1900–1909," Karina Reddy discusses American female fashion at this time: she remarks that "modest dresses, bodies molded by corsets, and ostentatious ornamentation dominated women's fashion throughout the first ten years of the century" (Reddy). Further, she notes that "[m]odesty was emphasized with day dresses covering the body from the neck to the floor and long sleeves covering the arms" (Reddy). John R. Neill, the original illustrator of *The Marvelous Land of Oz*, creates images that stay mostly true to this vogue modesty of the 1900s: the girls of

General Jinjur's army are clad in dresses that are buttoned up to their necks, covering the arms completely and loosely. However, the dresses depicted by Neill's illustrations do not touch the floor, but rather end just below the knee, showing off the knee-high boots each woman sports. This choice predicts the change in fashion later in the decade, where women began to wear clothing that was more practical for activities such as riding bicycles and working outside of the house (Reddy). Though this shortened dress may or may not have been considered modest for the time period, there is no other written description of the army's dress type in Baum's second novel.

The choice of dress, and what little Baum showcases of it, also bears a striking resemblance to the Aberdeen Guards. In April 1890, twelve daughters of the Grand Army of the Republic established themselves as the Aberdeen Guards, an auxiliary that intended to represent and uphold the history of the Army (*Our Landlady* 72). These women, "[d]ressed in red skirts, blue waists with gold braid trim, and red forage hats, […] drilled with lances topped with red flags" (*Our Landlady* 72) and many believe these women were the inspiration for Baum's representations of female armies in the future. In the annotated version of Baum's *Our Landlady*, Nancy Tystad Koupal relates how "General Jinjur and her jaunty and irreverent army of chattering girls most nearly resemble Baum's caricature of Captain Fannie Hauser and the female lancers of Aberdeen" (72). These elements of fashion and body type are used, then, to represent the strong female, not to overtly sexualize, though this has been argued in the can-can-esque portrayal in the stage performance. What Baum does overtly portray is gender expectation with the army's weapon of choice.

In Baum's novel, this army is able to infiltrate the Emerald City using nothing but wits and knitting needles as weapons. Knitting needles, stereotypically associated with women, are used in Baum's novel as a means of empowerment: these women are using this traditionally-feminized object to fight against the oppressive governing body. When the Guardian of the Gates confronts the army, he is attacked by an unconventional weapon:

> [H]e was surrounded by a crowd of girls who drew the knitting-needles from their hair and began jabbing them at the Guardian with the sharp points dangerously near his fat cheeks and blinking eyes. The poor man howled loudly for mercy and made no resistance when Jinjur drew the bunch of keys from around his neck [*Marvelous Land* 171].

Though he is not injured—the girls are only "dangerously near his fat cheeks and blinking eyes"—the Guardian of the Gates is still defeated by the knitting needles. This is not the only time in history where women have reclaimed knitting needles as a way to fight the government. In her article "Stitch by Stitch, A Brief History of Knitting and Activism," Corinne Segal tracks how women have used knitting as a means of protest, particularly in the United States. Segal notes how, "[f]or decades, knitting and sewing had provided a path to political involvement for women" and describes how women would hide war messages during the American Revolution in their yarn baskets to help the U.S. soldiers prepare for future attacks. In particular, Segal pulls from the Confederate poet Carrie Bell Sinclair's poem "Socks for the Soldiers" (1863) to show how knitting—specifically knitting needles—is used as a form of combat:

> Oh women of the sunny South
> We want you in the field;
> Not with a soldier's uniform,

> Nor sword, nor spear, nor shield;
> But with a weapon quite as keen—
> The knitting needle bright—
> And willing hands to knit for those
> Who for our country fight.

Though Sinclair's poem focuses on how women supported and fought in the Civil War through knitting and darning for soldiers, she is making the connection between war and knitting. Baum's all-female army makes the connection between knitting and fighting literal, as they physically fight the Scarecrow and the Guardian of the Gates with knitting needles. By giving General Jinjur and her army knitting needles as weapons, Baum calls upon the decades of resisting and fighting that women have endured through the domestic act of knitting.

Alongside the use of knitting needles, Baum adds language that comments specifically on the stereotypical roles of females at the time. When General Jinjur confronts the Guardian of the Gate for the keys to the kingdom, his response is sexist: "'Good gracious!' returned the surprised Guardian of the Gates; 'what a nonsensical idea! Go home to your mothers, my good girls, and milk the cows and bake the bread. Don't you know it's a dangerous thing to conquer a city?'" (*Marvelous Land* 170). The Guardian of the Gate, here, represents the oppressive patriarchy. The Guardian, instead of being afraid upon their arrival, tells the army to return to their domestic duties because they are in a dangerous situation, which can represent the political sphere in which women were not welcome. He is not concerned for his safety, but the safety of the girls: the question "[d]on't you know it's a dangerous thing to conquer a city?" turns the attention on the girls being in harm's way and he, in turn, is protecting them from this potential harm. General Jinjur, in response, does call herself defenseless in a performative manner. After she gathers the keys from the Guardian of the Gates, he pulls a gun from his person, threatening to use it (171). General Jinjur replies to his threat by asking, "'Why, how now? Would you shoot a poor, *defenseless* girl?'" (171, emphasis added). Here, Baum pokes fun at the idea of the defenseless girl. During Baum's life, women were breaking the stereotypes of the defenseless woman and striving to enact change, such as women's suffrage and the ability to work outside of the home. By including this performative interaction, Baum creates a satirical scenario that notes how incorrect the defenseless female stereotype has become.

The female warrior persists in Gregory Maguire's novel *Out of Oz*, the final volume in his *Wicked* series, where the world of Oz is in the midst of a civil war; the Emerald City army—also known as the EC—and the occupants of Munchkinland are fighting for power. General Jinjur is transformed in this text into General Jinjuria and her role, though she is present throughout the novel, is scarce. She is rarely mentioned, though the book is dependent upon a war effort that she herself is commanding. When she is mentioned, General Jinjuria is discussed only for her power as a general, with no discussion about her appearance, the defenseless female stereotype, or her feminine body. When described, she is noted as "a saucy young warrior princess" who has "kept [General] Cherrystone boxed up in Haugaard's Keep all year," by request of Mombey, the Wicked Witch of the North (Maguire 212). Though the term "saucy" does have some coy connotations, the term here can refer to her "impertinently bold and impudent" (Merriam-Webster) military prowess and how she is able to detain General Cherrystone through risk-taking. As such, she does continue to perpetuate the female warrior but begins to do so in a contemporary way.

When discussed by other periphery characters, General Jinjuria—in the imagination of those who wish her ill will—is banished to her worst confinement: domesticity. Madame Ginspoil of Shiz University elucidates:

> "She seems a right smart tartlet, to hold our army at bay all this time. If she's captured, she can be dragged here and made to tutor stupid young girls," seethed Madame Ginspoil. "Quite the suitable punishment. She can live on bread and water for what she has cost Loyal Oz in comforts.... I have chilblains, what with the reduction of coal allotments for our quarters. Chilblains, I tell you. I have refused to knit balaclavas for the troops this year. If they can't win the stupid war after all this time, they'll have no comfort from me" [Maguire 365–66].

It seems as though the ultimate punishment for General Jinjuria, in the eyes of Madame Ginspoil, is for her to return to domesticity and act as a teacher for the "stupid young girls" she herself has the pleasure to work with. The act of removing—"dragging," as she is apt to resist—General Jinjuria from her post and placing her in the domestic sphere as her penance for being a war criminal is an indirect comment on the warrior woman herself: those who fight for their beliefs may be punished through regressing into the confinement of the home—or boarding university, as Shiz is classified—to be stifled by their role as caretaker.

Caretaking and confinement to the home are main characteristics of the Angel of the House ideal, which was coined six years after "The Declaration of Sentiments and Resolutions" was published. First used by English author Coventry Patmore in his 1854 poem "The Angel in the House," this term is typically "used to refer to any woman of the [Victorian] period who embodied the ideal—the selflessly devoted and submissive wife and mother" (Hoffman 264). In her paper "'She loves with love that cannot tire': The Image of the Angel of the House across Cultures and across Time," Joan M. Hoffman describes how the Angel of the House figure fits into the society:

> From a feminist perspective, the social order being supported here by the institution of marriage and the angel-wife's place within it is most assuredly a conservative hierarchical one grounded in sexual repression within patriarchy. [...] She was an asexual being whose task in life was, paradoxically, to produce children. She was required to maintain a harmonious atmosphere in the household; [...] and to uphold the all-important bourgeois social values of order, peace, and happiness [265].

The idea of being a perfect subservient figure is also discussed by Stanton, Anthony, and Gage in "The Declaration of Sentiments and Resolutions," where they say that "she is compelled to promise obedience to her husband, he becoming, to all intents and purposes, her master—the law giving him power to deprive her of her liberty, and to administer chastisement." This Angel of the House figure must abdicate her autonomy and desires for that of her husband—and, subsequently, the patriarchy—which creates a subservient and docile woman.

Though the Angel of the House term was first used to discuss Victorian women, the subservient figure was conceived long before Patmore, and it continues to be used in relation to modern women, permeating discussions of fairy tales and their female protagonists (Hoffman 267). Many contemporary stories work through these unrealistic expectations for women. Movies such as *Pretty Woman* (1990) and *Shrek* (2001) subvert the typical Angel of the House motif (Hoffman 267), and writers such as Virginia Woolf note that "[k]illing the Angel in the House was part of the occupation of a woman writer" (279). In Baum's *Marvelous Land of Oz,* General Jinjur strays from the stereotype of the Angel in the House, though she does begin to submit to this role in Baum's *The Tin Woodman of Oz* (1918). In this appearance, Jinjur is a wife, a farmer, a homemaker, and a caretaker, though her tendencies to fight with household items persist as she whacks her unexpected visitors with a broom, her new weapon of choice (Baum 148). In Maguire's adaptation of General Jinjur, he depicts the strife that moving into a domestic role may cause General Jinjuria, as many readers may have believed of Baum's General Jinjur if not for her emergence in later novels. She is not an Angel of the House, and even Madame Ginspoil makes note of this.

Not only does Madame Ginspoil curse the efforts of General Jinjuria, she also curses the efforts of the EC as they try to defeat this mighty female warrior. She has "refuse[d] to knit balaclavas for the troops this year" as a protest to their war efforts. This becomes an ironic twist when compared to Baum's depiction of women, who fight with their knitting needles and have, historically, aided the war effort through their covert operations under the guise of knitting circles. She refuses to protest with knitting needles, therefore protesting the act of protestation that knitting has held. She resigns herself to the confines of Shiz University and depends on the war efforts of others to bring her comfort, playing the docile—yet deeply dissatisfied—confined woman, critiquing the war efforts and the women who participate in them.

All information readers receive about General Jinjuria is through stories told by the various characters in Oz; never does Maguire create a scene in which General Jinjuria's strength is depicted first-hand. The most information given about this war general is when Brrr the lion asks an older man at a café in Bright Lettins about how General Jinjuria can hold General Cherrystone in Haugaard's Keep. He responds,

> "Jinjuria, she could have held on to Haugaard's Keep, you know that. It's almost impregnable.... With their superior numbers the EC Messiars swarmed up the lakeside of the keep, see, and General Jinjuria's forces put on a handsome show of repelling them—but only as a lure.... She boxed up the Emerald City high command, General Cherrystone as they call him, and the cream of his forces too. She can't starve him out, as she can't prevent supplies from arriving on the lakeside, by flotillas of this sort or that. But she can prevent him from leaving by land... [S]he's got him cornered, like a cat playing with a larder mouse" [Maguire 263].

The speaker, instead of using the connotatively-charged term "beautiful" to describe General Jinjuria's war tactics, notes how it is a "handsome show." The choice to use "handsome" to describe military prowess does lean to the coding of violence and military action as male, but the decision to code male while concerning a female warrior does gloss over the otherwise obvious connotative dichotomy. Even the distinct choice to use the term "impregnable" when discussing Haugaard's Keep—the location over which General Jinjuria has dominion—subtly takes away the notion of the fertile, docile, and beautiful damsel in the tower. General Jinjuria, by holding this keep, is doing so as a warrior, not as the Angel of the House figure. She is neither sexualized being nor docile woman; she is successful fighter. Though she does "lure" as a siren lures men to their death, General Jinjuria is stripped of any language associating her with the stereotypically weak woman—or the Angel of the House—as she is compared to the predator cat toying with the mouse.

Oddly, this is not the only depiction of General Jinjur in a cat-and-mouse brawl. In Olga Grushin's novel *The Charmed Wife*—a Cinderella adaptation that follows a woman's break in reality—an army of mice fight off a kitchen cat threatening to destroy some of their own. In this adaptation, the General Jinjur character is seen in General

Gertrude, the leader of an all-female mouse army called the Valkyries. Brie, a young mouse whose life is threatened by the hungry kitchen cat, is saved by "[a] hundred roaring mice [who] poured out of every crack and crevice and attacked the beast, prodding its sides with forks, lobbing rinds of moldy cheese at its head, poking its paws with toothpicks, until it howled and bolted in a malodorous blur of rotten vegetables" (Grushin 50). Here, knitting needles are represented by the toothpicks, which mirror the seemingly frivolous accoutrement. For these powerful women, both are used for defense against greater forces of oppression or danger.

In Grushin's adaptation, General Gertrude and her army call themselves the Valkyrie. Valkyrie, in Norse mythology, are a band of warrior women "armed with [spears], who decide the fate of warriors in battle.... *Valkyrie* means 'chooser of the slain'" (Mark). Often, the Valkyrie are associated with their shape-shifting ability, turning into swans and other birds. Grushin takes this lore of the anthropomorphized female warrior and creates an army of mice who fight against the male kitchen cat's oppressive and deadly rule. Their female rule perpetuates as their army is only comprised of women. When asked where the male mice are, General Gertrude replies, "'Our men were all eaten by found beasts a long time ago, because men are weak and slow'" (50). The evidence of her claim is found only moments before when Brie, as she was traveling with her male companion Nibbles, watches as Nibbles is eaten by the kitchen cat before the Valkyrie arrives. Though Brie does initiate a fight for her life with the cat, the Valkyrie arrive in time to save her with their toothpicks—harkening back to the knitting needles and spears—and thereby save her, choosing her to enter their Valhalla—their army—if desired. Grushin, through her brief inclusion of General Gertrude, not only upholds the historical significance of the knitting needle in United States history, but dives further into the proto-feminist history of the Valkyrie, thereby hinting at global feminism.

This life with the Valkyrie calls to Brie, and she contemplates what her life could be if she joined this female army:

> And the timid Brie, who feared drafts and dust bunnies, looked in wonder from one strong, lean face to another—looked especially long into the bright eyes of a tall warrior with a jaunty red sash around her waist who stood shoulder to shoulder with Gertrude—and felt something equally strong and bright respond in her own breast, and saw another kind of life stretch before her, a purposeful, exhilarating life [Grushin 50].

Though she has lived in the confines of the castle under watch of her human owner, Brie catches a glimmer of what a life with "purpose" may look like: to Brie, in this contemplative moment, a purposeful life does not mean a domestic life. Brie has the option of choosing between a life as an Angel of the House figure, one of domesticity and docility, for a life of adventuring and thwarting social norms. She is encouraged to notice and enact change, such as Belsey and Moore advocate for, and she is encouraged to find a fulfilling life of her own design as an independent female. Though she does choose to return to life within her castle as a pet, she takes with her one of the female warriors and creates a matriarchal kingdom of her own design. She uses the wisdom of the Valkyrie to create change within her castle.

The greatest departure from the prior warriors can be seen in Danielle Paige's novella *The Straw King* (2015), where she introduces the all-female army as sexualized and violent:

> Rows and rows of girls, standing in military formation, stared back at [the Scarecrow]. They wore identical uniforms: tightly fitted leather leggings and pointy-toed stiletto heels with

flared minidresses made of chain mail. Each unsmiling mouth was painted the same shade of cherry red, and each girl's fingernails were polished a matching crimson. Each girl's glossy hair swung in a matching ponytail. *And they brandished matching pearl-handled silver pistols*, all of them pointed at the palace [emphasis added, 101].

Unlike the previous authors, Paige focuses heavily on sexualization in her descriptions of girls in her books. Each of the girls in Jinjur's army, though outfitted in protective armor in anticipation for battle, is dressed in an overly-sexualized manner, and Paige specifically draws attention to this. General Jinjur's authority, in particular, is associated with her sexualized appearance in Paige's novella: "Her chain mail minidress was shorter, her lipstick was redder, and her ponytail was higher. She had an unmistakable air of authority" (101). Instead of Baum's depiction of the pretty face marred by emotion or Maguire's depiction of handsome warfare, Paige's Jinjur gathers her authority through her dress and how it is heightened in comparison to the other girls' attire and attitudes. The emphasis on red accessories—a color associated with sexuality and reproduction—coupled with the stark and unnecessary attention to their bodies through tight and short clothing, invites readers to ruminate on their sexual natures as girls. Though their dress can be seen as weaponized—the sharply-pointed shoes as a fighting tool, the red symbolizing both the blood from battle and overt sexuality in appearance—Paige's descriptions of the army ultimately move away from the feminist satire that Baum created and Grushin withheld, entering into a place where sexuality and corruption mingle.

The choice to replace the knitting needles with pistols further destroys Baum's feminist message. Knitting as a means of fighting and resisting remains a current form of protest in the United States. On January 21, 2017, millions of people across the United States participated in the Women's March to protest President Donald Trump's misogynistic comments and actions toward women (Bynum). The Women's March "brought knitting into the international spotlight and lured newcomers to a symbol of activism that dates back hundreds of years" (Segal), where protesters knitted their own pink hats that resembled uteruses to address Trump's comment to "grab them by the pussy" as a means of controlling unruly women (Bynum 377). By knitting in peaceful protest, these activists used knitting needles as a weapon to fight an unjust ruler. Instead of further emphasizing women's history with knitting as protest—such as Grushin in her choice to keep the knitting needle imagery—Paige erases this history. Instead, she turns to the violent alternative, creating a world where women are only heard through violence and, according to Scarecrow, "cold-blooded murder" (109). Her depictions of General Jinjur and her army, then, lose the message of social change through peaceful protest that Baum created in his novel and, ultimately, the link to the suffrage movement, which was based in peaceful protest. Though Maguire moves closer to violence, he does keep the violence removed from the reader and does not elucidate which weapons General Jinjuria and her army favor. The movement from knitting needles to pistols creates a more violent story, which matches Baum's readings of violence in European fairy tales.

With his exposure to European fairy tales, Baum desired to make a distinct change to the fairy tale genre. Instead of using violence to scare readers, he uses small amounts of violence to address social and political change. Massachi in her paper "L. Frank Baum (1856–1919): Brains, Heart, and Courage" notes that though "Baum may not have left out morals, nightmares, or heartache, he did leave out unnecessary descriptions that may have detracted from children's enjoyment and increased their fear" (12). This is true for both the conquering of the castle and the Scarecrow's departure from Emerald City. General Jinjur and her army successfully "captured [the Emerald City] without a drop of blood being spilled" (*Marvelous Land* 172), which minimizes the child reader's fear of the fight and moves quickly through the battle to further the story line. This bloodless fight is reiterated when Tip, the Scarecrow, Jack Pumpkinhead, and the Saw-Horse escape from General Jinjur's invasion. They are attacked by a few of the girls in the army, where "one or two jabbed their knitting-needles frantically at the escaping prisoners. Tip got one small prick in his left arm, which smarted for an hour afterward; but the needles had no effect upon the Scarecrow or Jack Pumpkinhead" (*Marvelous Land* 179). Baum, when introducing violent scenes such as the Scarecrow's escape from the castle, quickly explains that the characters children are rooting for are safe, easing the fear and anxiety young readers may experience.

Like Baum, Maguire does not dip into violence in his description of the hold of Haugaard's Keep, though he does later reference the heads of soldiers in the water. His description of the action is removed and not graphic to the point of unnerving. He details the way that General Jinjuria "puts on a handsome show of repelling them" (263) instead of depicting the fight firsthand. This detachment of violent imagery also shows the detachment from the action itself; though General Jinjuria's feats are chronicled by the speaker, they are not described in detail. This retelling of action, removed from true violence and terror, stays true to Baum's aversion to great violence.

Though Baum desired to stay away from violence and ease the fear of his readers, Paige created an adaptation that focuses heavily on violence and creates scenarios where readers revel in fear. When General Jinjur and her army storm Emerald City, the order of events is drastically different:

> "It's time for a new era in Oz." [General Jinjur] leveled the pistol at the Royal Army's chest, and, still smiling, pulled the trigger. For just a second, time stood still. The Lion and the Scarecrow stared, gaping, at Jinjur's smoking pistol. The Royal Army's jaw dropped in shock. And then he looked down at the red stain spreading across his chest. He lifted one hand as if to touch the wound, his expression bewildered. And then, slowly, he toppled sideways and hit the ground with a thud, his eyes open. A glistening red pool spread outward from his inert body [109].

This scene both parallels and contradicts the stand-off in Baum's *The Marvelous Land of Oz*. While Baum's all-girl army threatened to use their knitting needles and achieved their goal without shedding blood, Paige's army takes the castle through murder and emphasizes the death of the Royal Army as he is shot by Jinjur. Though she is fighting to liberate Oz from a patriarchal structure, General Jinjur does so through violence, even when others have asked for negotiation. There is no element of Baum's feminist satire here, nor is there evidence of female empowerment; there is only violence and corruption in the way this army is painted.

When looking at violence, Massachi also notes that, in Baum's novels, "[t]he action every minute solves the scary parts as quickly as it brings them, in making them far less scary than if the reader lingered in fear through a lot of description" (12). Paige's adaptation does the opposite. In many scenes throughout her series, Paige draws out the violence, creating vivid scenes of horror and gore for her readers. This is particularly true when one of General Jinjur's soldiers murders the Munchkin Hibiscus, the Scarecrow's servant:

"Welcome to the new Oz." With a swift motion, she drew her knife across Hibiscus's throat. The Scarecrow cried out in horror as blood spurted from the gaping crescent wound. The soldier let the girl's body go. Her body teetered ghoulishly for a second and then fell to the ground with a sick thud [130–31].

As with the death of the Royal Army, Paige paints this murder in great detail, noting the body movement of the dying, the sounds of last life, and the way that life leaves the body. Instead of glossing over or disclosing discussions of violence as Baum and Maguire do, Paige takes her readers step-by-step through the process of these murders. Even characters such as the Scarecrow note the "cold-blooded murder" (109) occurring now, none of which was documented in the histories of Oz he has read. Through this wording, Paige is acknowledging the lack of violence and murder in the original Baum stories. No longer is the army representing female liberation; it is representing violence.

Trites states that "the greatest distinguishing mark of the feminist children's novel is that the character who uses introspection to overcome her oppression almost always overcomes at least part of what is oppressing her. Feminist children's novels, on the whole then, constitute a triumphal literature" (3). The General Jinjur adaptations offered by Maguire and Grushin parallel Baum's original message of social mobility and anti–Angel of the House warrior. However, General Jinjur and her army are oppressed by Paige's overly-sexualized representations of them. They are rooted in violence and sexuality, which loses the satirical and feminist stance Baum makes with these characters in *The Marvelous Land of Oz*. Therefore it is difficult to recognize this aspect of the series as feminist.

Clothing and accoutrement also play a large role in agency and female liberation throughout Baum's novels as his General Jinjur fights with knitting needles, which is a satirical yet empowering representation of women taking control and ownership over these household items attributed to their gender. Paige, again, muddies these moments in her Ozian retelling. She gives guns and tight clothing to Jinjur's army, which ultimately shows these female characters' corruption. Instead of transforming the clothing and accoutrement to reflect the same empowerment present in Baum's novels, Paige flouts these feminist notions and dives deeper into the sexualized and oppressed depictions of women. This creates a disconnect between her feminist depictions of the young female adventurer and her focus on clothing signaling sexualized and corrupt behavior; the first supports women, the second pigeonholes them into a "sex is bad" mentality. Further, Belsey and Moore note, "[h]istory itself has always been important to feminism, because it is history which provides us with evidence that things have changed. And if they have changed in the past, they do not have to stay as they are now" (2). Baum's novels, though still representative of a strong feminist lead character, do not uphold some of the newer definitions of feminism created in the twenty-first century. This historical context has morphed readers' expectations, yet many contemporary books remain imperfect in their depictions of feminism. It is paramount for readers to assess and question the depictions of "feminism," such as in Paige's *Dorothy Must Die* series. It is only through this lifelong questioning and challenging that generations can continue to evolve the definition of feminism, as there is still room to evolve this universal notion of feminism in literature.

Works Cited

Baum, L. Frank. *The Marvelous Land of Oz*. 1904. Fall Rivers Press, 2014.
_____. *Our Landlady*. Nancy Tystad Koupal, editor. University of Nebraska Press, 1996.

_____. *The Tin Woodman of Oz.* Illustrated by John R. Neill. 1918. Rand McNally & Co.

Beasley, Chris. *What Is Feminism? An Introduction to Feminist Theory.* SAGE, 1999.

Belsey, Catherine, and Jane Moore. "Introduction: The Story So Far." *The Feminist Reader*, Catherine Belsey and Jane Moore, editors. 2nd ed., Blackwell, 1997. 1–15.

Bynum, Caroline Walker. "The Women's March: New York, January 21, 2017." *Common Knowledge* 23, no. 3 (September 2017): 377–80.

"Feminism, n3." *Oxford English Dictionary Online*, March 2012, oed.com/view/Entry/69192?redirected From=Feminism#eid.

Hearn, Michael Patrick, ed. *The Annotated Wizard of Oz, Centennial Edition.* W.W. Norton, 2000.

Hoffman, Joan M. "'She loves with love that cannot tire': The Image of the Angel of the House Across Cultures and Across Time." *Pacific Coast Philology* 42, no. 2 (2007): 264–71.

Kent, Paula. "A Feminist Stroll Down the Yellow Brick Road: Dorothy's Heroine's Adventure." *The Universe of Oz: Essays on Baum's Series and Its Progeny*, Kevin K. Durand and Mary K. Leigh, editors. McFarland, 2010. 179–90.

Mark, Joshua J. "Valkyrie." *World History Encyclopedia*, https://www.worldhistory.org/Valkyrie/.

Massachi, Dina Schiff. "L. Frank Baum (1856–1919): Brains, Heart and Courage." *Shapers of American Childhood: Essays on Visionaries from L. Frank Baum to Dr. Spock to J.K. Rowling.* Kathy Merlock Jackson and Mark I. West, editors. McFarland, 2018. 3–15.

Paige, Danielle. *Dorothy Must Die Stories: Vol. 2.* HarperCollins, 2016.

Reddy, Karina. "Fashion History Timeline: 1900–1909." Fashion Institute of Technology, State University of New York, 31 December 2019, fashionhistory.fitnyc.edu/1900–1909/.

"Saucy." *Merriam-Webster*, https://www.merriam-webster.com/dictionary/saucy.

Segal, Corinne. "Stitch by Stitch, A Brief History of Knitting and Activism." *PBS*, 23 April 2017, www.pbs.org/newshour/arts/stitch-stitch-history-knitting-activism.

Stanton, Elizabeth Cady, Susan B. Anthony, and M.J. Gage. "The Declaration of Sentiments and Resolutions." *A History of Woman Suffrage*, vol. 1. Fowler and Wells, 1889, www.womenshistory.org/resources/primary-source/declaration-sentiments-and-resolution.

Treichler, Paula, and Cheris Kramarae. "Feminism." *Feminist Theory: A Reader.* Wendy K. Kolmar and Frances Bartkowski, editors. 3rd ed., McGraw-Hill Higher Education, 2010. 7–11.

Zipes, Jack. "Inverting and Subverting the World with Hope: The Fairy Tales of George MacDonald, Oscar Wilde, and L. Frank Baum," *Fairy Tales and the Art of Subversion: The Classical Genre for Children and the Process of Civilization.* Methuen, 1988. 97–133.

The Nome King

ANGELICA SHIRLEY CARPENTER

The 1939 MGM movie *The Wizard of Oz* made the Wicked Witch of the West the most famous villain in Oz, enlarging and wickedly enhancing her role from L. Frank Baum's novel *The Wonderful Wizard of Oz* (1900). People unfamiliar with the rest of Baum's thirteen Oz books don't usually know the Nome King, who is the series' most frequent villain. The Nome King, when he first appears in *Ozma of Oz* (1907), appears cute and seems good-humored, but soon reveals himself to be a cruel trickster. This Nome King doesn't kill people but he transforms them and/or imprisons them. Although the Nome King, like all the characters in Baum's sequel Oz books, is not well-known to readers in general, his cultural status was elevated when Disney Studios, mainstream America, decided to feature him prominently in the 1985 movie *Return to Oz*. Here, death is threatened and possible. In 2014 Danielle Paige's *Dorothy Must Die* series also borrows Baum's favorite villain. Here the Nome King is old, tall, thin, bald, and handsome, like an aging James Bond of villains. And with this series, touted as New York Times Bestsellers, the character seems to have moved further into the psyche of American readers. This essay will examine the Nome King as he is portrayed in several Baum Oz books, in the movie *Return to Oz*, and in Danielle Paige's four-part *Dorothy Must Die* series of young adult novels. Points of comparison will include format, magic, humor, the desire for power, gender issues, racism, abolition, kidnapping, violence, and death. The essay will also compare knowledge of the character among readers and reviewers.

Ozma of Oz (1907) is the third book in Baum's Oz series. In it, Dorothy, who did not appear in the second book, returns to Oz, although most of the story involves her adventures along the way. In this story Dorothy encounters Ozma of Oz, a fairyland ruler, who came to power in the second book. Ozma, accompanied by the Scarecrow, Tin Woodman, and Cowardly Lion, along with some new characters and the twenty-seven-member Army of Oz, is on a quest to rescue the Queen of Ev and her ten children from the Nome King, a neighboring monarch who has transformed them into ornaments. Dorothy, a talking chicken named Billina, and the mechanical man Tik-Tok join the mission.

L. Frank Baum simplified the spelling of the word *Gnome* to make it easier for children to pronounce. In the Oz world, Nomes are fairies who live underground, making jewels and forging precious metals and then hiding them. They resent the "up-stairs people" who dig for what Nomes consider to be *their* valuables. Gaining admission to King Roquat's underground domain, Ozma and her crew are surprised by the Nome King's twinkling eyes and comforting appearance—short and round, no taller than Dorothy.

"Why, he looks just like Santa Claus—only he isn't the same color!" whispered Dorothy to her friend [….] "Sit down, my dears," said the King, "and tell me why you have come all this way to see me, and what I can do to make you happy" […] "Your Majesty," said [Ozma], "I am the ruler of the Land of Oz and I have come here to ask you to release the good Queen of Ev and her ten children, whom you have enchanted and hold as your prisoners."

"Oh, no; you are mistaken about that," replied the King. "They are not my prisoners, but my slaves, whom I purchased from the King of Ev."

"But that was wrong," said Ozma.

"According to the laws of Ev, the king can do no wrong," answered the monarch […] "so that he had a perfect right to sell his family to me in exchange for a long life."

"You cheated him, though," declared Dorothy; "for the King of Ev did not have a long life. He jumped into the sea and was drowned."

"That was not my fault," said the Nome King, crossing his legs and smiling contentedly. "I gave him the long life, all right; but he destroyed it" [164–66].

When further talk seems pointless, Ozma threatens to conquer the Nome kingdom. Choking with laughter, Roquat leads the Oz party to a balcony overlooking a cave that stretches for miles. Then thousands of Nome soldiers march in, filling the cavern. "This," says the King, "is but a small part of my army" (170). Then Ozma's group changes plans, with the not-so-Cowardly Lion suggesting that he can pounce upon the King and tear him to pieces. "Try it," says the King, using his magic belt to freeze the beast in place. The Scarecrow suggests wheedling the King into giving up his slaves. "This is the most sensible thing any of you has suggested," says the King. "It is folly to threaten me, but I'm so kind-hearted that I cannot stand coaxing or wheedling" (172). However, the Nome King is a humbug, not the least bit kind-hearted, as young readers suspect by this point. "Are you willing to take a few chances and risk yourself, in order to set free the people of Ev?" he asks, and Ozma eagerly agrees (172–73). So he offers to let her party enter his palace, one at a time, giving each the power to transform the Ev ornaments back into people, provided they can guess which ones they are. And if they cannot guess in eleven tries, they themselves will be transformed into bric-a-brac.

Ozma goes first. When she sees how many ornaments there are, "the girl came to realize how dangerous was her task, and how likely she was to lose her own freedom in striving to free others from the bondage of the Nome King. No wonder the cunning monarch laughed good naturedly with his visitors, when he knew how easily they might be entrapped" (177–78). One by one, the members of the Oz party enter and guess, the King increasing the number of guesses allowed each time a new ornament is created. Only Dorothy manages to transform a purple cat ornament back into a young prince.

Billina is the key to this book's happy ending. Hiding under the Nome King's throne, she hears him discussing his color-coded ornaments with his Chief Steward: Ev ornaments are royal purple, Emerald City people are green.

When the hen lays her morning egg, cackling loudly, the King reacts unexpectedly.

"Don't you know that eggs are poison?" roared the King, while his rock-colored eyes stuck out in great terror.

"Poison! Well, I declare," said Bellina, indignantly. "I'll have you know all my eggs are warranted strictly fresh and up to date. Poison, indeed!" […]

"Take it away! Take it away at once!" [the king] shouted. […]

"I'll take the egg," said the Scarecrow. "I'm making a collection of Bellina's eggs" [207].

Billina, the last of the Oz party to guess, breaks the enchantments. Furious, the King changes terms, saying the prisoners may leave his palace, but not his dominions.

As he plans to hurl them into underground dungeons, the Scarecrow throws an egg, striking him in the eye. In the uproar that ensues, Dorothy manages to unbuckle the King's magic belt, fastening it around her own waist. Surprisingly, the King suffers no ill effects; he simply has egg on his face.

Dorothy quickly masters the power of the belt, opening a passage to the outside world. When the Nome King sends warriors in pursuit, she changes the frontrunners into eggs that stop the Nome army. The book ends with a feast in the Emerald City and then, using the magic belt, Ozma sends Dorothy back to Uncle Henry.

Ev and Oz are surreal, neighboring countries, but some features, like lunch boxes growing on trees, men with wheels instead of hands and feet, and Ozma's magic picture, which shows any person or place requested, come more under the "what if?" heading of fantasy. Magic, in this book, implies active use. As a fairy princess, Ozma has the power to work it (in later books she does), but in this novel she gets it from other sources. The sorceress Glinda the Good provides the magic carpet that allows the Oz party to cross the deadly desert safely to Ev. The Nome King's magic, seemingly controlled by his belt, is powerful, but it doesn't work on wood, as he learns when the wooden sawhorse, brought to life in the second Oz book, kicks him across the throne room while protecting Dorothy.

Power is important in all societies, even fairy lands.

The villainous Nome King (John R. Neill illustration from the *Oz Toy Book* [1915]).

Roquat is vain, greedy, materialistic, and power-hungry. Scholars like Suzanne Rahn consider him "a distinctly American kind of monarch—the industrial capitalist whose power resides in the monopoly he controls" (25). Like John D. Rockefeller, J.P. Morgan, and other famous giants of industry and finance who lived in Baum's time, the Nome King hoards wealth and property while collecting fabulous works of art which he alone enjoys. His workers and soldiers compare to American laborers who enriched robber barons of the Gilded Age, which immediately preceded the writing of the Oz books. The Industrial Revolution is charmingly reflected in Tik-Tok, a mechanical man who thinks, speaks, and moves, although only if he is wound up.

The Nome King rules over an all-male population. No explanation is offered for how thousands of Nomes came to exist without the involvement of females, but one thing is certain: they are all afraid of eggs. Why did Baum choose eggs as the Nomes' nemesis? The answer may relate to the author's mother-in-law, Matilda Joslyn Gage, who was a famous leader for the first fifty years of the women's rights movement. If readers don't recognize her name, there is a reason: after a falling-out late in Gage's life, her so-called friends Susan B. Anthony and Elizabeth Cady Stanton wrote her out of history. But that's another story. Gage lived with the Baum family off and on for many years. A well-known author herself, she enjoyed the stories Baum told his four sons and she encouraged him to publish them. Her influence can be seen in many Oz books. Her own most famous book, *Woman, Church and State* (1893), offers a radical history of how women have been oppressed for centuries by church and state. "Anciently," Gage writes, "motherhood was represented by a sphere or circle. The circle, like the mundane egg—which is but an elongated circle—contains everything in itself and is the true microcosm. It is eternity. It is feminine—the creative force, representing spirit" (8). Gage died in 1898, two years before the first Oz book was published, but the fact that Baum chose a matriarchal symbol to defeat the all-male Nomes is attributed by many scholars, including Gage' biographer, Dr. Sally Roesch Wagner, as a tribute to his mother-in-law and the women's movement.

Matilda Joslyn Gage, born in 1826, began her political activism as a child, going door to door in the 1830s in her home town of Cicero, New York, to collect signatures on anti-slavery petitions. L. Frank Baum, born in 1856 in Chittenango, New York (like Cicero, near Syracuse), was a child during the Civil War (1861–1865).

In their 2010 article, "The Ethics and Epistemology of Emancipation in Oz," Jason M. Bell and Jessica Bell look at Baum's series through the lens of his youth, "an age overshadowed by the great and bloody struggle that resulted in the abolition of slavery in the United States." In doing so, they find "a theme that is prevalent throughout the entire history of Oz. The effort to abolish slavery and establish diversity is essential to its heroes; the effort to institute slavery and race superiority is essential to its villains, and the strife between the two sides is a theme whose intensity and scale may serve to inspire a story for all ages" (225).

It seems likely that Baum's mother-in-law helped to inform his knowledge of enslavement. The Nome King's self-defensive arguments reflect points of view from Gage's own childhood, when the abolitionist movement was just getting started. When the Nome King argues that, by law, the King of Ev can do no wrong, he uses the law as real enslavers did, to justify the terrible practice.[1] When the Nome King insists he has made a fair deal to buy the Ev royal family, he echoes some early abolitionists who, even as they opposed slavery, felt that "owners" should be reimbursed for the loss of their property if they freed enslaved workers.[2] The myth of the kind master is debunked here, too.

> "Cruelty," says the Nome King, "is a thing I can't abide. So, as slaves must work hard, and the Queen of Ev and her children were delicate and tender, I transformed them all into articles of ornament and bric-a-brac. [...] Instead of being obliged to labor, they merely decorate my apartments, and I really think I have treated them with great kindness" [168].[3]

Then there is the subject of "race superiority," as mentioned above. Baum describes the Nome King as "a little fat man clothed in gray-brown garments that were the exact color of the rock throne in which he was seated. His bushy hair and flowing beard were also colored like the rocks, and so was his face" (163). This idea made sense to me as a child reader and has ever since. Not until working on this essay had I encountered Richard Tuerk's idea: "In *Ozma of Oz* readers can … see Baum's racism at work…. [I]n *Ozma of Oz* Baum emphasizes the color of the Nomes and the Nome King, and he does so in a way he does not in his later Oz books involving Nomes" (71). Or maybe, having established their color, Baum didn't feel the need to mention it again. Illustrator John R. Neill, following Baum's lead, depicts the King as round, cute, fluffy, and monochromatic. To bolster his theory, Tuerk points out that the Nome King often behaves like a naughty or spoiled child, an idea he claims fits "the racist idea that non-whites are like children" (71). Or perhaps L. Frank Baum, trying to amuse child readers, presented a powerful, magical, evil brat who gets away with more than they ever could.

Tuerk raises Joan Nagel's description of another early twentieth-century prejudice: "beneath their childlike exteriors, black men are barbaric creatures who lust to 'possess' white females, like Dorothy and Ozma." "Tuerk dials this theory back a bit by explaining that Baum makes the Nome King less 'hyperpotent' than the worst men of color, since he turns his prisoners into ornaments who cannot have sex" (71). To me, Tuerk's arguments prove that racism and lust are in the eyes of the beholder.

Baum wrote for children. Even his serious subjects are presented with light-hearted humor. The Nome King's meltdowns, when he hops around the throne room like a jumping jack, are hilarious and satisfying. "Rocketty-ricketts!" he says when Billina starts breaking enchantments. "Smudge and blazes!" as she continues. "Hippikaloric!" he screams in a fury and, in an aside to readers, Baum points out this "must be a dreadful word because we don't know what it means" (226–27).

In *Ozma of Oz*, the Nome King threatens to throw enemies into fiery furnaces or dungeons full of molten lava, but never follows through. In his second appearance, in the sixth book of the series, *The Emerald City of Oz* (1910), the King throws two advisers away for disagreeing with him and dispatches a third to the slicing machine, after which he will be fed to the seven-headed dogs. So this book begins with a new motive: a desire for revenge, with realized violence and without pretense that the angry Roquat is a nice fellow. His goal is to conquer and destroy Oz while retrieving his stolen magic belt. In his fourth adviser, General Guph, who hates nice people, the King finds a volunteer to tackle the project.

The Emerald City has a dual plot. In Kansas, Uncle Henry is about to lose the farm to foreclosure. At Dorothy's request (Ozma checks on her each day by magic picture), Ozma uses the magic belt to move the little girl, her aunt and uncle, and Toto, too, to live forever in Oz. Then Dorothy takes her relatives on a wagon tour of their new land.

Underground, the Nome King orders his miners to tunnel under the deadly desert all the way to Ozma's palace. To ensure that Ozites cannot defeat the Nomes by rolling eggs down the tunnel, General Guph recruits other evil creatures, who are unaffected by eggs, to help. These include Whimsies, whose elaborately decorated pasteboard heads cover the fact that their own heads (and brains) are small; Growleywogs, "of gigantic size, yet ... all bone and skin and muscle" (80); and Phanfasms, hairy men with the heads of animals. They all relish power and the chance to do harm and, once enlisted, plan to betray each other while enslaving the Oz people and the Nomes.

Luckily Ozma keeps an eye on the Nome King via her magic picture. The tunnel is nearly completed when the above-ground travelers (including Dorothy and her family) return to the palace and Ozma invites them to join her group of advisors. "I do not wish to fight," Ozma says. "I will not fight—even to save my kingdom" (268).

Some advisors consider leaving Oz for Kansas, taking emeralds in their pockets to use in paying off Uncle Henry's mortgage. But Ozma, as ruler, and Dorothy, now a princess of Oz, are determined to stay despite the threat of attack and enslavement. Aunt Em agrees. "I've been a slave all my life," she says, referring to her hard life in Kansas, "and so has Henry" (269–70). Here Baum suggests that they are two of the faceless workers whose work enriches bankers and other wealthy capitalists. Aunt Em may also have noticed that women run Oz, making it quite different from the United States patriarchy, and the limited role as a farm wife, that she is used to.

When the Scarecrow realizes that the tunnel will surface at the Forbidden Fountain on the palace grounds, he develops a plan. Using the magic belt, Ozma fills the tunnel with dust, making the attackers thirsty. When they emerge, they drink the Water of Oblivion, then look around, smiling pleasantly, having forgotten all they know.

> "You are the King of the Nomes," [Ozma] said.
> "Ah; I wonder what the Nomes are!" returned the King, as if puzzled.
> "They are underground elves, and that tunnel over there is full of them," she answered. "You have a beautiful cavern at the other end of the tunnel, so you must go to your Nomes and say: 'March home.' Then follow after them and in time you will reach the pretty cavern where you live."
> "The Nome King was much pleased to learn this, for he had forgotten he had a cavern. So he went to the tunnel and said to his army: 'March home!' At once the Nomes turned and marched back through the tunnel, and the King followed after them, laughing with delight to find his orders readily obeyed" [286].

Ozma sends the other creatures, who have also forgotten their wickedness, home and closes the tunnel. With this happy outcome, and with Dorothy and her loved ones safe in Oz, Baum intended to end the series. He has Glinda make Oz invisible, to protect it from the outside world. Unfortunately for the self-proclaimed Royal Historian of Oz, none of his other books sold as well as the Oz stories, so in 1913 Baum resumed the series, reportedly contacting the Ozites by telegraph.

The Nome King's third appearance comes in *Tik-Tok of Oz* (1914). The novel's plot resembles that of *Ozma of Oz* with good reason: Baum wanted to adapt *Ozma* into a stage show but he had sold the dramatic rights to characters from that book. So he invented a new, but similar, group of protagonists to rescue a transformed captive from the Nome King's beautiful metal forest. The musical *Tik-Tok of Oz* was moderately successful in the West, but was by no means a hit show. Ever adaptive, Baum reworked it into the eighth novel of his Oz series (Glassman).

In this book the Nome King has taken a new name, Ruggedo, after forgetting his old one. When he learns that conquerors are approaching his domain, he arranges for them to fall into the Hollow Tube through the world. The ruler on the other side sends them back, along with a young dragon named Quox, who falls asleep upon arrival. The others march on Ruggedo, who, at first, seems to succeed, capturing small groups as they enter his caverns.

Polychrome, the Rainbow's Daughter, is the last to arrive. Ruggedo is smitten. "I'll make a bargain with you, sweet Polly," he says. "Remain here and live with me and I'll set all these people free. You shall be my daughter or my wife or my aunt or grandmother—whichever you like—only stay here to brighten up my gloomy kingdom and make me happy!" (186). No lust seems involved in this offer, but the roles he suggests for Polychrome fit perfectly into his patriarchal view of the world, ignoring her unusual and considerable power as a fairy. Or they may reflect his need, as a naughty, lonely little boy, to be loved. We almost feel sorry for him here. Polychrome refuses and wakes up Quox, who removes Ruggedo's magic powers and proclaims his Royal Chamberlain, Kaliko, the new King. Ruggedo promises to behave himself as an ordinary Nome. Enchantments are broken, Quox quietly quits, and the main party goes on to a feast in the Emerald City.

Ruggedo returns, as evil as ever, in *The Magic of Oz* (1919), the thirteenth book in the series, published a month after the author's death. Ousted from the Nome Kingdom, the Nome King meets a gullible young man who has stumbled upon his father's magic word and the directions for pronouncing it. Baum warns in an aside,

> "Now, of course, I would not dare to write down this word so plainly if I thought my readers would pronounce it properly and so be able to transform themselves and others, but it is a fact that no one in all the world except [the father] had ever (up to the time this story begins) been able to pronounce *Pyrzqxgl* the right way, so I think it is safe to give it to you. It might be well, in reading this story aloud, to be careful not to pronounce *Pyrzqxgl* the proper way, and thus avoid all danger of the secret being able to work mischief [19–20].

[NB: I spent my childhood trying to pronounce *Pyrzqxgl*, alas, to no avail.]

Ruggedo and his companion, who are trying to conquer Oz, spend a good portion of this book as Li-mon-eags, beasts with the heads of lions, bodies of monkeys, wings of eagles, and tails of wild asses, with knobs of gold on the ends. The reformed, now revered, Wizard of Oz also appears in this book and others after returning to Oz in the fourth book, *Dorothy and the Wizard in Oz* (1908), where he learns real magic from Glinda. Many transformations later, the Wizard changes both villains into nuts (walnut and hickory). Later, standing by the fountain of the Water of Oblivion, he changes them back to their natural forms, at the same time making them very thirsty. This time, when Ruggedo forgets all, Ozma decides to keep him in Oz so that he can't relearn his old ways, as he must have done since *The Emerald City of Oz*, by returning to the Nome Kingdom. And maybe, as a feminist ruler, Ozma is used to putting up with clueless males.

Kindly, Baum gives the Nome King a happy ending. "And so the wandering ex-King of the Nomes found a new home, a peaceful and happy home, where he was quite content and passed his days in innocent enjoyment" (266). The last book in the series, *Glinda of Oz* (published posthumously in 1920), omits the character altogether.

The Nome King, like all characters introduced in Baum's later Oz books, was not well-known to readers in general when Walt Disney Pictures featured him prominently in the 1985 movie *Return to Oz*. And, surprisingly, the film did little to elevate his fame.

In a 2017 article, "How Disney Came to Define What Constitutes the American Experience," the *Smithsonian Magazine* says that Disney movies and theme parks have "played a dominant role in shaping the collective memory of American history." Early Disney films, "often set in a glorified 19th century rural American heartland … featured a hero … whose strong work ethic and bravery in the face of risk always found 'the little guy' and 'common man' triumphant over his foe" (Bemis). *Return to Oz*, which begins in 1899 Kansas, matches this setting and plot. Nine-year-old Fairuza Balk, appearing in her first movie, received rave reviews for her sensitive performance in the face of terrifying villains.

So what happened? Baum's characters from *The Wonderful Wizard of Oz*, and especially from the 1939 movie version starring Judy Garland, are American icons, recognized instantly in editorial cartoons, Halloween costumes, and sitcom fantasy sequences. Why didn't Disney's Nome King, in this sumptuous sequel, achieve the same cultural status? Simply put, the movie flopped. Costing $28 million to make (Harmetz), it lost $17 million in the domestic market (Burin). Critics called it bleak and nightmarish, terms which certainly apply to its beginning. The 1939 movie presented Oz as a dream, but in this film, as in the first Oz book, it is a real place. Still, in *Return to Oz*, no one believes Dorothy when she describes her fabulous adventure there.

After six months back in Kansas, the young heroine can't sleep or even get out of bed. Uncle Henry, also depressed, has managed to build only half a new house. Aunt Em (played by Piper Laurie), worn down by Dorothy's talk of Oz, needs help with housework. After seeing an ad for a new electric "healing" treatment for just about any malady, she takes Dorothy to a spooky-looking asylum (the interior resembles the set from the 1931 movie *Frankenstein*). Leaving Dorothy with a smarmy doctor (played by Nicol Williamson) and his second-in-command scary nurse (played by Jean Marsh), Aunt Em promises to return the next day, when Dorothy will have forgotten all that "Oz nonsense." (Director Walter Murch wanted to make a film based on L. Frank Baum's sequels, but he and co-author Gill Dennis dreamed up this shocking opening on their own. Baum would never have permitted a trusted grownup to betray a frightened child.) Luckily, with the help of another girl (played by Emma Ridley), Dorothy escapes before the doctor can hook her up to his machine. Caught in a flood, she clings to a chicken coop and reaches land with a talking hen named Billina.

From this point, *Return to Oz* follows the plot of *Ozma of Oz*. There are a few tweaks: the Nome King has already conquered the Emerald City, reclaiming the emeralds he believes are his and turning the residents to stone. He has also kidnapped the Scarecrow, leaving a fearsome witch named Mombi in charge. As in *Ozma*, Dorothy finds Tik-Tok and the mechanical man helps her fight off the Wheelers, in this movie, fiendish creatures with wheels instead of hands and feet. In *Ozma of Oz*, illustrator John R. Neill portrayed the Wheelers as foppish—barely alarming. Murch's psychotic cyberpunks are even scarier than MGM's flying monkeys (which were, in turn, more frightening than W.W. Denslow's illustrations of them in the first book).

Soon Dorothy, Billina, and Tik-Tok meet Mombi (Jean Marsh, again second-in-command to the main villain) in her Art Nouveau palace. This glamorous antagonist combines two characters: Langwidere from *Ozma*, and Mombi, an evil witch from the second book, *The Marvelous Land of Oz*. In *Return to Oz*, Mombi's thirty-one heads are stored—turning, nodding, and rolling their eyes—in glass-fronted cabinets. Mombi, who likes Dorothy's head, locks her up until it can grow to the right size for her to take.

Two more characters from the second book round out Dorothy's party in this film: a wooden man named Jack Pumpkinhead (also Mombi's prisoner) and the Gump, a flying creature the rest of them construct from found materials. Stealing Mombi's magic powder, Dorothy brings the Gump to life and he flies them away to the Nome King's mountain. As the protagonists land and approach the mountain, a rock wall appears exactly as described by L. Frank Baum himself in *Ozma of Oz*:

> In the gloom they could see strange forms flit across the face of the rock. Whatever the creations might be they seemed very like the rock itself, for they were the color of rocks and their shapes were as rough and rugged as if they had been broken away from the side of the mountain. They kept close to the steep cliff facing our friends, and glided up and down, and this way and that, with a lack of regularity that was quite confusing [157].

Through Claymation, which in 1984 was a fairly new stop-motion animation technique, the Nomes fade in and out of shifting rock surfaces, always jagged and chunky. At first the King is abstract, just an enormous head with a powerful voice. When angered, he magically opens a door to show his fiery furnaces. The movie provides a much scarier depiction of this hell than the book ever could, and the scene suggests that the King, described as looking like Santa Claus in Baum's novel, might, in this incarnation, be the devil.

When things go his way, he takes on a more organic body shape, gradually becoming recognizable as a human actor in rock-colored makeup. Then, pulling aside his rocky robe, he surprises Dorothy with his footwear—the ruby slippers. He found them, he explains, and they provide his magical powers. Director Murch paid MGM a hefty fee to use ruby slippers, from the movie, instead of silver slippers, from the first Oz book. Of course, Murch wanted to tie the two films together. Surprisingly, the Nome King taps his toes together in a dainty, feminine gesture. Could his power be less than a woman's? Whatever he has, it's not enough. "But you have so much," Dorothy says. "That's not the point," he replies (1:09:45–1:09:53). Having turned the Scarecrow into an ornament, the Nome King offers Dorothy and her friends the chance to enter his ornament rooms, one at a time, to try to guess which one he is. The friends go first and they fail. When Dorothy succeeds, freeing them all, the Nome King erupts in an earthquake of anger and destruction.

Looming overhead as a rock giant, the Satanic King decides to eat his prisoners. Holding Jack by the foot, he hoists the wooden man over his open jaws. Just then, Billina, who is hiding inside Jack's hollow pumpkin head, lays an egg that falls into the King's volcanic mouth. Dropping Jack, the Nome King shatters, starting with his eyeballs. "Don't you know that eggs are poison to Nomes?" (1:32:55–1:33:10) are his last, echoing words as he collapses into a heap of rocks while the cavern falls down around him.

Practical Dorothy grabs the ruby slippers, puts them on, wishes her friends to safety, and restores the Emerald City to its former glory. Learning that Mombi has imprisoned Ozma, the rightful ruler of Oz, Dorothy frees her, too. Then, surprisingly, Dorothy wants to go home. Ozma (Emma Ridley) uses the ruby slippers to send her, promising to keep an eye on her in Kansas and to wish her back any time she wants to come.

Danielle Paige addresses viewer's initial reluctance to embrace this version of Oz and its characters in her novel series, *Dorothy Must Die*. "'Oh, my god,' [Madison] whispered. 'I *hated* this movie.' 'What movie?' Amy asked. '*Return to Oz*? It's like showing a little kid *Clockwork Orange*. Fucked me up for life'" (*The End* 31). Even so, *Return to Oz* earned an Oscar nomination for its pre-computer-era visual effects, including puppetry, radio-controlled devices, front projection, animatronics, and Claymation. Now recognized as part of a group of dark children's movies of the 1980s, like *Labyrinth*, *Dark Crystal*, and *The Neverending Story*, *Return to Oz* has since earned a cult following. Nevertheless, the Nome King seems to have missed out here on his best chance to become a rock star.

Return to Oz is a romp in the theme park compared to Paige's *Dorothy Must Die* series of young adult novels. Published from 2014 to 2017, they take the "Dark Oz" subject matter of Gregory Maguire's *Wicked* series of novels (1995–2011) and the woman warrior theme of Suzanne Collins' dystopian *Hunger Games* trilogy (2008–2010) to new depths of depravity.

In book one, *Dorothy Must Die*, a tornado blows Amy Gumm (her surname pays tribute to Frances Ethel Gumm, better known as Judy Garland) to Oz from present day Kansas. But the Oz she finds is all wrong. Dorothy Gale, having returned to Oz, is Queen. This "super-evil bloodthirsty homicidal tyrant" (*End* 1), who talks like a foul-mouthed Valley Girl, rules Oz by magic, enslavement, torture, murder, and evil shoes. To escape her magic, monkeys cut off their own wings. Fashion and beauty details are more interesting with a vain female tyrant in charge, but Dorothy lacks the underpinnings of Baum's and Murch's male despots, who seem to be the rightful, or at least historically longstanding, rulers of their kingdoms.

Other familiar characters are also reversed. Glinda enslaves and tortures child miners, but there's little abolition in this book. The Scarecrow (nicknamed "Scare") performs Joseph Mengele–like medical experiments in his filthy laboratory. The Tin Woodman rules over the Scarecrow's survivors, gruesome hybrid creatures, part metal, part human, or mixtures of living beings. The Lion eats children. The miserable people of Oz wear PermaSmiles, which come in tubes and make everyone look happy.

With the help of good witches (they are probably good), Amy trains as a warrior and learns to do magic to prepare for tasks that only a special girl from Kansas can accomplish: remove the Tin Man's heart, steal the Scarecrow's brain, take the Lion's courage, and kill Dorothy. It takes her the second and third books, *The Wicked Will Rise* and *Yellow Brick War*, to complete this gory mission. Oh, and to kill Toto, too.

With so many evil people and deeds in these novels, the Nome King pales by comparison—literally. Bald, tall, and thin, he has a "pale hairless torso" (*End* 223), a slithering voice, bony fingers, and long silver nails filed to sharp tips. Baum's King, who was child-sized and specifically rock-colored, portrayed by Murch as a frightening giant(also rock-colored), in this series is the size of a tall adult Caucasian male. Some have suggested that Paige, an author of color, made Nomes white for reasons related to race. The King and his sentries, "pale as birds' eggs and lean as skeletons" (*End* 221), bring to mind white grubs who never see the light of day.

The Nome King makes his first appearance in Paige's third book in the series, *Yellow Brick War*, when Amy returns briefly to Kansas to look for Dorothy's other pair of magic shoes. Disguised as the assistant principal of her high school, the King reveals himself to Amy and her friend Madison: "Silver smoke billowed up from his feet. His body began to ripple and his skin peeled away in long strips that dissolved into silvery ooze" (264). He wants the shoes, too, but Amy keeps them and uses them to wish herself and her friend to Oz.

There, in the fourth book, Amy learns that Dorothy, presumably crushed under a collapsing castle, instead fell into the arms of the Nome King in his underground tunnel. Taking her home to his dominion, under Ev, he proposes marriage. Even though they kiss, the only lust they experience is a desire to kill each other. Both monarchs know that according to Ev marriage vows, magic bound to either spouse becomes community property once they are wed. And after that, the shared magic can be stolen with blood, so Dorothy realizes that the King will murder her for her shoes as soon as they say "I do."

The first three books in this series are written in first person, from Amy's point of view, but *The End of Oz* alternates between Amy and Dorothy. Hoping to distract and conquer the Nome King, Dorothy convinces him to hold their wedding ceremony at a huge masquerade ball (regrets will not be accepted, the invitations say). Amy, in the second pair of magic shoes, comes to the ball with her Oz boyfriend, Nox, her Kansas friend Madison, and Lang, the princess with many heads (Langwidere from the book *Ozma of Oz*). The Nome King hits Lang with a spear of magic red light but, before dying, she grabs his ruby sword. "You think you can use my own weapon against me?" he cackles (246), just before she stabs him to death. There are no eggs, poisonous or otherwise, in this ending, just a phallic plunge.

The story concludes as Dorothy, feeling a smidge of remorse for all the murder and mayhem she has caused, goes back in time to when she was a girl in the castle of the Wicked Witch of the West. When she dumps a pail of water over her own head, the world falls apart. Then Ozma, the rightful ruler of Oz, who has been enchanted through all four Paige volumes, is restored to the throne. Amy, Madison, and Nox go to high school in Kansas until Amy, who still has magic shoes, gets a call back to Oz. Realizing that she belongs in both Kansas and Oz, and certain that she can travel between them at will, she goes.

The *Dorothy Must Die* series contains elements of the Baum stories and *Return to Oz*. Paige's magic and settings often expand on Baum's to good effect. The power-crazed Nome King enslaves Munchkins, male and female, commands battle-scarred warriors, and relies on diggers, creatures with lights in their foreheads whose job is to hurt people. In these books, the Nomes seem to be all male. The King's furniture is carved with creepy elf-like characters that Dorothy decides are his ugly ancestors, so again we wonder, how do Nomes reproduce?

L. Frank Baum's Nome King is a cruel, but sometimes appealing, power-hungry trickster and enslaver who takes advantage of innocent people, even children. Despite Baum's stated desire in the first Oz book to write "a modernized fairy tale, in which the wonderment and joy are retained and the heart-aches and nightmares are left out" (*Wonderful* [5]), the author realized that a good adventure story requires a credible antagonist, scary predicaments, and occasional violence. But Baum does not dwell on evil. As his fatherly literary voice delivers the story, readers can almost see the twinkle in his eye. In *Ozma of Oz*, his Nome King is a complex character, a clever villain but also a source of humor. Dorothy stands up to him, secure in the knowledge that she is supported by friends and family, wherever they happen to live.

Return to Oz presents the same Nome King character as larger than life, more adult, much scarier, and completely humorless. Nicol Williamson portrays him with Shakespearean gravitas. Brave Dorothy still stands up to him, again with the help of faithful friends, but her Kansas relatives let her down. Director Walter Murch explained that the purpose of his movie was "to make kids realize that in some circumstances—sometimes in life, you're on your own and even the people who are there to protect you [can't]. Things go funny sometimes, so you have to be on alert" (Crotzer 9). That's a hard lesson to learn at age nine, and not what viewers expected from a movie sequel to one of the most positive (but sometimes scary) feature films ever made. Murch purposely links the movies by using ruby slippers, by having Kansas characters show up in Oz, and by making the Wheelers subservient to Mombi, as the Winged Monkeys are to the Wicked Witch of the West in both *The Wonderful Wizard of Oz* and the 1939 MGM movie.

The *Dorothy Must Die* series presents the Nome King as a weak character who is nominally scary, but not really frightening compared to other villains in the books. As nasty as these novels are, they match Baum's Oz books and *Return to Oz* in meeting Joseph Campbell's descriptors for the mythological journey of a hero in *The Hero with a Thousand Faces* (1949). Dorothy in the first two, and Amy in the third, separate from their regular lives, undergo rites of initiation, and return home, changed and empowered. All three engage in self-sacrifice for the greater good and the cultural order they work to uphold (Burger 18). The works of Baum, Murch, and Paige also match features of female heroic journeys as described in a new literary analysis, *The Heroine with 1,001 Faces* (2021) by Maria Tatar. In what Tatar calls a sequel to Campbell's book, she considers Jo March, Miss Marple, and even Lisbeth Salander to arrive at descriptors that apply to the Oz sagas considered here: curiosity, empathy, and a desire for justice or fairness (Beckerman).

The Nome King has appeared in many other stories and formats. Author Ruth Plumly Thompson, who was hired by Baum's publishers to continue the Oz series after his death, gave the King his own book in 1927, correcting Baum's spelling to *The Gnome King of Oz*. The King has appeared in comic books, graphic and standard novels, cartoons, animated television series, board games, computer games, and even a phone game. This list is far from complete. A Google search yields Nome King art prints, posters, and sculptures. Nome King cream wallpaper is no longer available—someone must have bought it all. Probably somewhere right now, someone is writing, drawing, or coding a story about the Nome King.

But in spite of everything, he remains a niche villain, appreciated mostly by fans of the Baum Oz books. An unscientific survey (asking around at meetings of the International Wizard of Oz Club) reveals that most of these readers consider *Ozma of Oz* to be the best of Baum's fourteen Oz books. And now we have mainstream media support: On October 15, 2020, *Time Magazine* named *Ozma of Oz* to its list of the "100 Best Fantasy Novels of All Time." Not *The Wonderful Wizard of Oz*, that "quintessential American fairy tale" (which I think should also have been included; after all, Lewis Carroll's two *Alice* books are both on the list), but *Ozma*. Surely the Nome King, one of L. Frank Baum's best characters, deserves a (thunder)clap or two for making this happen.

WORKS CITED

Baum, L. Frank. *The Emerald City of Oz*. Reilly & Britton, 1910
———. *The Magic of Oz*. 1919. Books of Wonder, 1999.
———. *The Marvelous Land of Oz*. 1904. Books of Wonder 1985.
———. *Ozma of Oz*. 1907. Books of Wonder, 1989.
———. *Tik-Tok of Oz*. 1914. Books of Wonder, 1996.
———. *The Wonderful Wizard of Oz*. 1900. Books of Wonder, 1987.

Beckerman, Gal. "The Heroine's Journey Gets Equal Time." *The New York Times*, "Books" page, 24 September 2021, p. C10.

Bell, James M., and Jessica Bell. "The Ethics and Epistemology of Emancipation in Oz." *The Universe of Oz: Essays on Baum's Series and Its Progeny*, Kevin K. Durand and Mary K. Leigh, editors. McFarland, 2010. 225–46.

Bemis, Bethanee. "How Disney Came to Define What Constitutes the American Experience." *Smithsonian Magazine*, 3 January 2017. www.smithsonianmag.com/history/how-disney-came-define-what-constitutes-american-experience-180961632/, accessed 15 September 2021.

Burger, Alissa. *The Wizard of Oz as American Myth: A Critical Study of Six Versions of the Story, 1900–2007.* McFarland, 2012.

Burin, Rick. "Hear Me Out: Why Return to Oz Isn't a Bad Movie." *The Guardian*, 12 February 2021. www.theguardian.com/film/2021/feb/11/hear-me-out-why-return-to-oz-isnt-a-bad-movie, accessed 15 September 2021.

Carroll, Joseph. "Violence in Literature: An Evolutionary Perspective." *The Evolution of Violence*. Springe, 2014. 33–52.

Collins, Suzanne. *The Hunger Games*. Scholastic, 2008.

Crotzer, Sarah K. "Outside Over There: In Praise of Walter Murch's *Return to Oz*." *The Baum Bugle* 64, no. 2 (Autumn 2020): 5–10.

Gage, Matilda Joslyn. *Woman, Church and State: A Historical Account of the Status of Woman Through the Christian Ages with Reminiscences of the Matriarchate*. 1893. Sky Carrier Press, 1998.

Glassman, Peter. "Editor's Note." *Tik-Tok of Oz* by L. Frank Baum. 1914. Books of Wonder, 1996. 10.

Harmetz, Aljean. "After 46 Years, Hollywood Revisits Oz." *New York Times*, 16 June 1985, Section 2, Page 1. www.nytimes.com/1985/06/16/movies/after-46-years-hollywood-revisits-oz.html, accessed 15 September 2021.

Hunter, Tera W. "When Slave Owners Got Reparations: Lincoln Signed a Bill in 1862 That Paid up to $300 for Every Enslaved Person Freed." *The New York Times*, 16 April 2019. www.nytimes.com/2019/04/16/opinion/when-slaveowners-got-reparations.html, accessed 15 September 2021.

Maguire, Gregory. *Wicked: The Life and Times of the Wicked Witch of the West*. ReganBooks, 1995.

Murch, Walter, dir. *Return to Oz*. Walt Disney Pictures, 1985.

"The 100 Best Fantasy Books of All Time." *Time Magazine*, 15 October 2020. https://time.com/collection/-100-best-fantasy-books/, accessed 15 September 2021.

Paige, Danielle. "BCBA Author Spotlight: Danielle Paige." *Black Children's Books and Authors: Our Stories Matter. YouTube*, uploaded by Justine Magazine. Published by Angie Nicole, 16 August 2016, https://bcbooksandauthors.com/bcba-author-spotlight-danielle-paige/, accessed 18 September 2021.

_____. *Dorothy Must Die*. HarperCollins, 2014. *Dorothy Must Die* series, vol. 1.

_____. *The End of Oz*. HarperCollins, 2016. *Dorothy Must Die* series, vol. 4.

_____. *The Wicked Will Rise*. HarperCollins, 2015. *Dorothy Must Die* series, vol. 2.

_____. *Yellow Brick War*. HarperCollins, 2016. *Dorothy Must Die* series, vol. 3.

Rahn, Suzanne. "Beneath the Surface of *Ozma of Oz*." *The Baum Bugle* 46, no. 1 (Spring 2002): 25–30.

"Slave Code: United States History." *Britannica*, www.britannica.com/topic/slave-code, accessed 15 September 2021.

"Slavery and the Constitution." *Bill of Rights Institute,* https://billofrightsinstitute.org/essays/slavery-and-the-constitution, accessed 15 September 15, 2021.

Tuerk, Richard. *Oz in Perspective: Magic and Myth in the L. Frank Baum Books*. McFarland, 2007.

Weld, Theodore. *American Slavery As It Is: Testimony of a Thousand Witnesses*. 1839. Arno Press and *The New York Times*, 1968.

Piecing Together
the Patchwork Girl of Oz

Gita Dorothy Morena

> Whee, but there's a gaudy dame!
> Makes a paint-box blush with shame,
> Razzle-dazzle, fizzle fazzle!
> Howdy-do, Miss What's-your-name?
> [Baum, 1913, 42]

The Patchwork Girl is one of L. Frank Baum's unique and lovable Oz characters, brought to life magically by a crooked wizard in *The Patchwork Girl of Oz* (1913). Like the fool in the tarot deck, she embodies a playful, spontaneous and lighthearted attitude that disguises the perceptive wisdom of her true nature. Although she is teased sometimes for being a silly girl or a "crazy quilt," as her story unfolds the Patchwork Girl becomes a wise and valued adviser and problem solver. Through her encounters in Oz, she demonstrates a part of us that comes to life when we recognize and integrate the diverse patches of our genetic inheritance—our family upbringing and our varied life experiences.

The mismatched image of patchwork is a simple and powerful way to illustrate the cacophony of feelings, thoughts, and associations that swirl in the invisible realms of our inner world. Recently, Ermeen Choudhury alluded to the metaphorical power of these patches in a publication of her poetry, saying: "The title of this collection, *The Patchwork Doll*, reflects the way I perceive my childhood self—composed of 'patches' of cloth cut from incongruous, clashing fabrics. I lacked the confidence to live in compete autonomy over my genuine self, often feeling helpless as I was stretched in multiple directions" (Choudhury, Preface). Seeing the shapes, colors, and pieces of patchwork as they multiply and connect in our life over time is the foundation from which we come to know ourselves.

As a Jungian psychotherapist and meditation practitioner, I see the Patchwork Girl as a symbolic image of the joy, vitality, and creativity that arises when the seemingly mismatched and patchwork experiences of life are understood, accepted, and integrated into a conscious acceptance of ourselves. She represents the freedom and *joie de vivre* that comes when we acknowledge the value of our unique perspective, personal insights, and depth of who we are. Although her unconventional thinking leads the Shaggy Man to call her "half crazy" (Baum, *Patchwork Girl*, 218), and Ozma to describe her as "bewildering" (Baum, *Patchwork Girl*, 217), the Patchwork Girl demonstrates the wisdom

Scraps, the Patchwork Girl (John R. Neill illustration from *The Patchwork Girl of Oz* [1913]).

and value of spontaneous intuition. At times her behavior appears somewhat foolish and mystifying to the logical, rational mind, but as she develops, the Patchwork Girl becomes a wise leader who can respond effectively to the needs of others. She is appreciated for her good judgement and ingenuity, her easy adaptability to changing circumstances, and her loyalty to Ozma and her friends in Oz.

Like all of us, though, the Patchwork Girl is not perfect: her exuberance can be irritating, her spontaneity problematic, and her self-confident attitude can be perceived as disrespectful and insulting. When she boasts to her Munchkin friend, Ojo, "I wonder if any of the people we shall meet will be as splendid as I am. I am bright and contented … while you are blue and sad," Ojo is offended and counters that perhaps she was given an overdose of brains (Baum, *Patchwork Girl*, 69). When she insults the Glass Cat with one of her whimsical rhymes, it angrily retaliates and threatens to "scratch off her suspender-button eyes" (Baum, *Patchwork Girl*, 73). As the Patchwork Girl matures and reflects on her behavior, she learns from her mistakes and exposes her vulnerability to become a trustworthy friend and valuable companion. She speaks with a universal wisdom that resonates with anyone on a path of self-discovery when she implores her friends, "Just let me discover myself in my own way" (Baum, *Patchwork Girl*, 72).

The Patchwork Girl was my mother's favorite Oz character, and she had a unique and special relationship to the Oz author. She was L. Frank Baum's first granddaughter, and when she was born, he named her "Ozma" and gave her a locket engraved with her name which she wore her whole life. Ozma and the Patchwork Girl become friends in the Oz stories, and are loyal, supportive, and protective of each other. When Ozma mysteriously vanishes in *The Lost Princess of Oz* (1916), the book that Baum dedicated to my mother, the Patchwork Girl solves the mystery of the Royal Princess' disappearance. Their friendship solidifies when the Patchwork Girl becomes a valued member of Ozma's advisory council in *Glinda of Oz* (1920), a book published after Baum's death in 1919.

My mother, Ozma, was a free and independent spirit, and as a child she often called herself "Scraps," the name the Patchwork Girl adopts for herself because she is "made of all scraps and nothing else" (Baum, *Patchwork Girl*, 61). As an adult, Mother described the Patchwork Girl as "fun, intelligent, and always getting into trouble," traits in her mind that resembled her grandmother, Maud Baum (Morena xvi). Like the Patchwork Girl, Mother saw her grandmother as a commanding, strong willed, and bright intellectual who was also a lot of fun. Maud loved to drive, and mother often told the story of how her grandmother "frequently put the car in reverse by mistake after coming to a stop." One time she did something strange while driving, and mother described how the car suddenly went around in circles, knocking the artificial flowers out of their vases in the back seat and scaring her half to death. She compared Maud's behavior to the sometimes reckless attitude of Scraps, saying, "You never knew what strange adventure awaited you with Maud at the wheel" (Mantele, "Memories of my Grandmother Baum," unpublished paper).

When she was sixteen, mother traveled with her grandmother to Chicago and described how they not only visited educational exhibits, but also "went to a German beer garden and sang a lot of old songs besides getting up to dance. She [Maud] could be a lot of fun and not always this bright intellectual woman that I had known" (Mantele, "Memories of my Grandmother Baum," unpublished paper). Reflecting on Baum's inspiration for writing stories about Oz, mother said her grandfather "wrote about the people and places he knew, transforming them into imaginary characters and strange places" (Mantele, "My Visit to Aberdeen," unpublished paper). Later in life, she realized the special connection she had with her lively grandmother might have also motivated her to adopt the nickname "Scraps" when she was young.

For me, my mother was the Royal Princess of Oz. I saw her as a strong-willed intellectual, with an authoritative and regal presence. As the empress of her kingdom, she expected others to follow her lead without question, and although there were moments when the curious, carefree, and fun-loving attitude of Scraps bubbled to the surface, she pursued her passion as a registered nurse with a focused determination. She volunteered as a school nurse until my brother and I left home, worked at Children's Hospital in Los Angeles for a number of years, and at the age of 75 obtained a master's degree in human behavior and worked with children who were grieving the loss of a family member. Perhaps Mother's attraction to Scraps' light-hearted attitude was an unconscious compensation for the serious and hard-working attitude that dominated her life.

When I was born, my mother named me Dorothy after the beloved heroine in Baum's first Oz book, *The Wonderful Wizard of Oz* (Baum, 1900). Although I changed my name to Gita years later when I needed to separate from the Oz legacy and begin my own spiritual journey, the landscape of Oz has been intricately woven into the fabric my life. As a child, I lived inside the magical fairy tale, and the Patchwork Girl made me laugh with her silly rhymes and playful pranks. Possessed with the archetypal energy of Dorothy, and fueled with the epigenetics of the strong women in our family, finding home has been about recognizing the essence of who I am. The Patchwork Girl's presence reminds me that I am a unique and lovable individual, especially when feelings of self-doubt and insecurity appear from the shadows. She encourages me to express myself in creative and spontaneous ways, to relax and wander lightly through life, to speak freely from my heart, examine my limitations honestly and connect with friends openly. As you explore the imagery of the delightful, lovable Patchwork Girl and follow her evolution through the Oz canon, I invite you to consider how she shows up in the experiences of your own life and relationships.

In the imaginary world of myths and fairy tales, heroes venture into uncharted territories, confront unexpected challenges, and stimulate exploration into the unconscious dimensions of the psyche. Marie Louise von Franz, author of *Interpretation of Fairy Tales,* says fairy tales "represent the archetypes in their simplest barest and most concise form … and afford us the best clues [for] the understanding of the processes going on in the collective psyche" (von Franz, 1). In other words, fairy tales reveal universal aspects of human nature that influence us all. Symbolically, they mirror psychological patterns of transformation and inner development, and reveal traits and energies in ourselves and our relationships that are hidden or misunderstood. In the language of metaphor, they are enchanting and entertaining ways to convey information about human nature and the mysteries of the inner world (Mitchell, 264).

Looking through a symbolic lens, Scraps shines in Baum's fairy tale as a multifaceted character who embodies the psyche in an original and creative way. Her patchwork weaves into a colorful pattern that visually expresses the characteristics of any individual, and her travels in Oz show how these patches integrate and develop into the wholeness of a complex personality. Carl Jung, a prolific writer and founder of analytic psychology, describes the psychological growth of a person as a process of "individuation" whereby a person naturally develops as a being "distinct from the general, collective psychology" (Jung 6:757). As individuation progresses, self-acceptance deepens and a person can access and assimilate inner experiences more easily, without resistance. The individual then experiences an expanded sense of wholeness, a profound relationship to the inner self, and an awakened consciousness that generates feelings of inner connection and integrity.

The Patchwork Girl can be seen as an animated image of Jung's individuation process. She has a deep sense of her own individuality and when she comes to life she looks into a mirror and proclaims, "I am an Original," and "I'm awfully glad ... that I am just what I am, and nothing else" (Baum, *Patchwork Girl*, 57). Metaphorically, looking in a mirror suggests a willingness to see things exactly as they are, and when the Patchwork Girl sees a reflection of herself, she accepts her originality totally. The nature of her diverse patchwork becomes visible as the stories of her adventures accumulate, and she becomes a complex example of a unique and liberated individual who accepts all aspects of herself. Hopefully, she will inspire you to express the beauty of your own individuality as you travel with her through Oz.

The Patchwork Girl appears for the first time in Baum's seventh Oz book, published a few years after he and Maud moved to their new home in Hollywood in 1910. Baum had planned to end the Oz series with his previous book, *The Emerald City of Oz* (1910), but his young readers insisted he write more stories from the magical fairy land, and he negotiated with Reilly and Britton to continue publishing Oz books. It's as if the Patchwork Girl jumps into life with vivacity so exuberant that it gives a fresh start to the Oz stories, as well as to Baum himself.

The appearance of this energetic character marks the passionate productivity of Baum's final years at Ozcot, the name of his Hollywood home. While he lived there, he published eight Oz novels,[1] the Little Wizard Series for younger children which included six "miniature" books,[2] and the *Little Wizard Stories of Oz*,[3] a book compiled of the previously published Little Wizard volumes. He also published several non–Oz books: ten under his own name,[4] twelve under the pen name of Edith van Dyne,[5] one under the name Floyd Akers,[5] two as Laura Bancroft,[6] and many other theatrical pieces that were never published or performed. In addition to his writing projects, Baum created a moderately successful stage musical, *The Tik-Tok Man of Oz* (1913), launched the short-lived Oz Film Manufacturing Company which produced five full-length silent films including *The Patchwork Girl of Oz* (1914), cofounded the Lofty and Exalted Order of Uplifters, a by-invitation group within the Los Angeles Athletic Club which was dedicated to "uplifting art and promoting good-fellowship" ("The Uplifter's Club"), tended an aviary of rare and exotic song birds, and won trophies for the chrysanthemums and dahlias he grew in his backyard garden (Baum and MacFall, 268–69). Baum was a busy and productive man while at Ozcot. He settled into a daily routine that included writing and gardening sessions until his health failed and he crossed the shifting sands in 1919 at the age of 63 (Baum and MacFall, 275).

Baum was known for his love of puns, jokes, and silly verse, and Scraps is a happy, helpful character who often bursts into song, dance, and whimsical rhymes. Although she sometimes irritates her companions with constant chatter, she often exposes an unacknowledged truth or bit of clever wisdom with lyrical verse and a play on words. When Ojo, the Munchkin boy who travels with her through Oz, asks about her spontaneous laughter, Scraps answers,

> "Your world pleases me, for it's a queer world, and life in it is queerer still. Here am I, made from an old bed quilt and intended to be a slave to Margolotte, rendered free as air by an accident that none of you could foresee. I am enjoying life and seeing the world, while the woman who made me is standing helpless as a block of wood. If that isn't funny enough to laugh at, I don't know what is" [Baum, *Patchwork Girl*, 68].

Scraps' response to Ojo, and her stream of frivolous verse and comical comments, is reminiscent of Baum's own wit and ironic humor. Mother remembers large family picnics and holiday gatherings at Ozcot filled with spontaneous bantering, outrageous puns, and outbursts of uproarious laughter (Mantele, "Memories of My Grandmother Baum," unpublished). Perhaps with the creation of the Patchwork Girl, Baum was coming into a deeper acceptance and appreciation for his own whimsical humor and the paradoxical effect it has on others.

Like a lovable rag doll, the Patchwork Girl is the embodiment of one of the oldest toys in existence, a treasured companion for a child's comfort and play. Bringing this well-loved rag doll to life awakens memories and feelings of protection, playfulness, enjoyment, and a child's connection with its mother. Scraps is mentioned in many of the Oz stories written after *The Emerald City of Oz*, and often chosen by followers as one of their favorite Oz characters. Years ago, the powerful influence of a patchwork doll was recognized by the American Seating Company, and Scraps was portrayed on a poster promoting student desks ("Patchwork Girl"). Later, the name Patchwork was used by two different organizations who were dedicated to serving disadvantaged populations: "The Patchwork Kids" was founded in 1997 to support the educational needs of children in Uganda, India, and Macedonia (patchworkkids.org), and "Patchwork Kids ABA" was formed that same year to serve teens and young adults on the autism spectrum (patchworkkidsaba.com). *The Patchwork Girl of Oz* is not credited as an inspiration for these organizations, but her rag doll image is recognized as a comfort and support for children around the world.

The creation of Baum's Patchwork Girl begins in the workshop of a Crooked Magician who secretly defies a law forbidding the use of magic and creates a powerful potion that can bring inanimate objects to life. This Powder of Life is the result of a mysterious, lengthy, and alchemical-like process of blending, heating, and dissolving a concoction of unnamed elements in a steaming cauldron for six years. With his first batch, the Crooked Magician animates a glass cat figurine, and with the success of his formula agrees to create a servant girl who can help his wife Margolotte with household chores. Margolotte sews a variety of mismatched fabric scraps together to make a full-size rag doll that she stuffs with cotton and adorns with pointed red leather shoes, braided brown yarn hair, silver button eyes, and gold-plated ears and fingernails. She gives the cotton-stuffed figure just a sprinkle of cleverness, and a more substantial dose of obedience, amiability, and honesty, hoping her creation will follow directions without resistance since "she will have to work, when she comes to life" (Baum, *Patchwork Girl*, 36).

Just as the second batch of the Powder of Life is nearing completion, the Munchkin boy, Ojo, and his beloved Unc Nunkie, knock on the magician's door seeking food and shelter for the night. Ojo is intrigued with the Patchwork Girl project, and although Margolotte does not want her servant to be too smart, Ojo reasons that "one cannot have too much cleverness." He secretly sprinkles powders into the rag doll from every jar in the Magician's "Brain Furniture" cabinet. He mixes large doses of Cleverness, Judgement, Courage, Ingenuity, Amiability, Learning, Truth, Poesy, and Self Reliance, and a small pinch of Obedience. In the excitement of the Patchwork Girl coming to life, a jar of Petrification Powder is accidentally knocked over and splatters onto Unc Nunkie and Margolotte, instantly turning them into marble statues. Although the Wizard finds a spell to counter their petrification, it requires some hard-to-find ingredients: a six-leaf clover, the left wing of a yellow butterfly, three hairs from the tail of a Woozy, a drop of oil from a live man's body, and a gill of water from a dark well. Everyone is quite distressed with what has happened, and the Patchwork Girl immediately demonstrates her cleverness and judgement by suggesting they search for the magical ingredients.

As Scraps prepares to leave the Magician's hut, he objects, saying, "You have no right to leave this house. You are only a servant, and have not been discharged." He explains that a servant is a "sort of slave," and insists Scraps cannot go since she belongs to Margolotte (Baum, *Patchwork Girl*, 64). With her quick wit and ingenuity, Scraps silences the Magician, saying she serves his wife by searching for the ingredients needed to bring her back to life. In this brief interaction with the Magician, the courage and depth of the Patchwork Girl's self-acceptance becomes visible and she defends her right to be free and independent. She was given a strong dose of self-reliance when she was created, and although she appears as carefree, poetic, and somewhat unpredictable, she fiercely fights for autonomy and her right to self-expression.

Scraps' declaration of freedom from the Magician marks the presence of an anti-slavery theme that runs through many of Baum's books and is especially visible in the character of the Patchwork Girl (Bell 232). She repeatedly proves herself to be an intelligent and determined freedom fighter, passionately opposing any form of oppression or slavery, and repeatedly defending her right to be autonomous and independent. Scraps insists she will never live with the Magician and his wife, and when she sees a Woozy who is confined in a fenced yard, she is adamant that they free him from his imprisonment. Later, when the group enters the territory of the Horners, Scraps finds their chief proudly following the rigid and dogmatic rules of a leading bachelor who requires young girls always to be polite, sit quietly, and never make a joke. She is outraged at the patriarchal men who control the tribe and dominate the women, and boldly proclaims, "That old bachelor who made the rules ought to be skinned alive!" (Baum, *Patchwork Girl*, 290).

Later, Scraps meets Diksey, perhaps Baum's play on the word "Dixie" (Bell 232), who has started a war with the neighboring Hoppers by insulting them with an inappropriate joke. Scraps attempts to resolve their feud by encouraging Diksey to explain his comment and, when he does, peace between the kingdoms is reestablished. Scraps is a woman ahead of her times, for she not only defends her own right to be free, but also confronts conflict and advocates unabashedly for equality, justice, and liberty for all oppressed people. Later, after she and her friends find the ingredients for the magic spell that releases Margolotte and Unc Nunkie from the slavery of petrifaction, the Wizard declares Scraps to be a free person who "may live in the palace, or wherever she pleases, and be nobody's servant but her own" (Baum, *Patchwork Girl*, 338).

After Baum died, Ruth Plumly Thompson continued the Oz series, and in 1927 Scraps' role as a freedom fighter further develops in *The Gnome King of Oz*. She is kidnapped by the Quilties after their Queen Cross Patch the Sixth dissolves in pieces, and the Spool of Succession leads them to Scraps. When she arrives in Patch, a land of quilt makers and seamstresses, Scraps is furious that she has been captured. In a rage, she strikes out at her captors screaming, "You villain ragman, take me back. How dare you hurl me in a sack?" (Thompson 28). The Quilties are delighted with Scraps' "fine temper," and celebrate their new Queen shouting, "Hurrah for the Queen of the Quilties" (Thompson 28).

Scraps is initially intrigued with the thought of being a Queen; however, she refuses to do any of the expected work and as a result is imprisoned in their palace. Then, as fate would have it, she learns the evil King Ruggedo has broken out of exile and plans to conquer the Emerald City. She finds a way to escape with her new-found friends and warn Ozma about Ruggedo's plan, and in the process demonstrates her growing capability as a leader. She also shows her sensitivity to the needs of others, and her skillfulness with using song and rhyme to survive. When King Ruggedo is captured, Scraps shares the details of her adventure with Ozma and her royal entourage, and is proclaimed a hero by the inhabitants of Emerald City. The relationship between Scraps and Ozma deepens as their mutual dedication to maintain peace in Oz intensifies. Together, their combined characteristics of skillful communication, lighthearted spontaneity, discernment, and compassionate leadership become a model for those who promote non-violence, equality and liberation.

Although Scraps appears as a figure from Baum's imagination, she is reminiscent of the fiery temper of his mother-in-law, Matilda Joselyn Gage, a dedicated freedom fighter who worked in the political arena as an activist, abolitionist, and early suffragist. Her scholarly—and at the time controversial—book, *Woman, Church and State*, documented in great detail the oppression of Western women in the name of religion, and initiated an investigation into the patriarchy's domination and devaluation of women (Gage). I imagine Scraps as an example of Matilda's fierce dedication to the freedom and emancipation of all people, and an example of the strength, independence and creative intelligence of the feminine that was becoming more visible at the turn of the twentieth century. Like the American psyche from which she originated, Scraps' composition of mismatched patches can be seen as a reflection of the diverse melting pot of American culture. Her strong independent spirit is an inspiration for women to shed the shackles that have bound them and speak openly from the depths of their personal feminine perspective.

Matilda spent several months every year with Maud and Frank, and it is easy to imagine them sitting around the table discussing their ongoing projects and thoughts about current affairs. When she heard Frank telling the children his magical tales of Oz, Matilda and her daughter Maud insisted he publish them. It is as if Matilda's energy merged subconsciously with Frank's and materialized in the stories that contained so many feminine heroines: Dorothy, the courageous and determined young adventurer; Ozma the generous and benevolent ruler; Scraps, the carefree and lighthearted optimist; and Glinda, the magical matriarch and Good Witch of the South. As I reflect on these characters, I marvel at how the essence of their fairy tale personalities also appear in the women of our family. Matilda is like Glinda, the visionary who inspired women's liberation. Mother is represented as the Royal Princess Ozma, who encouraged the family values of freedom and independence. And I am Ozma's daughter Dorothy, an innocent young girl who travels her own Yellow Brick Road to find her way home to herself. The energy of Scraps, the Patchwork Girl, is a vibrant and colorful thread that twirls through each of us.

In Baum's original story, the Scarecrow is immediately smitten when he meets Scraps, and boldly declares, "You are the most beautiful sight my eyes have ever beheld" (Baum, *Patchwork Girl*, 169). They are attracted to each other instantly, and delight in each other's presence as their friendship blossoms. When the Scarecrow hears Scraps is in the Emerald City, he shares his excitement with Ozma saying, "I met a charming girl on the road and wanted to see more of her, so I hurried back" (Baum, *Lost Princess*, 217). The meeting of the Scarecrow and Scraps is reminiscent of Baum's first meeting with Maud in December 1881. His sister Harriet insisted he meet a young woman of her acquaintance who was "independent, with a mind and will of her own … and lots of fun" (Baum and McFall 43). Baum agreed reluctantly, and when they were introduced, his aunt Josephine commented causally, "I'm sure you will love her." Then Frank took

Maud's extended hand and responded gallantly, "Consider yourself loved, Miss Gage," to which the quick-witted Maud replied, "That's a promise. Please see that you live up to it" (Baum and McFall 43). Baum did live up to his promise, and after an amorous courtship he and Maud were married November 9, 1882 (Baum and McFall 45).

Long after Scraps meets the Scarecrow in *The Patchwork Girl of Oz*, Gilbert Sprague describes how their relationship evolves when they fall under the spell of a Love Magnet in *The Patchwork Bride of Oz* (Sprague). Scraps accepts the Scarecrow's somewhat abrupt and awkward proposal of marriage, and the inhabitants of Oz gather to celebrate and prepare for their wedding. However, within a few weeks after they settle into a small cabin in Gillikin Country, the newlyweds each realize they want to spend time in their separate homes: Scraps in the Emerald City and the Scarecrow in the land of the Winkies. Although they are happily married, they agree "to go our separate ways for a period of time, then when we feel the pang of missing each other … return here to our love nest" (Sprague 38). Scraps does not hesitate to express her inner truth and inclinations, even as her heart opens and she joins with the Scarecrow. She continues to value her individuality and freedom, and honors her love by telling the Scarecrow how she feels. Over time, the Patchwork Girl's initial appearance as a flighty, carefree young girl shifts into a wiser, more mature woman who values her connections and speaks her mind freely. It is as if the Powder of Life enlivened her to become an example for twentieth-century women to speak their truth and maintain their independence while simultaneously deepening their friendships and personal relationships.

Although the Patchwork Girl is portrayed as a positive and agreeable personality in Baum's original stories, the complexity of her character emerges as the vulnerability of her dark side appears in John R. Neil's book, *The Runaway in Oz*. Written in 1943 and published more than 50 years later (in 1995), the characteristically optimistic and playful Scraps exposes a challenging and painful aspect of her inner world. She creates a ruckus by giddily bouncing off walls and sliding down palace banisters, and is chastised by Jellia Jamb who demands Scraps leave the palace. In her haste to go, Scraps collides with the Tin Woodman who in exasperation yells at her, "Sometimes you're just too much" (Neil 7). Then she runs out of the palace defiantly, jumps onto her spoolicle, crashes it into a Dragonette crossing the road, and later explodes into a fit of rage when Jenny is unable to help her with an outfit for the evening banquet.

In a flurry of anger and humbled by disgrace, Scraps decides to run away and looks for a Weather Witch who can blow her into the wind so she can cross the Deadly Desert and leave the land of Oz. At one point she joins a group of students and righteously asserts that learning by experience is her favorite way (Neil 50).However, she avoids self-reflection, and after spending a week in a castle in the air, is catapulted explosively into an enchanted orchard. She lands on the Royal Quince and Quincess, the King and Queen who control the garden, and with their dying breaths they command their subjects, the "conse-quinces," to avenge their deaths (Neil 211). A horde of dire conse-quinces stream toward Scraps, throwing thorns and smoke balls at her before they explode and die. Scraps' beautiful patchwork is torn and stained black with soot, and she is overwhelmed with shame, disgust, and humiliation. Although the farmers proclaim her a heroine for defeating the destructive quinces, the brilliant colors of Scraps' dress and the vibrant sparkle of her personality are ruined. She wallows in the darkness of her humiliated state and hides from friends who want her to return to the Emerald City for healing.

Eventually, Scraps covers herself with a sheet so no one will see her disgrace and returns to the palace, where Ozma repairs her dress and restores her spirit. In the loving presence of Ozma and her friends, she can acknowledge her faults and recover her sense of well-being. Later, Ozma asks Scraps what she intends to do, and after some deep soul searching, she replies, "I admit that the Emerald City is a grand place to spend a little time, but the rest of the world is grand too. I've only seen a little of it. So I guess I'm not quite finished running away" (Neil 239–40). Although she loves Ozma and wants to stay in the Emerald City, Scraps is unwilling to give up her freedom. She finds a way to honor her deepest desire to travel, while also recognizing that running away to avoid unpleasant feelings has negative consequences.

The Patchwork Girl's portrayal as a liberated and independent woman continues in the Warner Brothers cartoon series *Dorothy and the Wizard of Oz* (2017–2020). She is a successful seamstress who lives in the palace, operates her own independent business, and has a close relationship with the Scarecrow. In this story, the Scarecrow continues to be infatuated with Scraps, and appears to lose his mind whenever he is near her. When Wilhelmina the Witch observes their relationship, she assumes Scraps has cast a magic spell on the Scarecrow and that her business success is the result of having captured his brain power. Wilhelmina kidnaps Scraps hoping to steal her magical potion and secure the Scarecrow's brain power for herself. Wilhelmina does not realize "brain power" can only be found inside oneself. She is caught in a misguided belief that power resides in the masculine and assumes women cannot be successful without it. Trapped by the conditioning of the male patriarchy, she exemplifies the self-doubt and fear that has victimized women for centuries and still hides surreptitiously in the inner world of many successful, self-assured women. In the cartoon series, the Scarecrow, a symbolic representation of Scraps' inner masculine or animus function, stops Wilhelmina's threatening sabotage. Scraps is released from the dark negativity of Wilhelmina, and with her strong sense of self affirms the integrity of her own power and inner strength. Perhaps the struggle between Wilhelmina and Scraps depicts an internal conflict that plagues many women today as they free themselves from the entanglement of past oppression and patriarchal conditioning.

A dark and vulnerable aspect of Scraps' inner world is further exposed in the graphic novel *The Royal Historian of Oz* (Kovac and Hirsch). When she is chosen as a team member to go to America and retrieve stolen Oz magic, Scraps is overpowered by another Wicked Witch who is possessed with a desire for power and control. Although she deflected the Magician's attempt to enslave her in *The Patchwork Girl of Oz*, now Scraps is unable to defend herself against the controlling witch-like darkness that enters her inner world. Her ability to be a leader and help her friends when they are in danger crumbles when she leaves the safety of Oz, and she finds herself in the vulnerable position of needing to be rescued herself. She is unable to resist the evil intentions of a dark and mysterious force, and needs the support of her friends to free herself from the Witch's intrusion into her inner world. Ozma comes to the rescue and mobilizes her team to save Scraps and the stolen Oz treasures. It is as if Kovac is describing an unconscious realm of the psyche where the archetypal forces of power and greed can become overwhelming and controlling. Carl Jung believed that dark, unconscious forces exist in all of us, and must be recognized and integrated as we grow and mature (Jung, *Letters*, 236–37). Perhaps Scraps' experience in America is a disturbing reminder of this challenging process. She shows us how negative energies can blindly intensify and control our behavior, and how the support of friends and mentors is necessary to redirect their influence.

Shelley Jackson creatively explores another aspect of the Patchwork Girl's darkness with her Gothic hypertext, *Patchwork Girl*, written in the software application "Storybook" (Jackson). She looks at the Patchwork Girl as a Frankenstein-like creature whose body parts are pieced together in the story's narrative, as well as in the reader's interaction with the hypertext. Like a literary collage, the hypertext contains links that carry the reader into a web of associations and contributions that are designed to explore the lives of women whose "corpses have contributed body parts to the [Patchwork Girl] creature" ("Patchwork Girl [hypertext]"). Although a patchwork of body parts is a disturbing image, it reminds me how generations of past freedom fighters have formed an invisible web of women warriors to break the chains of oppression and tyranny. Jackson's work is part of this invisible network of freedom fighters, and is often cited as an example of "cyberfeminism" ("Patchwork Girl [hypertext]"), a movement that calls for the dissolution of gender and racial hierarchies in the internet, cyberspace, and new-media technologies. Women warriors around the world connect on the web "to hack the codes of patriarchy" and overcome racial and gender privilege (Scott). In Jackson's hypertext, the Patchwork Girl is an inspiration for women to acknowledge their patches of experience and come together to expose the tendrils of patriarchal domination that weave through the world of technology.

As Scraps evolves through the years of Oz publications, she becomes a strong, unassuming, and highly valued character, devoted to the welfare of Oz and able to move freely in a variety of different and often difficult situations. She comes to life with an exuberant, creative, and spontaneous energy, and evolves into an intuitive, compassionate, and valued friend and advisor. As she matures through the Oz canon, the Patchwork Girl develops self-control and awareness, while maintaining a delightfully lighthearted, liberated and playful attitude. Her individuation process integrates light and dark aspects of her psyche as she transforms into an admirable and inspiring model for all of us. As a free and independent spirit, she expresses an integration of the multifaceted qualities of brain power given to her, and is an inspiration for discovering and accepting the beauty of our own individuality.

Works Cited

Baum, Frank Joslyn, and Russell P. MacFall. *To Please a Child: A Biography of L. Frank Baum, Royal Historian of Oz.* Reilly & Lee, 1961.
Baum, L. Frank. *The Emerald City of Oz.* Reilly & Britton, 1910.
_____. *Glinda of Oz.* Reilly & Lee, 1920.
_____. *The Lost Princess of Oz.* Reilly & Britton, 1917.
_____. *The Patchwork Girl of Oz.* Reilly & Lee, 1913.
_____. *The Tic Tok Man of Oz* (Musical). Oliver Morosco, prod. Majestic Theater, Los Angeles, 1913.
_____. *The Wonderful Wizard of Oz.* George M. Hill, 1900.
Bell, Jason M., and Jessica Bell. "The Ethics and Epistemology of Emancipation in Oz." *The Universe of Oz: Essays on Baum's Series and Its Progeny*, Kevin K. Durand and Mary K. Leigh, editors. McFarland, 2010. 225–45.
Choudhury, Ermeen. *The Patchwork Doll.* Kindle ed., 2020.
Decker, Thomas, Bert Ring, Rhoydon Shishido, and David Teague, dirs. *The Oz Kids:* Virtual Oz. Episode 8. Hyperion Animation, 1999.
Gage, Matilda Joslyn. *Woman, Church and State.* Charles H. Kerr &, 1893.
Jackson, Shelley. *Patchwork Girl.* Eastgate Systems, 1995.
Jung, Carl G. *The Collected Works of C.G. Jung.* Bollingen Foundation, 1954.

_____. Letter to Kendig B. Cully, 25 September 1937. *Letters*, vol. 1.1973. 236–237.

Kovac, Tommy, and Andy Hirsch. *The Royal Historian of Oz*. SLG Publishing, 2011.

Mantele, Ozma Baum. "Memories of my Grandmother Baum." Unpublished.

_____. "My Visit to Aberdeen." Unpublished.

Mitchell, Meredith B. "Learning about Ourselves Through Fairy Tales: Their Psychological Value." *Psychological Perspectives, A Quarterly Journal of Jungian Thought* 53, no. 3 (2010): 264–79.

Morena, Gita Dorothy. *The Wisdom of Oz: Reflections of a Jungian Sandplay Therapist*. North Atlantic Books, 1998.

Neill, John R. *The Runaway in Oz*. Books of Wonder, 1995.

"Patchwork Girl (hypertext)." en.wikipedia.org, 10 December 2019.

"Patchwork Girl: Scraps in Other Media." en.wikipedia.org, 18 July 2021.

"The Patchwork Kids." patchworkids.org.

"Patchwork Kids ABA." patchworkkidsaba.com.

Scott, Isabella. "A Brief History of Cyberfeminism" www.artsy.net, 13 October 2016.

Singleton, Kexx, Charles Visser, Kuni Tomita, and Brad Goodchild, dirs. *Dorothy and the Wizard of Oz*. Boomerang SVOD, 2017–2020.

Sprague, Gilbert M. *The Patchwork Bride of Oz*. Books of Wonder, 1997.

Thompson, Ruth Plumly. *The Gnome King of Oz*. Ballantine, 1955.

"The Uplifters Club." en.wikipedia.org, 26 September 2020.

von Franz, Marie Louise. *Interpretation of Fairy Tales*. Spring Publications, 1970.

Afterword

Frank and His Imagination

ROBERT BAUM

Note to the reader: Before you read the following Baum family tale about my great grandfather, you need to know that his garden at Ozcot was part and parcel of his imagination. You are among the *very* few who have been privileged to hear this tale. Please understand that you are dealing with the Wizard himself and his totally unique imagination, which can take you one step over the line between fantasy and reality. Please realize he was *not* always sure which was which, so I will let you decide for yourself which this story is.

* * *

Ozcot, in California's Hollywood, became more than a home to Frank and Maud in 1910. It was a castle fit for a wizard and his queen. It was a magical portal to his limitless imagination and a wonderful garden retreat for L. Frank Baum and his host of unique characters. He also grew a field of prize-winning dahlias and chrysanthemums there. It became an homage to his childhood home at Rose Lawn near Syracuse, New York. It boasted a lily pond for princely frogs and solitude, a chicken coop for some fowl characters, and a grand pergola where guest writers might ply their craft undisturbed.

Should you stroll by Ozcot on any given day, you might find the Wizard himself tending to his prize dahlias or exterminating a weed that dared to intrude. Or perhaps you would find him lost in imaginative bliss, busily recording his characters' actions in his characteristic longhand, or maybe just conversing with a passing bird. You had no doubt that you were privileged to be witnessing what might be the birth of a new chapter from the Land of Oz(cot). What you did not see was the Wizard deep in consternation at the need for a new story. You did not realize that despite all the trappings that could induce imagination that surrounded the Wizard, he had writer's block. He was stuck in reality!

A typical day for Frank would include getting up early, reviewing and editing yesterday's work, eating breakfast with his sweetheart Maud, and enjoying a morning of gardening and imagining in his Oz-some royal "studio." Suddenly all this normalcy was disrupted, the flow of literary genius was … stymied. No editing, no rewrite, no new Ozzian saga to feed his publisher's presses and his readers' book shelves—only an author's frustration with his characters.

Maud always knew when Frank was frustrated with his writing. She sensed his

173

acute distress and voiced her concern. "Frank, you have to eat something. You have to keep up your strength," she told him one day with genuine compassion.

"Thank you, sweetheart. You are right as usual. I just cannot find a way to work through this problem," he responded.

"What is causing it?" she asked.

"Well, the simple answer is I just can't get my characters to agree on the direction my new story needs to go," he said with resignation. "I have made compromise after compromise and they ... they are frustrating me so...." Frank stopped talking and looked at Maud.

She read his face and understood his problem completely. She had been through this before.

"Frank Baum, you get out there and use your wonderful gift of imagination to solve this battle with your characters. Remember all those early childhood memories of Rose Lawn you have shared with me? Think back and try to remember what inspired you. Be that small boy again, lying entranced on the living room floor, reading about new worlds and ideas and places."

Frank got up from the kitchen table smiling at Maud and gave her a hug. "Thanks for the shot of confidence, sweetheart. You are so wonderful." Nothing else needed to be said. Their mutual bond was again working its magic.

Once in his garden, Frank picked up his hoe and set out to do battle ... with the weeds and with his writer's block. He soon became lost in his childhood memories of the Scarecrow that had scared him so, and his mother's calming words of wisdom when he had nightmares about the Scarecrow chasing him.

"Frank, try talking to the Scarecrow. Find out his story and then maybe he will not seem so scary," she said. He smiled as he remembered the long hours spent in the field talking to the Scarecrow, but without any answer. He chuckled with a wry smile as he relived their conversation when the Scarecrow finally did answer him!

Frank made his way toward the chicken coop, sensing that they were hungry. All of them clucked and squawked as he threw the mash to them. "Good morning, Frank, 'bout time you fed us. Understand you and the Scarecrow got a clash of minds. Good luck, Frank. We know you two will get 'er solved."

"Thanks, Billina," he answered. Retrieving his hoe, Frank went right back to his weeding. He began working his way toward the side fence where he noticed one of his trees needed some care. Setting the hoe aside, he tended to the tree's tangled branches. "There, that should make you feel better," he told the tree.

"Thanks, Frank. Those twisted branches were hurtin' a might," it responded.

"You're welcome," Frank said as he reached for his hoe and went right back to weeding.

Suddenly Frank stopped and leaned on his hoe. Voices ... was he ... hearing voices? He just could not tell for sure. It sounded like ... a conversation ... but...? He stood quietly for a moment listening, but heard nothing more. After looking around the garden again, he resumed his walk, weeding when he saw the need. Nearing his prize bed of dinner plate sized dahlias, he stopped. He had built supports for these fragile flowers, but the wind last night had undone some of them. Without hesitating, Frank went to the small garden shed just behind the pergola and got a hammer, several wooden stakes, and some twine. Returning to the flowers in need, and with the skill of a consummate flower grower, he soon had all the flowers properly supported once again.

Standing back, Frank checked over his handy work. These dahlias were part of a

A parade of Oz characters (John R. Neill illustration from *The Scarecrow of Oz* [1915]).

careful crossbreeding program of his own creation. He even went so far as to name a special one after Ozcot. He had high hopes they would win him a blue ribbon or two in the annual Hollywood Women's Club flower show later this year.

Frank hesitated once again. He swore he heard voices that seemed to say, "Thank you." He looked directly at the biggest dahlia in front of him. Was it looking back at him? No, it could not be that the flowers were…. No, that just was not possible. But then, this *was* the royal garden of a wizard.

Picking up the hammer and twine, Frank returned them to the shed and decided to sit in the shade of the pergola and take a short rest. Besides, he had a few new thoughts forming in his imagination—perhaps a solution for his new Oz story. As he walked up the single step to the pergola, his mind began to listen to the new thoughts coming.

A loud voice suddenly brought him back to the present. It was Maud calling from the back door. "Frank, oh Frank! There is a young lady here to see you. She says she spoke to you the other day about an interview for her publication?"

This news totally discombobulated Frank. He hesitantly replied, "Send her back to the pergola. I was … eh … expecting her?" He made a quick search of his memory and had absolutely no inkling of ever speaking to anyone about an interview. And now of all the inconvenient times to have to stop and….

"Well, I declare. If it isn't the one and only bona fide L. Frank Baum, in the flesh *and* in his Oz-some garden to boot! I am, well, the luckiest lady alive, if I do say so myself!"

Frank was completely taken aback by her unexpected and unique arrival. Being the perfect gentleman, Frank rose to greet the young woman and direct her to the chair across the table from him. He extended a helping hand as the guest walked up the single step and stood by the offered chair. Sensing Frank's bewilderment, the visitor introduced herself in a quieter voice.

"Hello, Mr. Baum. I am Edith Smith, reporter for the Fairytale Guild of New York."

She quickly sat down in the offered chair and retrieved a business card from her small clutch and handed it to Frank. Upon reading it he noticed that the ink seemed damp.

"Pardon me, madam, but do I know you from somewhere?" Frank slowly questioned the young lady now examining his puzzled expression.

"Well, I sure do hope so, Frank," she quickly responded. "I sure hope so. How many times have you and I sat at this very table, right here in this gorgeous pergola in your Oz-garden and written another in that fascinating girls series, *Aunt Jane's Nieces*? But that is all beside the point right now, Frank Baum! Do you have any idea at all what it has taken to get me here? Do you?"

She looked him straight in the face, her eyes piercing right into Frank's very being. He sat transfixed and totally taken aback by her actions and words. He could only sit there ... staring at Edith Smith? His imagination felt like it would burst with all the questions now flooding into it.

He finally collected himself enough to speak coherently. "You are ... my...."

"Come on, Frank. You are on the right track. Think now!"

"You are ... my imagination? But how is that possible? You are in *my* reality, Edith van Dyne? You are one of my pseudonyms. I do not understand what is happening here."

"Simple, Frank Baum. I may be just a pseudonym to you, but I am also a part of your imagination. After all, *you* make me up! We were in hopes you would catch on to what was happening to you and your imagination, Frank. That is why I became visible to everyone. We need to talk. You have a serious problem to overcome right now. We have come together in order to help you through your writer's block and this silly self doubt you have about being a good children's author."

Frank could only stare blankly at Edith van Dyne for what seemed an eternity while what she had just said began to sink in. His facial expression slowly showed that he was beginning to understand the events he was now experiencing. "By *we*, I am assuming you mean all of my characters?" Frank asked.

Now it was Edith van Dyne's facial expression that made Frank realize exactly what was happening to him. He was operating in both reality and fantasy at the same time. "Frank, sorry to have shocked you this way, but it is in your best interest—in all of *our* best interests—for you to realize that you, reality, and your imagination are one! You have no idea what you and your imagination have started. I am not at liberty to show you the future, but just take it from me, Frank Baum; it is most Oz-some. You are the catalyst for so many new and wonderful ideas and authors and ... but I digress, Frank. We must get you through this Ozzian crisis and back on the Yellow Brick Road again."

Slumping in his chair, Frank looked as though his world had just gone crazy. Edith was becoming genuinely concerned when to her amazement Frank straightened up and began to chuckle and grin at the same time.

"If I were not experiencing this right here in my garden, my own Ozcot garden." Stopping mid-sentence, Frank carefully looked around his garden and surroundings. As he did, he now saw clearly all of his past characters as if they were actually standing about the garden watching and listening to Frank and Edith's conversation.

"Frank, are you all right?" questioned a wide-eyed Edith van Dyne. She could sense that Frank now had begun to fully comprehend the transformation he had just gone through. Sensing her apprehension, Frank spoke directly at her.

"Edith, this has been a revelation. I can see many of my characters standing about the garden, all worried about *me*. Now I understand how all my brief forays into the world of fantasy have made me a real part of my own imagination."

Frank allowed himself to totally become absorbed in his new understanding of who he was. Smiling from ear to ear, he simply said, "Thank you, Edith, for making *me* possible."

Frank could not stop himself from grinning. He suddenly laughed and looked around him. All of his characters were grinning and laughing with him. Even Edith had a big smile on her face. Both of them now had tears of happiness running down their faces. Frank felt like a giant weight had been lifted from his being and Edith was over-joyed that the author's uncertainty and doubts had now been conquered. Everything was now Oz-some!

Turning to the Tin Woodman, Frank smiled as he spoke. "I can recall the day I made you in a window display for one of my Baum's Castorine customers. I remember vividly thinking that I had forgotten the most important thing I had come for and that was to advertise our Axle oil. I recall I placed several cans next to your stovepipe legs and, wouldn't you know it, one leaked a few drops of oil on you and POOF! You came to life full of steam and clattering so and waving that ax around! You scared me half to death. I thought I was a goner for sure, but then I realized you were just a product of my imagination. I can tell you now that you have become much more than just a character. You have become a lifelong friend and companion. You have stood by me and helped all of us through some hard times." Frank wiped a tear from his eye.

"Thanks for the compliment, Mr. Baum," the Tin Man replied. "I am going to cry if you continue to carry on so! Can't have me rusting in your garden, now, can we?"

"Dorothy, you have been a wonderful daughter-in-imagination to Maud," Frank told one of his favorite creations. "You have been a welcome break from our four sons. I do not know how to thank you enough."

"Give her a big hug from me," Dorothy replied. "I am glad I can make her days brighter. Besides, she is a wonderful role model. She is strong, smart, and caring, and she values education so. I just love her."

"And you, Cowardly Lion," Frank continued. "What would I do without your cour-age? When I get discouraged, I just roar and snarl. Makes me feel better and scares my bad feelings away. You remind me a great deal of my dad—a lot of roar but, in reality, full of kindness and understanding. He exposed me to so many new and wonderful new ideas."

"Ah, shucks, Mr. Baum, I am just a big scaredy cat at heart. I am the one who should be thanking you for making me a part of this wonderful Oz saga you have conjured up. You have given me life, hear me ROAR! Makes me proud to be a 'mane' character and help all your readers."

Frank's gaze now turned to the Scarecrow, who was sitting on the edge of the Lily Pond wall. "Ah, my man of straw, what a true friend you are to me! You may have started as a bad dream in my childhood, but we have shared so much since becoming friends. It was with your help and guidance that I was first able to find all the rest of you and write such a wonderful story about your adventures in a land far away."

"Mr. Baum, I owe you my continued existence," the Scarecrow said. "If you had not been persistent and followed your mother's advice, we might not have begun our dia-logue in that cornfield. You might say you were the *brains* of that conversation! You have a lot of wonderful stories to write about."

Suddenly, both Edith and Frank sat bolt upright, each with a look of bewilderment. All of Frank's assembled characters were disappearing.

"Frank, are you all right?"

Frank woke with a start to his wife's words. Quickly pulling himself together, he answered. "Yes, sweetheart, I'm fine. Guess I dozed off there for a minute or two. I think I need to come in and cool off." As Frank rose and walked toward the house, he met Maud coming out to check on him.

"Frank Baum, you had me worried. You were working out here in your garden and in this hot sun. You know you need to wear your hat on days like this!"

"I am sorry, sweetheart, I was weeding and I guess I just sort of lost track of things." He gave his wife a big hug, one that surprised her with its suddenness.

"That's from Dorothy and the gang. They send their best," Frank said with a wink.

Maud stopped and gave her husband a puzzled look. Frank knew Maud suspected something was afoot, but he knew she had no inkling of what he had just been through. "Frank Baum, something has changed. I am sure of it. What has gotten into you? You seem so much more…."

Grinning from ear to ear, Frank interrupted her. "I have solved my problem with my characters, Maud. I am going to let them help me write my new Oz book!"

Maud gently pushed back on Frank. "Have you gone daft on me? What do you mean 'let them help me'? Sometimes I think your imagination is going to get you in big trouble!"

The two of them walked arm in arm through the garden to the backdoor. Climbing the steps, Frank let Maud enter first. Before he followed, he gave a backward glance to all of his characters who now had reappeared, and with a wink of his eye said, "And sometimes my imagination may get me *out* of trouble!"

Bibliography

Further Oz Readings, Fiction and Nonfiction

DINA SCHIFF MASSACHI

Nonfiction

The Baum Bugle. International Wizard of Oz Club.

Burger, Alyssa. *The Wizard of Oz as American Myth: A Critical Study of Six Versions of the Story, 1900–2007.* McFarland, 2012.

Carpenter, Angelica Shirley. *Born Criminal: Matilda Joslyn Gage, Radical Suffragist.* South Dakota Historical Society Press, 2018.

Durand, Kevin K., and Mary K. Leigh, eds. *The Universe of Oz: Essays on Baum's Series and Its Progeny.* McFarland, 2010.

Gage, Matilda Joslyn. *Woman, Church and State.* 1893. Humanities Press, 2002.

Harmetz, Aljean. *The Making of The Wizard of Oz.* Knopf, 1977.

Hearn, Michael Patrick, ed. *The Annotated Wizard of Oz, Centennial Edition.* W.W. Norton, 2000.

Hearn, Michael Patrick, ed. *The Wizard of Oz.* Critical Heritage Series. Schocken Books, 1983.

Koupal, Nancy Tystad, ed. *Baum's Road to Oz: The Dakota Years.* South Dakota Historical Society Press, 2000.

Langley, Noel, Florence Ryerson, and Edgar Allan Woolf. *The Wizard of Oz: The Screenplay.* Michael Patrick Hearn, editor. Delta/Dell, 1989.

Michel, Dee. *Friends of Dorothy: Why Gay Boys and Gay Men Love* The Wizard of Oz. Dark Ink Press, 2018.

Nye, Russel B. "An Appreciation." *The Wizard of Oz and Who He Was.* Martin Gardner and Russel B. Nye, editors. 2nd ed., Michigan State University Press, 1994.

Riley, Michael O. *Oz and Beyond: The Fantasy World of L. Frank Baum.* University Press of Kansas, 1997.

Rogers, Katharine M. *L. Frank Baum: Creator of Oz.* St. Martin's Press, 2002.

Scarfone, Jay, and William Stillman. *The Road to Oz: The Evolution, Creation, and Legacy of a Motion Picture Masterpiece.* Lyons Press, 2019.

Swartz, Mark Evan. *Oz Before the Rainbow: L. Frank Baum's The Wonderful Wizard of Oz on Stage and Screen to 1939.* Johns Hopkins University Press, 2000.

Tuerk, Richard. *Oz in Perspective: Magic and Myth in the L. Frank Baum Books.* McFarland, 2007.

Fiction

Farmer, Philip Jose. *A Barnstormer in Oz, or, a Rationalization and Extrapolation of the Split-Level Continuum.* Phantasia Press, 1982.

Maguire, Gregory. *Wicked: The Life and Times of the Wicked Witch of the West.* HarperCollins, 1995.

Paige, Danielle. *Dorothy Must Die.* New York: HarperCollins, 2014.

The "Famous Forty" Oz books

Baum, L. Frank (Lyman Frank), and W.W. Denslow. *The Wonderful Wizard of Oz.* Dover, 1960.

Baum, L. Frank (Lyman Frank), and John R. Neill. *Dorothy and the Wizard in Oz.* Reilly & Lee, 1908.

_____. *The Emerald City of Oz*. Reilly & Lee, 1910.
_____. *Glinda of Oz*. Reilly & Lee, 1920.
_____. *The Land of Oz: A Sequel to The Wizard of Oz*. Reilly & Lee, 1904.
_____. *The Lost Princess of Oz*. Reilly & Lee, 1917.
_____. *The Magic of Oz* . Reilly & Lee, 1919.
_____. *Ozma of Oz*. Reilly & Lee, 1907.
_____. *The Patchwork Girl of Oz*. Reilly & Lee, 1913.
_____. *The Road to Oz*. Reilly & Britton, 1909.
_____. *The Scarecrow of Oz*. Reilly & Lee, 1915.
_____. *Rinkitink in Oz*. Reilly & Lee, 1916.
_____. *Tik-Tok of Oz*. Reilly & Lee, 1914.
_____. *The Tin Woodman of Oz*. Reilly & Lee, 1918.
Cosgrove, Rachel R. *The Hidden Valley of Oz*. Reilly & Lee, 1951.
McGraw, Eloise Jarvis, and Lauren McGraw Wagner. *Merry Go Round in Oz*. Reilly & Lee, 1963.
Neill, John R. *Lucky Bucky in Oz*. Reilly & Lee, 1942.
_____. *The Scalawagons of Oz*. Reilly & Lee, 1941.
_____. *The Wonder City of Oz*. Reilly & Lee, 1940.
Snow, Jack. *The Magical Mimics in Oz*. Reilly & Lee, 1946.
_____. *The Shaggy Man of Oz*. Reilly & Lee, 1949.
Thompson, Ruth Plumly, and John R. Neill. *Captain Salt in Oz*. Reilly & Lee, 1936.
_____, and _____. *The Cowardly Lion of Oz*. Reilly & Lee, 1923.
_____, and _____. *The Giant Horse of Oz*. Reilly & Lee, 1928.
_____, and _____. *The Gnome King of Oz*. Reilly & Lee, 1927.
_____, and _____. *Grandpa in Oz*. Reilly & Lee, 1924.
_____, and _____. *Handy Mandy in Oz*. Reilly & Lee, 1937.
_____, and _____. *The Hungry Tiger of Oz*. Reilly & Lee, 1926.
_____, and _____. *Jack Pumpkinhead of Oz*. Reilly & Lee, 1929.
_____, and _____. *Kabumpo in Oz*. Reilly & Lee, 1922.
_____, and _____. *The Lost King of Oz*. Reilly & Lee, 1925.
_____, and _____. *Ojo in Oz*. Reilly & Lee, 1933.
_____, and _____. *Ozplaning with the Wizard of Oz*. Reilly & Lee, 1939.
_____, and _____. *Pirates in Oz*. Reilly & Lee, 1931.
_____, and _____. *The Purple Prince of Oz*. Reilly & Lee, 1932.
_____, and _____. *The Royal Book of Oz*. Reilly & Lee, 1921.
_____, and _____. *The Silver Princess in Oz*. Reilly & Lee, 1938.
_____, and _____. *Speedy in Oz*. Reilly & Lee, 1934.
_____, and _____. *The Wishing Horse of Oz*. Reilly & Lee, 1935.
_____, and _____. *The Yellow Knight of Oz*. Reilly & Lee, 1930.

Films & Television

Fleming, Victor, dir. *The Wizard of Oz*. MGM, 1939.
Hall, Todrick. *Straight Outta Oz*. *YouTube*, 12 March 2017, www.youtube.com/watch?v=4mUSwHhJ6zA.
Löfvén, Chris, dir. *Twentieth Century Oz* (originally called *Oz* and also called *Oz—A Rock 'n' Roll Road Movie*). Greater Union, 1976.
Lumet, Sidney, dir. *The Wiz*. Universal Pictures and Motown Productions, 1978.
Murch, Walter, dir. *Return to Oz*. Walt Disney Pictures, 1985.
Raimi, Sam, dir. *Oz the Great and Powerful*. Disney, 2013.
Semon, Larry, dir. *The Wizard of Oz*. Chadwick, 1925.
Singh, Tarsem, dir. *Emerald City*. National Broadcasting Company (NBC), 2016–2017.
Thatcher, Kirk R., dir. *Muppets' Wizard of Oz*. Fox Television Studios, 2005.
Turner, Otis, dir. *The Wonderful Wizard of Oz*. Selig Polyscope Co., 1910.
Willing, Nick, dir. *Tin Man*. RHI Entertainment and the Sci Fi Channel, 2007.

About the Contributors

Robert **Baum**, great-grandson of L. Frank Baum, is a long-standing member of the International Wizard of Oz Club. As an avid Oz collector, he has shared his collection and findings with many authors and researchers. He was a technical advisor on the movie *Dreamer of Oz* and, with his wife Clare, has traveled extensively presenting their show *Frank and Maud* to numerous audiences, cruises, schools, Oz events, and conventions.

J.L. **Bell** studies the American Revolution in New England, but over the years he has written numerous articles for the International Wizard of Oz Club's *Baum Bugle*, including the first detailed analysis of a surviving L. Frank Baum manuscript. He edited *Oziana*, the club's creative magazine, and received several club awards for Oz short fiction. He also contributed to the essay collection *Dick Grayson, Boy Wonder* (McFarland, 2015).

Angelica Shirley **Carpenter** co-authored *L. Frank Baum: Royal Historian of Oz* (1992) with her mother Jean Shirley and has written books about Matilda Joslyn Gage, Frances Hodgson Burnett, Robert Louis Stevenson, and Lewis Carroll. Curator emerita of the Arne Nixon Center for the Study of Children's Literature at California State University, Fresno, she is a former president of the International Wizard of Oz Club and a frequent contributor to the *Baum Bugle*.

Paige **Gray** is a professor of liberal arts and writing at the Savannah College of Art and Design. She specializes in young people's literature and culture and has published work on a variety of texts. She is the author of *Cub Reporters: American Children's Literature and Journalism in the Golden Age* (2019). Other research areas include nineteenth-century and early twentieth-century American literature and journalism and media studies.

Katharine **Kittredge** is a professor of English at Ithaca College and the author of scholarly articles on texts ranging from *Kick-Ass* to the *I Hate to Cook Book*. Her areas of interest include eighteenth-century British literature, children's literature, science fiction and gender studies. She was a coordinator of the ITHACON comic book convention and coordinates a feminist pop culture conference called *Pippi to Ripley*.

Mary **Lenard** is a faculty member at the University of Wisconsin–Parkside, where she teaches nineteenth-century British literature and children's and young adult literature. She is the author of *Preaching Pity: Dickens, Gaskell, and Sentimentality in Victorian Culture* (1999). She has presented several papers on the Oz books and studies their significance in their original historical and cultural context.

Robert B. **Luehrs** taught European intellectual history and the history of early modern Europe at Fort Hays State University for 46 years. He serves as a mentor and counselor for young faculty there. He has published articles on a variety of topics, including deism, eighteenth-century utopianism, nineteenth-century religious skepticism, early horror films, detective fiction, the folklore of witchcraft, and the Oz stories.

Dina Schiff **Massachi** lectures in the University of North Carolina at Charlotte's English and American studies departments, where one of her favorite classes to teach is on *The Wizard of Oz*. A specialist in children's literature, she has written and presented numerous academic essays on L. Frank Baum's masterpiece, and she also studies utopias and dystopias.

Dee **Michel** is the author of *Friends of Dorothy: Why Gay Boys and Gay Men Love* The Wizard of Oz (2018). He has presented about the Oz/gay connection in the United States and the UK, including a speech at Boston's Youth Pride in 2006, "The Cowardly Lion and Courage to Be Who You Are." He writes regularly for the *Baum Bugle*.

Gita Dorothy **Morena** is a transpersonal psychotherapist, author, university instructor, and seminar leader. Her great-grandfather, L. Frank Baum, provided a rich tapestry of fairy tales which she draws upon to exemplify the power of symbolic imagery. Her book, *The Wisdom of Oz* (1998), sheds light on *The Wonderful Wizard of Oz* as a tale of individuation and spiritual awakening.

Shannon **Murphy** has presented her work in children's literature, folklore, and adaptations at conferences across the United States. Her first exposure to *The Wonderful Wizard of Oz* was the film as a child, but in her academic fairy tale studies, she made a departure from her German and Irish folk background to tackle the history of Baum's work. Her other areas of interest include feminist theory and horror studies.

James **Satter** is a former book editor who teaches reading and math at Sylvan Learning Center. He has presented lectures and led workshops about fiction and popular culture at regional conferences. He is also a freelance game designer for Great Scott Press.

Walter **Squire** is an associate professor of English and director of the film studies program at Marshall University. His specializes in American literature and critical theory. He has published articles on literature of the Loray Mill textile mill strike, American mad scientist films, cinematic depictions of teachers, Disney adaptations, and *The Wonderful Wizard of Oz*.

Mark I. **West** is a professor of English at the University of North Carolina at Charlotte, where he holds the title of Bonnie E. Cone Professor in Civic Engagement. He has been teaching courses on children's and young adult literature since 1984, and he has written or edited sixteen books. His articles have appeared in various national publications, including the *New York Times Book Review*, *Publishers Weekly*, *Americana*, and *British Heritage*.

Index